IN THE FIRING LINE:
VIOLENCE AND POWER IN
CHILD PROTECTION WORK

WILEY SERIES

in

CHILD CARE AND PROTECTION

Series Editors

Kevin D. Browne
School of Psychology
The University of Birmingham, UK

Margaret A. Lynch
Newcomen Centre
Guy's Hospital, London, UK

The Child Care and Protection Series furthers the understanding of health, psychosocial and cultural factors that influence the development of the child. It also examines early interactions and the formation of relationships in and outside the family. This international series covers the psychological as well as the physical welfare of the child and considers protection from all forms of maltreatment.

The series is essential reading for all professionals concerned with the welfare and protection of children and their families. All books in the series have a practice orientation with referenced information from theory and research.

Other books in the series:

Michelle Aldridge & Joanne Wood	Interviewing Children: A Guide for Child Care and Forensic Practitioners
Ann Buchanan	Cycles of Child Maltreatment: Facts, Fallacies and Interventions
Dorota Iwaniec	The Emotionally Abused and Neglected Child: Identification, Assessment and Intervention
David Quinton	Joining New Families: A Study of Adoption and Fostering in Middle Childhood
Jacqui Saradjian	Women who Sexually Abuse Children: From Research to Clinical Practice

Forthcoming title

Kevin Browne, Dr Helga Hanks, Dr Peter Stratton and Dr Catherine Hamilton:
Early Prediction and Prevention of Child Abuse: A Handbook

IN THE FIRING LINE: VIOLENCE AND POWER IN CHILD PROTECTION WORK

Janet Stanley and Chris Goddard
Monash University, Victoria, Australia

JOHN WILEY & SONS, LTD

Copyright © 2002 by John Wiley & Sons Ltd,
Baffins Lane, Chichester,
West Sussex PO19 1UD, England

National   01243 779777
International   (+44) 1243 779777
e-mail (for orders and customer service enquiries):
cs-books@wiley.co.uk
Visit our Home Page on http://www.wiley.co.uk
         or http://www.wiley.com

Other Wiley Editorial Offices

John Wiley & Sons, Inc., 605 Third Avenue,
New York, NY 10158-0012, USA

WILEY-VCH Verlag GmbH, Pappelallee 3,
D-69469 Weinheim, Germany

John Wiley & Sons Australia, Ltd, 33 Park Road, Milton,
Queensland 4064, Australia

John Wiley & Sons (Asia) Pte Ltd, 2 Clementi Loop #02-01,
Jin Xing Distripark, Singapore 129809

John Wiley & Sons (Canada) Ltd, 22 Worcester Road,
Rexdale, Ontario M9W 1L1, Canada

Library of Congress Cataloging-in-Publication Data

Stanley, Janet.
    In the firing line : violence and power in child protection work / Janet Stanley and Chris Goddard.
        p. cm. — (Wiley series in child care and protection)
    Includes bibliographical references and index.
    ISBN 0-471-99884-2 — ISBN 0-471-99885-0 (pbk.)
        1. Child welfare workers—Violence against—Australia—Victoria.   2. Social work with children—Australia—Victoria.   3. Abused children—Australia—Victoria.   4. Child abuse—Australia—Victoria.   I. Goddard, Chris (Christopher)   II. Title.   III. Series.
    HV802.Z8 V5265 2002
    362.76'8'09945—dc21

                                                            2001046657

British Library Cataloguing in Publication Data

A catalogue record for this book is available from the British Library

ISBN 0-471-99884-2 (cased)
ISBN 0-471-99885-0 (paper)

Typeset in 10/12pt Palatino by Dorwyn Ltd, Rowlands Castle, Hants
Printed and bound in Great Britain by Antony Rowe Ltd, Chippenham, Wilts
This book is printed on acid-free paper responsibly manufactured from sustainable forestry, in which at least two trees are planted for each one used for paper production.

CONTENTS

ABOUT THE AUTHORS

Dr Janet Stanley has researched child maltreatment and family violence for 12 years while associated with the Child Abuse and Family Violence Research Unit, Monash University, Australia. Currently, Janet also undertakes research consultancies with the National Child Protection Clearinghouse, which has a particular interest in the prevention of child maltreatment. Janet has published in leading international and Australian journals.

Associate Professor Chris Goddard has worked as a child protection worker in the UK and Australia. He is the author of a number of books and more than 50 journal articles on child welfare, and he has written for the media on child protection issues. His research on child protection has led to a government inquiry and to major reforms to services. Chris is the Head of Social Work at Monash University, and Director of the Child Abuse and Family Violence Research Unit in Australia.

ACKNOWLEDGEMENTS

This book is about violence towards child protection workers and the ability of the child protection system to protect children who have suffered abuse, assault and neglect. Many people have contributed to our research in many ways.

Our first and most significant acknowledgement is to the child protection workers who took part in the research. The demands of their work, and their working conditions, are described in this book. The fact that they were prepared to participate, in the face of such pressures, says a great deal about their commitment to children. We would also like to thank the Department of Human Services for granting permission for the first stage of the study.

The funding for this research came from three sources. The Victorian Health Promotion Foundation provided the major financial support, both for the earlier pilot study and the research reported in this book. Australians Against Child Abuse also provided financial assistance for the Child Abuse and Family Violence Research Unit at Monash University, where the research was undertaken. Finally, Monash University also assisted with a writing-up award.

On a more personal level, many people have assisted throughout the project. Thanks go to our colleagues Neerosh Mudaly, Adam Tomison and Joe Tucci in the Child Abuse and Family Violence Research Unit, and to Joy Karton in Social Work. A special thanks goes to Bernadette Saunders from the Child Abuse and Family Violence Research Unit who gave up her time to read the book and offered valuable editorial and content comments. Finally, none of this would have been possible without the support of our respective families, who allowed us to forsake other duties, to disappear, and write 'the book': John, Chris and Kate, and Lydia, Tom, Michael, Sandy and Julia.

Janet Stanley and Chris Goddard

1

CHILDREN AND WORKERS IN THE FIRING LINE: MESSAGES FROM THE CASE FILES AND INTERVIEWS

INTRODUCTION

The failures of child protection services have preoccupied health and welfare professions and the media for nearly three decades. During the writing of this book, many child abuse cases appeared prominently in the newspapers. The *Daily Mail* (25 March 2000) asked the question that has repeatedly challenged child protection services in the UK, the USA, Australia, New Zealand and elsewhere: 'How were these parents allowed to remain in charge of . . . children?' (Jones 2000: 8). The main headline, in letters nearly five centimetres tall, took readers 'Inside the house of hell'. Similar stories appeared at the same time in the USA and other countries – see, for example, 'Brianna report cites chaos in 7 D.C. agencies' (Horwitz & Higham 2000: A01) and, in New Zealand, 'Never again: How we all failed James Whakaruru' (Collins 2000).

As we put the finishing touches to the book, the terrible death of Victoria (known as Anna) Climbie dominated the news in the UK. The headline in *The Independent* asked 'How did it happen again?' (Wolmar 2001). *The Observer* wanted to know 'Why did no one try to save this bright, happy girl?' (Bright & McVeigh 2001) in a headline spread across two pages. In equally large letters, a headline in *The Sunday Times* provided the 'answer' generally accepted by the media in such circumstances: 'Social work bosses backed bungling that let child die' (Ungoed-Thomas & Collcutt 2001) while the lead story on the front page of *The Daily Telegraph* declared 'Failures left tragic Anna to cruel fate' (Clough 2001a: 1).

This media coverage has a major impact. Every such death provides the opportunity to revisit previous tragedies. Bright and McVeigh (2001: 9), for example, gave details of Maria Colwell, Jasmine Beckford and Kimberley Carlile. In the same paper, Levy 'recalls scandals of child abuse since the Maria Colwell case . . .' (p. 9). The coverage may also become international. *The Guardian Weekly* gave the story similar prominence: 'For Anna, a new life ended in pain, fear and filth' (Gillan 2001: 8). A major broadsheet in Australia carried the large headline 'Murdered by her carers' (Clough 2001b: 11). All this media coverage created what *Community Care* described in an editorial as '. . a terrible week for child protection' (*Community Care* 2001a: 17).

The reaction to such news also tends to follow a predictable path:

> 'The government yesterday ordered an urgent inquiry into lessons to be learned from the murder of eight-year-old Anna Climbie after months of "truly unimaginable abuse" went unheeded . . .' (Gillan & Carvel 2001)

Inquiries into the murder of children, after child protection intervention, focus closely on the procedures in place – see, for example, 'NSPCC calls for complete overhaul of child protection procedures' (Carvel 2001).

While it is too early to form a judgement in the Victoria Climbie case, this book provides a new perspective on the failures of child protection services in their attempts to protect children who have been maltreated. We suggest that hostage theory, a new theoretical approach, can contribute to our understanding of why some child protection failures occur. In brief, hostage theory proposes that there may be an association between the trauma and isolation experienced by child protection workers and re-abuse of children known to protective services. It also proposes that the full impact on the protective worker of *all* violence occurring in, and involving, the family, needs to be understood. This book, in other words, makes an important connection between child protection failure and another issue receiving increased international attention: violence against social care staff. In Canada, Philp (2001) described high levels of violence against child protection workers. In the UK, the release of the report of the National Task Force on Violence against Social Care Staff (2001) prompted another editorial in *Community Care* (2001b). Hostage theory suggests that this actual and threatened violence may contribute to child protection failure.

Research on hostage theory, based on an extensive pilot study (Stanley & Goddard 1993a, 1993b), was undertaken in Victoria, Australia. The research utilised exploratory, descriptive and qualitative research designs. (Further details about research design and methodology are provided in the Appendix.) In short, the research involved rigorously reviewing the case files of 50 children known to have been abused, and interviewing 50 child protection workers.

AN OVERVIEW OF THE BOOK

The book is set out as follows. Chapter 2 examines the shifting foundations of child protection. Particular attention is paid to developments in Victoria, Australia. This provides both an example of an historical perspective on protective services and some insights into the context of research reported in this book. Chapter 3 critically re-examines some of the material on child deaths and explores the omissions. Chapter 4 reports on non-fatal child protection failure and presents findings from our study. Aspects of the social worker–client relationship are reviewed in Chapter 5, together with a summary of the increasing understanding that this relationship may be marked by intimidation and violence towards the social worker in some cases.

Chapter 6 reports on two further factors which have received little attention in the child protection literature. The first of these is the context of violence which may surround severe child assault and neglect. There is increasing interest in the physical assaults reported against social workers. The second factor concerns the physical, intellectual and emotional isolation of the protective worker. Further findings from our study are presented. Chapter 7 explores hostage theory and Chapter 8 relates the major study findings in relation to hostage-like behaviour in child protection workers.

The final three chapters of the book explore possible solutions to some of the problems raised. Chapter 9 comprises reflections upon the major theories developed in the book. Chapter 10 explores the issues from the perspective of professional supervision, again drawing out significant findings from our study. Chapter 11 concludes the book by reviewing one of the cases in the light of the research findings.

THE VALUE POSITION ON WHICH THE BOOK IS BASED

The book is written from a strong value-based perspective about the position of children in society. The authors believe that every child has a right to live in an environment that fosters her or his physical, social, emotional, spiritual and educational development. From the perspective of child protection this entails:

- stopping current assault, abuse and/or neglect;
- preventing future assault, abuse and/or neglect from occurring;
- ensuring that the child has a sense of security and attachment with an adult who cares for the child and can fulfil a 'guiding' parental role, offering the child direction and boundaries;
- ensuring that the child has the basic essentials in life such as physical health, suitable accommodation, emotional and financial security, education and job training;
- ensuring that the child protective process is not abusive in itself; and
- repairing the emotional and psychological scars left by past assault, abuse and/or neglect.

Finally, the authors also believe that child protection workers and others working in social care have a right to work in a physically, emotionally and psychologically safe environment.

A WORD ABOUT LANGUAGE

The majority of child protection workers in Victoria are women and the sample in our study reflects this. Unless the issue of gender is significant to a specific point being made, all protective workers are described using the feminine pronoun. In this book we conform to common practice by using the categories of physical abuse, sexual abuse, psychological and/or emotional abuse, and neglect. However, we believe that this method of categorisation of the abuse of children has some major disadvantages. In particular, it takes no account of the most important dimension, the impact of the assault, abuse or neglect on the child. These categories also make no allowance for some forms of abuse, such as the witnessing of domestic violence, nor do they indicate severity. The authors replace the word 'abuse' with 'assault' where this relates to what is usually known as physical abuse. While the authors also have reservations about the word 'abuse' being used as an umbrella form to describe many other adverse events which a child may experience, the term is maintained in this book for the purpose of clarity.

CASE SUMMARIES AND QUOTES FROM PROTECTIVE WORKERS

We now present some case summaries and quotes from protective workers. It should be noted that throughout the book the names of the children and any other identifying details have been changed to preserve anonymity. Any resemblance to real persons is a coincidence.

Robert

Robert was 10 years old at the time of our research. His case file described only the last year of child protection intervention. Robert had previously been subject to a court order (a legal requirement that he receive some form of protection against maltreatment) but his earlier files are missing. Information contained in his current file suggests that he has been subject to physical assault, sexual and psychological abuse, and neglect. The following account is taken from his current case file.

About a year earlier, Robert told his mother that he was being sexually abused by his step-father. His mother said that there was nothing that she could do about it. In total, Robert reported this history of abuse to five professionals. He rang a telephone 'help-line' on two occasions, and was 'strapped' by his step-father for doing so. He told his local doctor. He rang child protection services. He also confirmed the abuse during the eventual police interview. Shortly after the police interview, however, Robert wrote a detailed retraction of his statement to the police about the abuse. Some months later, he wrote another retraction.

There was little detailed information on the file about Robert's mother. She had had a previous relationship with a man who was described as a 'heavy drinker' and a 'very violent person', who repeatedly 'bashed' and 'threatened' her. Robert's mother had attempted to leave her current relationship on several occasions, sometimes taking the children with her but at other times leaving them with her partner. In addition to these regular separations the family changed accommodation frequently. When she left her partner on the last occasion, mother was threatened with violence by her partner's relatives if she did not return. When she finally went back to the house, she was 'severely' beaten by her partner who told her that she would be 'killed' if she left him again. In spite of this extreme violence, mother stated that her partner was a 'loving man' who respected her. She excused his aggression and violence on the grounds that she had been 'flirting' with another man. Mother did say that she was 'always nervous', however, but she did not understand why. She categorically denied to authorities that Robert had been sexually abused by her partner.

There was also surprisingly little information on the file about Robert's step-father, the alleged perpetrator. He was described as a 'heavy drinker'. There had been police involvement on a number of occasions as a result of his assaults on Robert's mother. He had been intimidating and verbally abusive to protective workers, and had also threatened to 'blow up' the local protective services office. The step-father's brother and sister also lived in the same house. Robert's mother had been threatened by them and they had also made threats of violence towards the protective workers. Robert had a younger brother and sister but there was no evidence on the file of any assessment of their welfare.

The family vigorously contested all court proceedings relating to Robert. There was tension within protective services as a result of one court hearing. In this hearing, protective services' own legal representatives came to an agreement with the family's solicitor to return Robert to his home, in spite of opposition from the protective workers themselves. Robert was returned under a legal order which required the workers to supervise his well-being at home with his mother and step-father. The magistrate at the court hearing was 'aggressive' in the face of the protective workers' opposition to the supervision order.

There was also extreme tension between the police and protective services. The police had planned to complain formally about protective services' initial handling of Robert's reports of abuse. In turn, protective services expressed 'serious concern' that the police had arrived at Robert's school in uniform to interview him without protective services, or any other support person, being present during the interview. The police decided not to prosecute Robert's step-father for any offences.

Robert reported the sexual abuse by his step-father to the family's general practitioner. In his statement to the court, the GP stated that he did not believe Robert was capable of writing his initial retraction without substantial adult 'assistance'. The doctor received an 'intimidating' letter from the family's solicitor, and he and his colleagues had also been threatened with violence by the step-father. The GP clearly stated that he was not prepared to visit the home on his own.

Robert's mother, step-father, and step-father's siblings had all made numerous complaints, principally about protective services, to a number of senior politicians and government officials, who in turn instigated official inquiries. They had also written to complain about police involvement in the case. In all these complaints they denied that Robert had ever been abused.

There was some information on the file about the family's involvement with the broader community. One neighbour reported that she had seen Robert 'cringe like a beaten dog' in the presence of his step-father. She also reported that all three children were rarely allowed outside the home. The neighbour expressed fears for her own safety if the step-father found out that she had given any information. Another neighbour reported that Robert's mother was completely 'dominated' by the step-father and his relatives. After Robert retracted his reports of abuse, he and his mother visited neighbours and other people in the community to allow Robert to apologise for accusing his step-father.

During this protective service involvement, Robert spent a period of one week with a foster family. The foster father reported to the police that he was terrified of the step-father and his relatives and that they had threatened to assault him and leave him with serious injuries. The foster father received a letter from the family's solicitor threatening defamation proceedings if he continued to 'talk'. A court hearing returned Robert to his home on an interim basis with the condition that the step-father leave the family home. However, following a visit two weeks later by protective services, the step-father was apparently living at home in contravention of the court order. Prior to the next court hearing, Robert was placed in a motel overnight.

Two psychologists assessed Robert. The first reported to the court that he believed that Robert had been sexually abused and that he was suffering from an 'accommodation syndrome'. The second assessment confirmed that Robert had been physically assaulted and emotionally abused. This psychologist reported that Robert was suffering from 'a fairly high level of fear'. This report recommended that the step-father, and his brother and sister, receive counselling, and that the step-father specifically receive counselling for 'sexual problems'. Two referrals were made apparently as a result of these psychological assessments. The first agency advised protective services that they were 'unable to take on this family'. The second agency declared that this family was not suitable for any available counselling and that it was not appropriate that they see Robert as he was still living with the perpetrator of abuse. It appeared that neither Robert nor any other member of the household received any counselling.

There was clear evidence in the file that the assessment of the protective workers changed as time passed. The initial assessment concluded that Robert was 'at risk of significant emotional harm due to sexual abuse'. Subsequent assessments found that there was 'the likelihood of significant physical harm'. The workers, however, concluded on the file that a thorough family assessment was not possible because of the 'adversarial' nature of any meetings with the family.

The last visit recorded on the file graphically described the aggression experienced by the worker. At one point, she found herself sitting in a

chair with three adults 'standing in close proximity'. They were aggressively making 'derogatory' remarks about protective services and the
worker herself. The worker described this on the file as 'an intimidating,
verbally abusive scene'. She recorded that she was upset and felt 'extremely intimidated and overpowered'. The file recorded seven changes
of key protective workers in one year. At the time of the research, the
eighth worker had just resigned. The researcher was told that another
worker had resigned specifically because of this family. The final record
on the file stated that access to the house had been denied on the last
attempted visit. There was no evidence in the file that any further contact
had been made with Robert for five months. There were no indications in
the file that any other action was planned to protect Robert in the future.

Phoebe

The following timetable provides a brief summary of protective services'
involvement with Phoebe and her family.

1992	June	After her birth, Phoebe was almost immediately referred to protective services, on the grounds of neglect and domestic violence.
	August	Abuse was described as 'unsubstantiated' and the file was closed.
	September	Phoebe was referred to protective services.
	October	Abuse was again described as 'unsubstantiated' and the file closed.
1993	July	Phoebe was referred to protective services. She was found to be neglected.
	August	Phoebe was referred to protective services. No action was recorded in the file.
	September	The protective file was closed.
	November	Phoebe was referred to protective services, who confirmed that she had suffered physical assault and psychological abuse. Phoebe was placed in foster care.
1994	February	Children's Court proceedings were concluded. Phoebe was returned home on an interim legal order (a legal requirement that she is given some form of protection against maltreatment), after nine weeks in foster care.
	June	As of this date, no visits to the home had been recorded since March.

Phoebe was referred to protective services soon after she was born. She was almost two years of age when the researcher read her file. Once again, there was little information on important aspects of her circumstances. Phoebe lived in a house with her young mother, her five siblings, a male described as a 'boarder', and a 15-year-old female. During Phoebe's short life, there had been repeated concerns about physical assault, psychological abuse and neglect. Phoebe's physical injuries included cuts, bruises, welts and a split lip. There had also been concerns about her dirty condition, inadequate nutrition, and being left alone in the house. Phoebe had been a witness to domestic violence and drug use. She was described as a 'withdrawn and sad toddler' who did not interact well with other children at the day care centre. She was also displaying a number of behavioural problems, including head-banging.

Phoebe's mother was described in the file as a 'prostitute'. She and her various male partners had drug and alcohol problems. She had attempted suicide on a number of occasions. On one occasion, she took an overdose while pregnant. On another, she slashed her wrists. There had been multiple episodes of domestic violence. One assault caused a miscarriage. The police had been called to the house in response to many of these attacks. The researcher learnt that mother had stabbed one partner, but this was not recorded on the file.

Phoebe's mother had threatened violence against protective workers and others many times. On one visit to the protective services' office, mother was described as 'swearing and gesticulating' at the protective worker. She also damaged furniture on this visit. On another occasion, while Phoebe was in foster care, a new protective worker, a colleague and the police visited mother's home. During this visit, mother threatened to get a gun and shoot the protective workers. At one point the police had to intervene physically to defend the protective workers when mother attempted to assault them.

Even when there was no direct contact, mother sent a number of threatening and intimidating letters to the protective workers. A protective worker told the researcher that these threats were never taken seriously enough. During the eventual court proceedings, Phoebe's mother, other relatives and friends yelled at the protective worker and threatened retribution. In spite of police presence in the building, mother assaulted the protective worker, who had to be taken to hospital for treatment. The protective worker was described in the file as 'planning to press charges' and the assault had been formally reported to the police, but the outcome of any proceedings was not known at the time of the research. As a result of this assault, it had been decided that the protective workers should not visit the house alone. The worker who had been assaulted continued to be the key protective worker. The researcher was told that solo visits soon recommenced.

There was very little information about Phoebe's father on the file. He had been charged with attempted murder, found guilty, and received a suspended sentence but was not living at home at the time of the research. There was no evidence on the file of any assessment of Phoebe's five siblings, nor was there any indication of any protective services intervention on their behalf. The file stated that a 15-year-old girl was living in the home. There was no record of any assessment or intervention on her behalf. This was concerning, given the information on the file about the 'boarder'. He is described as a drug user with a number of convictions for alcohol and drug-related offences. He had also served three months', and six months' imprisonment for two offences of aggravated cruelty and served a 12-months' community-based order for sexual penetration of a 15-year-old female.

Other agencies had been involved with Phoebe's family and had made a number of referrals to protective services about Phoebe. Mother had received material help, including food vouchers. Other counselling and support services had also been provided. Protective services organised day care five days a week for Phoebe, which commenced shortly after she was born. A member of the child care staff had noticed injuries to Phoebe for nearly 12 months but had not made a report. The file noted that: 'No explanation could be given as to why these injuries had not been reported. It was very obvious, however, that [day care staff member] was very anxious about her own safety.'

Gail

Gail was 5 years of age when she was first referred to protective services. At the time of the research she was 14 years old. Once again, the protective services' file appeared to lack significant information.

Gail was subject to court proceedings at the age of 8 years, apparently on the grounds of sexual abuse. She was placed with relatives in another part of Australia but returned to live with her mother at the age of 10. Gail ran away from home when she was 12 years of age. Her sister had run away two months earlier. When Gail was found by the police, she refused to return home.

Gail revealed extreme physical violence and psychological abuse since being returned to her mother's care two years earlier. She described abuse by her mother, step-father and another male relative. She described being beaten on the head and body. On one occasion, she reported that she had lost consciousness as a result of the assaults. She described her mother's incessant verbal abuse and insults. She said that her mother had 'kicked' her out of the house on many occasions. Gail also reported that she had been sexually abused. There appeared to be some confusion on the file as to whether this sexual abuse referred to the earlier assaults when she was 8 years old, or whether they referred to her current situation. Gail told protective workers that she didn't 'want to be hit any more'. Three younger children, aged 9, 3 and a baby remained at home. Gail reported that the younger children had also been assaulted and 'thrown across the room'. Gail also described how her mother had been beaten by her partners.

Gail was initially housed in a short-term residential institution. While it was difficult to get a clear picture of all circumstances from the file, it appears that Gail maintained her refusal to return home. She was placed under a Guardianship order (a legal requirement which removes parental guardianship for a set period of time). Gail's mother, however, made continued attempts to have Gail returned to the family. Gail's placements provide a record of repeated disruption as she was frequently moved from one short-term placement to another, and occasionally placed with relatives. On other occasions, she was recorded as staying with friends, but at the time the file was read by the researcher, she was homeless.

In spite of her repeated attempts to get Gail returned home, threats and intimidation marked mother's contact with Gail. On occasions, she was physically violent to Gail; she was described as rejecting, vindictive and hostile to Gail; and yet continued to seek contact with her. She refused to allow Gail to have contact with her younger siblings, even though Gail asked for this on several occasions. She insisted that Gail should be 'punished' for everything that she had done to hurt her mother, and on a number of occasions threatened to kill Gail.

Mother's relationships with protective workers were no less hostile and threatening. She was frequently abusive to protective workers; refused to keep appointments and refused to take phone calls from them. On other occasions, she made highly abusive and threatening phone calls to the protective services' offices and threatened to kill protective workers on a number of occasions. She made these death threats directly to the workers, or by leaving messages with other workers. She also made repeated threats to sue the workers for harassment. She vigorously opposed all court proceedings concerning Gail's future care.

Gail's health and behaviour deteriorated. She presented to hospitals with various 'psychosomatic' complaints and made a number of apparently unsuccessful attempts to get counselling. By the time she was 14 years of age, she had been subject to sexual and physical assaults from perpetrators outside the family. She had also been involved in various criminal activities, including drug offences and theft with a weapon. She had harmed herself on a number of occasions and refused to attend school.

In the 17 months that the protective file had been re-opened (from the time that Gail ran away from home at 12 years of age until the research at age 14 years) Gail's case had been allocated to no less than five protective workers. For seven months, it appeared that her case was unallocated. There was no record on the file of any protective service assessment or intervention on behalf of Gail's younger siblings.

Richard

At the time of the research, Richard was aged 5 years and his half-brother was 3 years old. The children lived with their father, and occasionally with a female partner of father. The children had also lived from time to time with grandparents and other members of the extended family.

Richard had been reported to protective services at the age of 4 years. He was found to be neglected and psychologically abused. He was inadequately fed and clothed and was unwashed. His care was described as lacking any routine and he was frequently locked alone in a room. In the house he had often witnessed extreme violence which included death threats and the destruction of property. Richard was described as developmentally delayed. He had poor speech and was not toilet trained.

The file described Richard's father, and many other members of the extended family, as suffering from intellectual disabilities. Richard's father had chronic drug problems and a 'psychiatric disorder', about which no further details were recorded. He was unemployed and had an extensive criminal record, including the illegal possession of a firearm. Family members often engaged in extensive verbal and physical violence towards each other and there was a report of sexual relations between some of the father's adult siblings. The child's natural mother and a friend had an Intervention order (a legal order placing specified restrictions on contact between two people for the protection of one of the parties) against the father, and the father had an Intervention order against his father.

Violence was not confined to the family. Father had been aggressive towards the police, family support agencies, and the protective worker. The family's general practitioner described the family members as having 'borderline psychoses' and 'little intelligence'. The doctor described the situation as 'dangerous' and refused to visit the family home without police protection.

After his referral to protective services, Richard was placed in foster care as no member of the extended family was willing to take him. Four weeks later, Richard was returned to his father on a court-ordered supervision order that required protective services to monitor Richard's welfare in his own home. A family support worker provided intensive support for two weeks and day care was then organised for Richard. He was also referred to child psychiatric services but the referral was not accepted. It was apparently intended that Richard's father receive psychiatric services but this had not occurred six months later when the file was read. Once again, there was no record of any assessment or intervention regarding Richard's half-brother, aged 3 years. At the time of reading the file, there was no record of any contact with the family for three months, nor was there any report of Richard's welfare in this period.

Extracts from the Interviews with Protective Workers

The worker reported that she had been threatened with a gun, had been assaulted once, had received numerous death threats, and had been twice threatened with a knife. On one occasion, a man had produced a knife from his sock. On another occasion, a member of a client's family had 'pulled a knife' even though there were police present. This person was gaoled, but the worker was 'dreading' his release as she felt he was a danger to the community. (Worker 6130)

After one court hearing, this worker described how she had gone straight home but her supervisor had returned to the office. When the supervisor later left the office, she noticed two men in the back lane. The supervisor suspected that they were waiting for the worker. (Worker 6350)

A worker described an armed hold-up at her office. Another worker had been held hostage with a gun at her head. A number of files were stolen in the raid. The man believed to be responsible was still free and continued to 'stalk' and 'harass' workers. He had also threatened to 'take out' some workers. The protective services office was closed as a result of this hold-up and its effects on the protective workers. The workers were moved to a new location. (Worker 4120)

The worker told of how she had faced a child's father who was 'raging with a screwdriver in his hand'. (Worker 1130)

The worker told of how a man, who had threatened to shoot workers in the past, had stood in the door of the interview room and refused to let her out. (Worker 1180)

This worker described an attack by a family member who also used an ashtray to threaten and intimidate her, saying, 'I could easily pick this up and split your head open.' (Worker 5410)

One worker described an occasion when it took five policemen to hold a man down while the worker was removing a baby and two young children from his partner. She was afraid the mother would hit her. She said she felt particularly apprehensive because the woman looked very similar to someone who had assaulted her in the past: 'I was surprised how frightened I felt . . . I had a clear idea I would be hit.' (Worker 1170)

This worker described being in an office with a man who had sexually abused a child. She said that she knew that this man was 'a nut' but no one was willing to help. The man 'exploded in the conference room . . . He picked up a chair, held it at my head, and said, "I'm going to kill you".' The perpetrator was a serving police officer. The police provided protective surveillance of the worker's home. They also provided surveillance at her children's school. The worker had serious doubts about her safety, given the perpetrator's occupation. At a later date the man was seen in the protective services car park, writing down car registration numbers. (Worker 5280)

A worker described how she was frightened in circumstances where she thought she would be safe. On one occasion, she removed a child from his home and took him to hospital to be examined. The child's mother, her partner and his brother later arrived at the hospital. The worker said she was frightened by their 'physical presence' and by their threats of legal action. She said no one in the hospital offered her any support. (Worker 2130)

CONCLUSION

The case summaries and the information from the interviews with protective workers, presented above, were chosen to illustrate some of the obstacles in the path of child protection. This book examines many of the difficulties inherent in attempting to protect children from further harm. It offers no simple solutions but rather stresses that many of the obstacles are interrelated. If children are to be better protected we need to acknowledge fully the complexity of the task we face.

2

THE SHIFTING FOUNDATIONS OF CHILD PROTECTION: THE CONTEXT OF THE VICTORIAN STUDY

INTRODUCTION

This chapter provides an overview of the shifting foundations of child protection. We pay particular attention to developments in Victoria, Australia, in order to provide the essential context of our research. Few areas of endeavour can be as complex as protecting children who have been abused. The field of child protection is also remarkable because of the rapid and major changes it has undergone. Although reference can be found to neglect and cruelty to children throughout written history, broad 'scientific' interest in the subject has only taken place over the last 40 years. During this time the literature has grown exponentially. The foundations have shifted from a belief that child abuse occurred infrequently, to one where it is thought to be experienced by many children; from a belief that it was perpetrated by people who were mentally ill, to one where it is also perpetrated by 'normal' people.

Interest in protecting children has shifted from an evolving nineteenth-century understanding that children required protection outside the family in the form of education and labour laws, to a current commonly held, and certainly Australian, position that child protection is almost exclusively about protecting the child from specific forms of maltreatment within the home. The assault, abuse and/or neglect of children in third-world countries is often overlooked as an issue within the field. Contemporary Western society holds ambivalent and conflicting views about children. Child protection has moved from the domain of small charity-based organisations to a government-controlled process which is large, highly bureaucratised and legalistic. At times, especially in relation to the death of a child, child protection is prominent in the media, with significant policy consequences.

Thus, judgements about the welfare of the child are always intertwined with politics, economics, values, cultural attitudes and available knowledge, as well as being heavily steeped in emotion. A failure to consider all contextual influences or to examine the issues from the child's perspective has led to research and practice oversights and errors. Artificial boundaries are placed around, and define what is and what is not, child maltreatment. Language used to describe children, and the assault, abuse and neglect of children, sometimes reduces their status and importance, and often sanitises and minimises their experiences as well as the criminal nature of the events (Goddard & Saunders 2000). A lack of research and academic discussion in the field has often resulted in knowledge development and practice 'fashions' which are not necessarily grounded in research and good practice principles. This historical context, some of which is reviewed in this book, is fundamental to understanding child assault, abuse and neglect, and child protection.

AN HISTORICAL PERSPECTIVE ON PROTECTIVE SERVICES

An Overview

A study of the history of child abuse reveals behaviours and practices which, while condoned or ignored at the time, would presently be considered unacceptable in most Western cultures. The dominant view throughout much of history has been that the parent or child's carer has absolute rights over the child. At times these extended to the right of parents to subject their children to harsh punishments, physical mutilation, infanticide and extensive labour (Goddard 1980).

It is argued by some that a gradual attitudinal change towards the intrinsic rights of children began in association with a reduction of infant mortality. In mid eighteenth-century Britain, between 50% and 75% of children died before they reached 5 years of age (Jones, Pickett, Oates & Barbor 1987). As conditions for adults improved, so did the conditions for children, although they often lagged behind.

It is usual to place the scientific 'discovery' of child assault, abuse and/or neglect in the mid-1940s when paediatric radiologists in the United States investigated long-bone fractures in children of 'unspecific origin' (Caffey 1946). The first article to gain wide attention was published in 1962 by Kempe and his colleagues in the *Journal of the American Medical Association*. Howitt (1992) argues, however, that the medical profession knew about child assault, abuse and neglect for much longer than this but chose not to recognise it as such. (Social work itself has a long history of protecting children, as will be seen in Chapter 5.) The work of Caffey and his colleagues was undertaken at a time when it was socially possible to 'reconstruct' the facts into a different framework.

The Recent History of Child Protection in Victoria

A brief overview of the recent history of protective services in the state of Victoria, Australia, is now presented as a case study of the development of protective services, as background to the research described in this book and as an aid to understanding the complex environment within which protective workers may be required to work. The reader's attention is drawn to the themes that can be extracted from this history. These include: the repetition of structural change including the context within which the changes occurred; the restrictions placed on free speech; the difficult working conditions for protective workers; and, most importantly, the repeated discovery that children were not being adequately protected.

Two articles in the 10 December 1966 issue of the *Medical Journal of Australia* (Bialestock 1966, Birrell & Birrell 1966) mark an Australian 'watershed' in the re-discovery of child abuse and/or neglect (Goddard 1988a: 21). The articles described the physical characteristics of child assault and sought to draw attention to the issue. In 1968, following this attention, the Victorian government set up an inquiry into child abuse and/or neglect, followed by protective legislation in the early 1970s. In contrast to early directions in child protection, this new legislation was aimed not at working conditions and education but at protecting the child from his or her family, an issue which still remains the dominant concern (Howitt 1992).

The recent history of protective services in Victoria has left a legacy that the only certainty is that of continuous change. The processes of when the government should intervene to protect a child, how this should be done, and within what structure, have all undergone major changes since the 1950s (Paterson 1990). These changes have been marked by a series of government inquiries and extensive departmental restructuring. In Victoria, many of these shifts in the child protection system have been instigated by purposeful campaigns in the media, particularly the print media

(Goddard 1996a; Loane 1997). As many of the recent changes have not been formally documented, the authors draw some of the following information from media reports.

By the 1970s, the Victorian Social Welfare Department was adopting a policy of de-institutionalisation and returning children to their homes (Liddell 1993). Child protection was contracted to the Children's Protection Society and the police (Social Welfare Department 1970). In 1976, an inquiry resulted in a name change to the Department of Community Welfare, with a broader departmental emphasis on community welfare rather than the removal of children from their families (Markiewicz 1996).

In 1982, the government commissioned another major review of child welfare practice (Carney 1984) and the report found many areas to criticise in child protection, such as the:

> '. . . lack of cooperation between agencies; lack of accountability of the
> system; inexperienced staff; inadequate protection of children; and inade-
> quate safeguards given to the rights of children and their families'. (God-
> dard, Liddell & Brown 1990: 587)

In 1984 and 1985, there were further reorganisations of the department, resulting in an integration of parts of the Department of Health and the Department of Community Welfare Services, to form the Department of Community Services. Responsibility for child protection was removed from the Children's Protection Society, and the new Department of Community Services and the Victorian Police were given joint responsibility for this role.

Despite these adjustments, extensive concerns were still expressed by some people about child protection. Such reservations led Goddard (1988a) to write *Dual Tracks and Double Standards* in a deliberate move to provoke a major media campaign. In this book he called for a Royal Commission into the 'deeply flawed' protective services (Goddard 1988a: 86). He criticised the dual-track system as unworkable. He noted: the lack of cooperation between other services and child protection; the high turnover and lack of experienced staff; the failure to protect children adequately; the lack of accountability within the system; the massive system changes which did not lead to improvements; the failure to research child protection; and the failure to learn from overseas experiences. Goddard also drew attention to a number of child deaths caused by parental assault. Moreover, there appeared to be no obvious effort within the department to learn from these deficiencies (Goddard & Carew 1993). Goddard and Carew were also disturbed by the poor work conditions and high stress levels found in child protection workers.

At the end of the 1980s the departmental head wrote of the problems:

'Child protection . . . was marginalised in corporate life. . . . Child Protection suffered in the competition for resources. CSV's [Community Services Victoria's] poor performance in the field became a public scandal in 1988.' (Paterson 1990: 3)

Academics wrote:

'. . . the Child Welfare Practice and Legislation Review appears to misunderstand the nature of practice and the dilemmas and conflicts involved in child protection and related services, (and) . . . the Victorian State Government (has a) . . . reluctance to accept responsibility for child protection and to provide adequate resources . . .' (Goddard et al. 1990: 588)

Goddard's book (1988a) resulted in a major media campaign in *The Age*, a leading daily paper in Victoria, Australia. Entitled, 'Our Children, Our Shame', the campaign continued for six days in July 1988 (Loane 1988). On 7 July 1988 the government announced that protective services would receive 118 additional staff and a $7.2 million increase in budget (Goddard & Carew 1993; Loane 1997). The same year, Justice Fogarty was asked by the Victorian government to chair another inquiry into protective services. The findings of this inquiry largely repeated the recommendations outlined in *Dual Tracks and Double Standards* (Goddard 1988a). It was recommended that the dual-track system should cease, leaving the department with sole responsibility for child protection services. It recommended that all referrals of children who had been assaulted, abused and/or neglected should be accepted, that a central register of abuse and/or neglect cases be established, and that a 24-hour service be provided. Suggestions were made about improvements to administrative structures in Community Services Victoria (CSV) and that attention be given to the problem of high staff turnover (Fogarty & Sargeant 1989). A 'single-track' service was progressively implemented between 1990 and 1993, although delayed and hampered by funding gaps (*The Sunday Age* editorial 1991).

In 1989, new legislation, the *Children and Young Persons Act 1989*, was enacted. This Act provided for a separation of the services to children in need of protection and juvenile offenders; provided greater accountability, standards and protection of parental and children's rights; and provided new categories of protection, including a 'permanent care' option for children (Liddell & Goddard 1995).

In 1992, the conservative Liberal State Government was elected in Victoria, bringing with it tight budgets, further departmental restructuring and policies of privatisation and managerialism. Child protection did not

escape the changes, undergoing another major restructuring and becoming subsumed in the Department of Health and Community Services
(H&CS). It was subject to new policies of privatisation, competition and
performance-based funding (Mitchell 1996). New management structures
were put in place and local offices were amalgamated into a few, large,
regional offices. There was a rapid closure of residential services and a
build up of home-based services. Many welfare agencies were closed,
forced to reduce their services or to amalgamate with other organisations
(Mitchell 1996). According to Mitchell, resultant competition between the
agencies led to a compromise in service quality and the field being defined by H&CS administrators, with minimal consultation. He suggests
that welfare policy and programmes were being developed for economic
reasons, rather than growing from research and practice experience.

The 1990 murder of Daniel Valerio, a child known to Victorian protective
services, was followed by another extensive media campaign which led to a
'staged' introduction of mandatory reporting laws (Goddard 1994, 2001;
Goddard & Liddell 1995). Medical practitioners, nurses and police were
required to report physical assault and sexual abuse from November 1993
and teachers were required to report from July 1994; the planned inclusion of
other professionals, however, has not occurred to date. Mandatory reporting,
and the surrounding publicity, has resulted in a large increase in child abuse
reports (Angus & Hall 1996, Department of Human Services 1997).

The findings arising from a further review of child protection, undertaken
by Justice Fogarty, were published in October 1993. He acknowledged
that there had been some significant improvements, such as a 24-hour
service, the phasing out of the dual-track system, and an increase in staff
numbers and retention rates, but the report remained critical of other
aspects, particularly services to adolescents (Liddell & Goddard 1995).

In November 1993, child protection workers from two offices instigated
work bans against budget cuts, believing that the cuts would place children's lives in jeopardy because of insufficient resources, excessive work
loads and dangerous practices (Pirrie 1993). The debate in the print media, which at times became heated and personal, was joined by major
political and legal figures (Boreham 1993; Hughes 1993).

Academics continued to express their concerns about Victorian protective
services. Liddell and Goddard (1995) expressed the view that, while a
number of problem areas in protection were addressed, other problems
had been created. Their concerns centred on a failure to come to terms
with how a protection system can function adequately in a climate of cost-
cutting and a reduction in government intervention. They also expressed
concern about the continuous restructuring in the department, the

increase in bureaucratisation and the procedurally driven process of child protection, as well as increased pressures and control on private welfare agencies. Specific concerns were expressed about adolescent welfare and the overwork and under-support of child protection workers. Similar concerns were being expressed in the British child abuse literature. For example, Dominelli (1996) and Parton (1996) expressed the belief that welfare policy-making and resource allocation have now become dominated by men. Adherence to administrative processes has been given priority in organisational changes, and the assessment of outcome effectiveness has received little priority.

Major concerns about child protection continued to be expressed in the media. For example, in January and February 1995, *The Age* published a series entitled 'The Lost Children'. Articles highlighted the plight of adolescents under the care of the department (for example, Tuohy 1995, Tuohy & Freeman-Greene 1995). Concerns were expressed about work standards, child deaths, budget cuts leading to service reduction, and the extent of inquiries and restructuring of the department. While the government allocated additional funds for investigation of child abuse and neglect, there was repeated criticism of reductions to out-of-home accommodation for children, counselling agencies and the preventative services (see, for example, Mitchell, quoted by Pegler 1996a).

Many of these criticisms were accompanied by concern about the lack of consultation with the community. The Victorian tabloid paper, the *Herald Sun*, reported that:

> '. . . bullying and intimidation had increased, . . . protective services had become a "monster" that's responsive only to itself, . . . it's a culture of fear and intimidation.' (Critchley 1996: 12)

These concerns were supported by some private welfare agencies who were fearful about cuts in departmental subsidies in retaliation for making comments about the protection system (Pirrie 1994).

> 'A climate of fear exists in Victoria about open debate on this topic – the leaders in the field are running scared of losing State Government funding.' (Father Norden, quoted by Pegler 1996a: A2)

Milburn (1994: 17) reported that many social care agencies had been 'cowed' by threats of funding cuts and 'letters of chastisement from department bureaucrats' after they had spoken out about policy decisions. Continuing problems in the child protection system were highlighted in a number of Goddard's articles in the press in 1996 (see Goddard 1996c–e).

That year, considerable publicity was also given to the murder of a taxi driver by a 14-year-old boy and his friend, both of whom were under state care (Mottram 1996a). The child had absconded from departmental accommodation 26 times in two years. One staff member commented that he was 'powerless to control' this boy who also intimidated other residents, assaulted his brother and brandished a knife at a worker. The trial judge described the protection system as 'lamentably inadequate', to which Victoria's Premier is reported to have suggested that there had been no indication that the child was violent (Farouque 1996: A2, Mottram 1996a: News 13).

In February and March 1996, industrial action was taken by child protection workers in relation to pay claims. On 8 March, a large number of workers were stood down from work and the remaining workers walked off the job (Pegler & Martin 1996). On 26 March, 8000 members of the Public Service Union took strike action to support the child protection workers (*The Age* editorial 1996a), but the department, now known as the Department of Human Services (DHS), bought a series of half page advertisements in a leading daily newspaper condemning the strike (for example, Department of Human Services 1996).

A further major review of the DHS by the Auditor General, begun in 1994, was released in June 1996 (Auditor General, Victoria 1996). A draft copy, leaked to a newspaper, reported evidence of 'serious flaws' in the system. It revealed that the DHS was involved in 'system abuse' of some children and some children were returned to violent, abusive homes (*The Age* editorial 1996b: A22). The review reported that:

> 'Scores of children in State Government care are running out of control, committing serious crimes, terrorising youth workers and flouting court orders without reprimand.' (Mottram 1996b: 1)

Mottram (1996b: 1) reported that an investigation by *The Sunday Age* found that children under state care were involved in serious crimes, 'including murder, rape and armed robbery'. The Auditor General reported that, between 1989 and 1995, only a quarter of the deaths of children under the care of child protection services in Victoria were investigated. The report also found that the workers were stressed, overworked and inexperienced and noted a high turnover of workers and poor work conditions (Painter & Martin 1996).

The death of children under departmental care continued to receive extensive media attention, receiving full front-page coverage in the *Herald Sun* (Pirrie 1996). Amanda Clark died in June 1994, Dillion Palfrey in May 1995 and Katy Bolger in October 1996 (Gleeson & Coffey 1996). All cases had been known to the department for an extended period of time, two being closed just prior to the child's death (Pirrie 1996: 29). The blame was often passed onto the individual child protection worker; for example, it was reported that the worker in charge of Dillion Palfrey's case:

'. . . had not had his higher duties position renewed ". . . because he had been involved in a number of cases where his decision-making, particularly relating to risk assessment, was assessed as deficient".' (Davies 1996: 1, 2)

Towards the end of 1996, a Royal Commission into Victoria's child protection system was again called for, this time by Justice Fogarty who stated that the death of 92 children in care since 1990 was too high (Yallop 1996). This call was supported by others, such as the Chief Justice of the Family Court, who commented that 'arguably child protection systems are failing children' (Milburn 1996: A3).

A further restructuring of the department began in 1996. A major component of this has been the requirement that non-government organisations competitively tender for service provision contracts with a set time-period. Emphasis has been placed on a 'case-management' approach with individual client packages of services with a directly costed budget. Departmental documents outline a desire for outcome measurement (Department of Human Services 1997, Youth and Family Services 1999).

Liddell and Liddell argue that, while there are some positive signs of improvement in the protection service, many criticisms can still be made. Fundamentally, they believe that new systems and programmes are being imposed on a structure which is already flawed. They point to *The Age* newspaper's reporting on the continuing embargo on public comments on government policy. This was enforced through the threat of loss of government funding (Liddell & Liddell 1999). Liddell also draws attention to the increasing government control and bureaucratic management practices that have accompanied the commercial contracting process of non-government agencies. He describes the 'capture and neutering' of the non-government sector and the social workers who work in this sector, resulting in an 'alarming and depressing scenario' which stifles initiative and creativity (Liddell 1997: 422).

'Child protection and care systems, right around Australia, are in a sad and sorry state. Every state and territory [in Australia] has reviewed all or part of its protection and care provisions in the past few years. All have added to the confusion rather than solving the problems, partly through well-meaning attempts that have addressed isolated symptoms rather than comprehensively addressing basic causes.' (Liddell & Liddell 1999: 106)

During the writing of this book, another investigation of the state's child protection system was undertaken by *The Age* newspaper. The reports, under the title, 'Broken Lives' featured as the lead story on a number of occasions (see, for example, Goddard 2000, Davies 2000, 2001).

ISSUES AND LESSONS FROM HISTORY

Blind Spots, Selective Attention and Value Confusion

The previous discussion shows that Victoria's child protection system is subject to major pressures and frequent changes. History reveals selective and sporadic attention, blind spots and denial coexisting with the researchers' and the community's struggles towards an understanding of child abuse.

The specific commissions or omissions which are defined as child maltreatment are determined at any point of time by historical, philosophical and cultural, as well as scientific factors. At present, the concept of 'child abuse' tends to be viewed as relating only to the 'Western developed' countries. Western society largely ignores accounts which report that in Africa about 40% of all 5- to 14-year-old children work, that one-third of the children in the world are undernourished, and that about one million children in Asia are victims of sexual exploitation (Saul 1997, *The Age* 1996c). This ability to deny is reflected in the following extract:

> 'A key Commonwealth department has argued strongly against imposing import bans to tackle exploited child labor, saying the action could jeopardise Australia's regional trade.' (*The Age* 1995: 6)

Even within Australia, behaviours currently viewed as 'child abuse' are narrow and selective. The field of child abuse is almost exclusively centred around the issue of specific, unacceptable forms of interaction between parental figures and children, mainly behaviour that adversely affects the child physically and psychologically, neglects basic needs, and exposes the child to sexual behaviour and sexual abuse. Even within these behaviours, some, such as psychological abuse and neglect, are often overlooked in research and practice. Commonly, these issues are viewed in terms of a single (or more than one) specific event. Issues such as other criminal activities, poverty, poor health, poor educational systems, youth unemployment, homelessness, substance abuse, mental illness, and institutional and system abuse, are usually still excluded. This continues despite the fact that Gil drew attention to many of these issues in 1975.

Within the areas that Western society has defined as abusive, the point at which the behaviour becomes abuse, or the extent to which society is willing to risk danger to the child before intervening, is very unclear

(Daro 1988). There has been little research into practice, and the field is far from introducing effective treatment and prevention programmes (Corby 1993). The study of the assault, abuse and/or neglect of children is a field of scientific endeavour that draws on many different disciplines, all bringing their own perspective and differing philosophical bases to the subject. While this adds complexity, it also presents an opportunity to increase understanding and formulate more effective interventions.

The Use of the Medical Model, and the Legalisation and Bureaucratisation of Child Protection

As illustrated in this brief history of protective services in Victoria, and as noted in Chapter 1, child abuse and child protection now attracts considerable political and media attention in Western societies. One impact of this has been that the community's demand for response to the serious assault, abuse and/or neglect of children has often overtaken understanding within the field. This lack of understanding creates a vacuum, with the risk that the protective system will be moulded to fit the current dominant philosophy (Howe 1996). In the current climate in Victoria, managers rather than professionals are seen as crucial, and market principles, in association with staff performance and business plans, have become central to work practices (Corby 1987, Parton 1996). Associated with this has been repeated organisational change. Manageralism has also resulted in outcomes being measured in corporate terms, rather than based on measurements relating to the improved welfare of the child who has been assaulted, abused and/or neglected. People have almost become commodities, and marketing language is used where outputs are 'purchased', and 'performance targets' unrelated to a child's welfare are sought (Youth and Family Services 1999). The Victorian *2000–01 Budget Estimates* describe the 'Performance Measures' of child protection services as follows:

'*Quantity*
   Notifications to child protection services . . .
   Daily average number of placements . . .

Quality
   Protective cases resubstantiated within twelve months of case closure . . .
   Daily average number of clients receiving a specialist support service . . .
   Proportion of placements that are Home Based Care . . .

Timeliness
   Protective intervention cases closed within ninety days . . .'
                               (Department of Treasury and Finance 2000: 84)

Improvement in a child's welfare is only given recognition in one of these measures. Indeed, it is unclear whether the targeted outcome is to increase or decrease the figures attached to some of these measures.

Parton (1996: 10) believes that, particularly in the last decade, corporate philosophy has also led to 'a reconstruction of social work' in general. Social work has been fragmented into tasks and the work divided into discrete episodes of intervention which are unrelated to previous episodes and have 'no history, pattern or direction' (Clarke 1996: 91). For example, there has been the development of a central notion of 'structured risk assessment' in child protection which seeks to establish the children most at risk of future assault, abuse and/or neglect. This has led to the replacement of complexity and uncertainty with the simplicity and certainty of standardised procedures and apparently 'all-inclusive' lists (Goddard, Saunders, Stanley & Tucci 1999). There has, however, been a move towards reducing and packaging child protection practice skills into competency statements which define actions (O'Hagan 1996).

A number of writers express concern about these trends, where skills, knowledge and discretionary powers have, or will be, replaced with standardised practices, which stereotype situations without '. . . any real understanding of the complexity of practice, or practice dilemmas nor the moral and political nature of practice' (Cooper 1993: 28). Such standardised practice is '. . . antithetical to depth explanations, professional discretion, creative practice, and tolerance of complexity and uncertainty' (Howe 1996: 92).

These developments have occurred at the same time as reductions in the share of public spending on welfare, and 'a generalised hostility towards state intervention' (Clarke 1996).

The medical model had a major influence on early child protection practice. This 'medicalisation' of child protection, among other influences, individualised the issue of the assault, abuse and/or neglect of children (Howitt 1992: 21). It also perceived abuse as an event rather than a relationship or interactional issue. This model is now increasingly being replaced by a legalistic one (Parton 1991). Wattam (1992) believes that it is increasingly the legal definition of evidence that determines the facts of the case and whether the assault, abuse and/or neglect is serious enough to warrant intervention. Wattam believes that this legalistic development places in jeopardy the rights of the child, as the child is now likely to be viewed as evidence and the best interests of the child may be in conflict with gaining legal evidence. Thus, with the law becoming the arbitrator of what is abuse, it may only be those cases with legal consequences that are singled out for attention (Lynch 1992). As a consequence, the definition of abuse is narrowed, and chronic neglect and psychological abuse, the most difficult to establish in a court case, may be overlooked. There is also the risk that no action may be taken by the child protection worker until the assault to the child is 'serious' enough, or the child has received severe physical injury, to enable the case to stand up legally.

> 'The whole system of referral, investigation, conference and registration, prosecution and treatment is designed to filter out the "least serious" cases.' (Wattam 1992: 10)

Valentine (1994: 81) also writes of this legalistic trend and argues that 'legalistic rights' rather than 'therapeutic needs' pervade child protection practice. She believes that such a legalistic and adversarial style of working can be used as a defence against work stress. By focusing on 'rights', on procedure, on written agreements, and working in this very concrete way, there is an attempt to control the nature of the relationship between social worker and parent, and between parent and child. Valentine notes that all parties may collude in this strategy to avoid unconscious dynamics. This legalistic response has been noted in Victoria: Mitchell (1996: 80) writes that the protective process is 'mechanistic' and 'overwhelmingly concerned with the administrative and legal decision'.

CONCLUSION

The Victorian child protection system has undergone frequent and major changes. The changes have been prompted by economic and political forces, and by media coverage. In this, the Victorian system appears to have characteristics similar to other child protection systems. The uncertain and complex political and moral context of child protection in the UK, for example, is described by The Violence Against Children Study Group (1999). As Buchanan (1996: 15) notes, the British media also prefer 'simple truths' even where it is clear that none exists.

This brief history of child protection in Victoria illustrates the pervasive pressures and constant changes at every level of the system. In this context, it is easy to understand how violence against child protection workers can be overlooked. The poor working conditions of the workers, the limited opportunities of workers to express their views, the increased emphasis on procedurally driven practice, and repeated media coverage, all combine to disempower those in the front line.

Much of the pressure for procedurally driven child protection practice has been prompted by child death inquiries and the resultant media coverage. Significant texts from the USA, the UK and Australia are critically analysed in the following chapter.

3

THE FAILURE TO PROTECT: CHILD DEATHS DUE TO FAMILIAL ASSAULT OR NEGLECT

INTRODUCTION

In this chapter we review some of the significant publications from Australia, the UK, and the USA on child deaths from assault and/or neglect. Writing in the UK, Sanders has declared that it is 'almost impossible to overestimate' the influence of child abuse deaths on child protection systems (1999: 160). There have been few studies, however, into very serious – but non-fatal – cases of assault and/or neglect of children (see Chapter 4). We acknowledge that the cases examined in reports on child deaths are different to some degree to the cases analysed in our research. As stressed in the US material, however, death of, or serious injury to, a child may indeed be simply a matter of chance (see below).

The study on which this book is based was undertaken in Victoria, Australia. Australia does not have uniform child protection legislation (for a fuller explanation, see Goddard 1996a) nor is there a uniform system for inquiring into child deaths caused by familial assault. We start by examining recent reports on child deaths from two Australian states, Victoria and New South Wales.

THE VICTORIAN CHILD DEATHS REPORT 1997

A Victorian Child Death Review Committee (VCDRC) was established in 1996 and provides an annual report of its work, the *Annual Report of*

Inquiries into Child Deaths: Protection and Care (VCDRC 1997, 1998). The terms of reference include the review of all deaths of children who die while clients of child protection, or within three months of case closure, the identification of risk factors, and the evaluation of service and system responses. The 1997 report is 82 pages long but 20 pages are taken up with tables set out in the Appendices. In total, 17 of the pages are completely blank. The practitioner seeking guidance will concentrate on pages 31–43 which draw out themes and issues.

The Victorian Child Death Review Committee makes this point:

> 'As these themes are based purely on cases where death occurred, they represent a limited view of the child protection system. Just as the health system is no longer judged purely on mortality rates it is not appropriate to judge a child protection system solely on the inquiries conducted into client deaths.' (VCDRC 1997: 31)

The problem for the researcher and practitioner (see Chapter 9) is that where no other research is undertaken, this limited view is the only one available.

Eight themes and issues are identified in this section of the report. Four of those themes, the incidence of Sudden Infant Death Syndrome (SIDS), death by accident in the home, adolescent alcohol and drug use, and children with a medical condition with severely shortened life expectancy, are not directly relevant to the thrust of this book. The remaining themes are analysed below.

Service Provision Issues

In this very brief section, the VCDRC (1997: 33–34) reviews staffing and structural issues within protective services. Under the sub-heading 'staffing', the key concerns are described on page 33 of the report as:

> '. . . being clearly related to the relative inexperience, education, and training of staff charged with investigating child abuse allegations, and the quality of support and supervision with which they are provided.'

Other issues identified include high turnover of child protection workers, low morale, staff development and training opportunities, the failure to follow protocols and practice standards, the nature of the education that staff have received when they join the child protection system, and issues concerning recruitment of staff.

This summary is all that appears in this section. There is no critical analysis, for example, of exactly what 'high turnover' means or what 'staff development' opportunities exist. The next two paragraphs appear to be written with damage control in mind:

> 'The VCDRC accepts that even if the Department could recruit, train, and retain protective workers who complied totally with the protocols, it would not prevent child abuse or the deaths of children. . . . the VCDRC accepts that the review of cases where death has resulted presented a very limited picture of departmental service delivery and practice standards as a whole. It agrees that departmental standards about supervision, and implementation of practice guidelines and protocols are essential components for monitoring the quality assurance of the system.' (Ibid.: 33)

The sub-theme of structural issues is presented in a more critical light. The impact of mandatory reporting in Victoria (introduced in part in November 1993) and the introduction of a computer record system, are said to have had 'dramatic' repercussions on workloads (although again no data is provided). Management structures are described as 'inefficient'. In one unidentified case, an 'effective' service was not possible because 'an inappropriate number of staff were granted recreation leave' (ibid.: 34).

Risk Assessment

The section on risk assessment (ibid.: 34–37) reports a failure to undertake 'effective assessment' in 11 child deaths. In particular, inadequate assessment of 'relevant cohabitants' in the family and the roles of other agencies were also noted. Comprehensive assessments are described as 'the cornerstone of a successful child protection system', in turn providing 'the basis for determining risk of harm' (ibid.: 35).

Sub-sections of this theme are identified. The first, the culture of optimism, is said to have applied to the death of infants where:

> '. . . the workers appeared to overestimate the capacity of the parents to care for the child and to respond to parent education intervention.' (Ibid.: 35–36)

Work with adolescents, by contrast, is reported to be informed by a culture of pessimism that 'resonated with an inevitability of a poor outcome' (ibid.: 36). Accidents, drugs and suicide overwhelmingly caused the deaths of adolescents. The authors do not intend to explore these in this text, but note that there are significant connections that require further, detailed research.

Coordination and Collaboration with Other Service Providers

The relationships between child protection services and other agencies were described as another cause for concern, and:

'Characterised by poorly articulated plans, poor communications, and lack of effective and stated review/feedback mechanisms and expectations.' (Ibid.: 38)

A further 11 issues were drawn from the cases. These included a lack of review and monitoring, poor communication, mutual misunderstandings and lack of clarity in case closure.

Death due to Trauma

Since 1989, when child death inquiries were first instituted (as a result of the media pressure described in Chapter 2), 17% of deaths were attributed to trauma inflicted by a parent or carer. In a number of cases parents are reported to have made threats to kill or harm their children prior to their death. The committee recommends that such threats 'should be treated with the same seriousness as *actual harm*' (ibid.: 40; emphasis in original).

Overview

The VCDRC summarises the factors that are said to have an impact on service delivery to the children and young people who died. These are said to include: a lack of adequate assessment; parents with an intellectual disability; a lack of inter-agency coordination; work pressures; confusion about practice requirements; case closure (four cases had been closed prior to the death of the child); and drug problems in the parents.

THE VICTORIAN CHILD DEATHS REPORT 1998

The 1998 Victorian report (VCDRC 1998) appeared in a larger format but with only 65 pages. While the 1998 report has fewer blank pages than the 1997 report, the emerging themes and issues are again contained in a small proportion (12 pages) of the publication. Five themes are said to be 'distilled' from the cases examined (ibid.: 43–54). Three of these are described as a 'continuing elaboration' of those raised in the 1997 report. The recurring themes are described as: service delivery to adolescents; coordination and collaboration with other service providers; and continuing service provision issues. The two new themes are permanent placements and the family focus of casework intervention. While recognising the interconnectedness of issues relating to adolescents, as in the analysis of the 1997 report above, we will focus on the remaining themes that are relevant to our research.

Collaboration and Coordination between Service Providers

The 1998 report acknowledges that this issue was commented upon 'at length' in the 1997 report. In fact, comment in the themes and issues section comprised little more than one page (VCDRC 1997: 38–39). The report quotes from *Beyond Blame* (Reder, Duncan & Gray 1993) and states that there has been 'little improvement in this crucial area . . . to date' (VCDRC 1998: 49).

The 1998 report repeats the concern that:

> 'Without a clear definition in regard to monitoring, roles and respon-
> sibilities, a diffusion of accountability occurs creating a situation whereby
> no one can be held accountable for the level of service to the client.'
> (VCDRC 1998: 49)

In spite of the stress placed on this area, again barely a page is devoted to it. One major issue is added to the material provided in the 1997 report: the failure to include teachers in the case-planning processes.

Continuing Service Provision Issues

Once again, in this section, the impact of mandatory reporting and the introduction of a computer record system are said to have contributed to increased pressures on individual workers and management (VCDRC 1998: 50). High worker turnover in the 1998 report appears to have acquired an air of inevitability, while low morale (identified as significant in the 1997 report) is not mentioned.

Permanent Placement

The first page of this section comprises contextual quotes from the relevant legislation and from protective services' practice guidelines (VCDRC

1998: 51–52). The second, and final, page provides some analysis of the concerns arising from two cases. This theme stresses that where:

> '. . . reunification is not possible, the client via a Permanent Care Order is afforded a level of long term security in terms of accommodation and care that other Orders do not offer.' (Ibid.: 52).

The two cases referred to both concerned adolescents who had been placed for more than two years, and who both came from abusive and rejecting parents. The 1998 report states that many placement options in the extended families 'had been investigated without success' (ibid.: 53). The Children's Court and protective workers appear to be prevented from 'comfortably making recommendations and decisions' that ensure permanency of placement and remove guardianship rights from the family (ibid.: 53).

Family Focus of Casework Intervention

This theme stresses the workers' preoccupations with the 'dysfunctional' families rather than on the child or young person:

> 'It is not uncommon for reports to comment on a worker's failure to listen to particular concerns raised by children and young people.' (Ibid.: 54)

The report, interestingly in our view, stresses that casework should focus on the client 'rather than becoming enmeshed with the family' (ibid.: 54).

Overview

The 1998 report provides very little in terms of critical analysis, and the absence of case material makes this almost impossible. The committee describes itself as having 'grappled' with the issue of incorporating case summaries in order to 'give full justice to the complex nature of protective intervention' (ibid.: 8).

The committee expresses concern (ibid.: 8) about:

> '. . . the adverse impact of media treatment of the Panel's reports on child protection workers and the families of the deceased. It is also our view that such action by some sections of the media has the potential to undermine both the inquiry process and the effectiveness of this committee . . .'

An equally significant facet of the 1998 report is outlined on pages 26 to 28. The report notes that the inquiries into child deaths summarised in the publication were on occasions hindered by 'inability to access medical records relating to the subject of the inquiry' (ibid.: 26). This finding is highly ironic given the attention paid to inter-agency cooperation. Protective services in Victoria are but one part of a large organisation, at present called the Department of Human Services, that also provides hospital and other health care:

> 'In two instances it seemed that a decision to refuse access was made after the hospital sought a ruling from their legal advisers . . . it is of concern that in these instances a valid reason existed for the request, and the refusal was akin to one arm of the human services system blocking the activities of another part of the system.' (Ibid.: 26)

THE NEW SOUTH WALES CHILD DEATH REVIEW REPORT

The first major report of the New South Wales Child Death Review Team was published in 1997. The report (NSWCDRT 1997) is an attempt to create public accountability and to review all child deaths in the Australian state of New South Wales. The report examines in some detail the deaths of some children who were known to the state's protective services (the Department of Community Services). The aim of the report is stated in the Foreword (p. 1):

> '. . . to increase awareness of the circumstances and systemic factors surrounding these deaths leading to agency practices which will more effectively prevent child deaths in subsequent years.'

The deaths examined occurred between January and December 1996. Systemic factors in protective services included:

> . . . unmanageable caseloads, unallocated cases, insufficient training, and inadequate de-briefing and supervision of frontline workers.' (Ibid.: 80)

The report quotes from Reder, Duncan and Gray (1993) to demonstrate that these problems have been found elsewhere.

A total of 24 cases are examined. The causes of death had been variously described as 'homicide', 'non-accidental' or 'undetermined'. All 24 children reviewed had been known to protective services. In 11 cases there had been one or more confirmed referrals; in eight cases there had been prior unconfirmed referrals; in four cases referrals were made 'shortly before' the child died; and in the remaining case the child's sibling had been the subject of a referral (NSWCDRT 1997: 83).

The report identifies five issues and provides recommendations for each. Four of these are summarised below. A fifth, the lack of adequate out-of-home care services for adolescents, is not directly relevant to our research.

Information Not Taken as a 'Notification' and Inadequately Recorded

The report finds that there were several instances of reports being made to protective services where information was recorded only on handwritten forms and not officially recorded in the protective services' Client Information System:

> 'The practice prevents the cross-referencing, collation, and analysis of information from different . . . offices, and inhibits any one office or officer being able to see the total picture of the child's social circumstances.' (NSWCDRT 1997: 85)

One particular value of the NSWCDRT report is that, in contrast to the Victorian reports, it provides case extracts to illustrate the points being made. Three case summaries are provided for this first theme: Jeremy, Teresa and Alistair, and are referred to below. The recommendations made under this issue concern recording and standardising intake procedures.

The case of Jeremy concerns the failure of protective services to respond to a report from a health professional. Jeremy (aged 3 weeks) had been found in the care of a 12-year-old on one occasion and, a few days earlier, his mother (who had a history of intravenous drug use) had been observed to have slow speech and red eyes. The information was not classified as a 'notification' (referral) and was not regarded as sufficient to justify any intervention. This view was held in spite of another referral. Jeremy died of a head injury a few days later (ibid.: 86).

Teresa's family was provided with support after her birth but a number of issues were 'not adequately addressed' (ibid.: 87). These included Teresa's sibling receiving double doses of medication at the hands of her mother and the children being seen in a 'filthy state'. Of particular significance to our study, Teresa's father was reported to persistently call the children 'fucking bitches', Teresa's mother stated that she felt like killing one of the children (during a visit by a protective worker) and, one week later, the mother attempted suicide. Teresa died when she was 6 months of age, just two weeks after her mother's suicide attempt (ibid.: 87).

Alistair's case also highlights the coexistence of other violence. The case extract is quoted in full:

> 'Alistair's mother was known to DCS[1] officers. She had been abused as a child and was at times violent to other adults. When Alistair was about six months of age, his mother informed DCS that he had sustained bruises some weeks before, having been hurt by a friend of hers. The DCS file indicated that DCS suggested Alistair's mother charge her friend with assaulting the baby. The mother declined because she admitted she had also "beaten" this friend and was herself fearful of being charged.
>
> DCS took no action following the admission by Alistair's mother that the baby had been assaulted. Two months later, Alistair died from injuries consistent with having been severely shaken when in the care of another friend of his mother.
>
> After Alistair's death, his mother informed DCS that she had understated the extent of Alistair's previous injuries – in fact, there had been extensive bruising to his face and head – because she was fearful that Alistair would be removed from her care. She had not sought any medical attention for him at that time. She told DCS that she had noticed a cigarette burn on his ear and that these injuries only occurred when Alistair was minded by her other friend. Later enquiries revealed that this friend had previously injured another child by shaking.' (NSWCDRT 1997: 88)

Inadequate Risk Assessment

The report suggests that a number of child death reviews reveal superficial assessments. The problems are said to include: the minimisation of the seriousness of information; the failure to understand the significance of information; the failure to follow up concerns; premature case closure after parental denial; the failure to visit or sight the child; and a lack of access to professional expertise (ibid.: 92).

Cassie's case, the first cited in this section, involves allegations of domestic violence and drug abuse. Cassie, born with a physical disability, was the subject of an anonymous referral at age 3 months. It was alleged that Cassie was left with unsuitable people, that she was neglected, and that her mother, who used drugs and was herself a victim of violence, verbally abused her (ibid.: 93). A second referral, from another named caller, reported similar concerns one month later: Cassie was neglected, verbally and physically abused by mother; mother was using drugs; and Cassie's father was violent to mother (ibid.: 94).

---

[1] Department of Community Services is the name of protective services in New South Wales, Australia.

In Rebecca's case (ibid.: 95), mother presented 3-week-old Rebecca to a hospital saying that she could not cope with the baby's screaming. Rebecca's mother had attempted suicide shortly before the baby was born, and was diagnosed as depressed, unstable, immature and socially isolated. Three weeks later, the case was closed. At 5 months, Rebecca died. (Although the death was classified as Sudden Infant Death Syndrome, this view was challenged by a later forensic opinion.)

Joseph, the sixth child, died at age 21 months at the hands of his father, who then committed suicide:

'The file indicated that Joseph's father had a history of violence, had threatened others, and had threatened to kill Joseph's mother and her family if she left him.' (Ibid.: 96).

Reports to protective services were viewed as arising from custody disagreements, and a doctor accepted that a fractured clavicle, one month before Joseph's death, was the result of a fall from a table (ibid.: 96).

Case Extract Seven, Robert, is a mere six-line summary of a boy who drowned after being left unsupervised near a pool. There are no indications of other violence (ibid.: 97).

Petra, the eighth child cited, died when aged 4 months. Petra's mother had a history of drug abuse and 'related criminal charges' (ibid.: 97). Case 9 involves the death of an adolescent killed by a car while running away from residential care. Nicholas (case 10) died after three fractures had led to three previous hospital visits. There is no mention of other violence.

There is one particular section of this part of the report that is particularly relevant to our work (ibid.: 97–100). Information given to protective services, it is noted, tends to be minimised and this minimisation is not confined to anonymous referrers and Family Court cases. In one case cited, the personality of a referring health worker is said to have been used as an excuse for minimising the seriousness of the case. The report quotes from the file:

'. . . the "local [protective services] assessment of one of the health workers was that she finds 'child protection' issues in everything and tends to 'cry wolf'. As a consequence, her assessments are discounted as they were in this case . . ." In fact, this particular health worker was not involved with the family . . ..' (Ibid.: 97)

Inadequate Monitoring of Children at Risk of Assault or Neglect after Referral to Other Agencies

The report states that the majority of cases, after abuse or neglect is confirmed, are referred to other agencies for ongoing services (ibid.: 108). Although the policy of protective services was to maintain contact after such referrals, in most cases there was little contact.

Issues in the early investigation of unexpected child deaths

This discussion of minimisation, we suggest, is related to the final issue discussed in the report. The need for thorough death scene investigations and a full understanding of the child's clinical and social history is stressed. In some cases, the report states, no social history was given to the forensic pathologists, or the history that was provided was itself 'minimised' (ibid.: 120). The report emphasises the importance of such an approach, stating that the post-mortem results will determine the extent to which the death is investigated. Three cases are cited as examples in the report: two were classified as SIDS deaths, while the third was so classified early in the investigation even though all three had been re-ported to protective services in the weeks leading up to the death. The report states that:

> '. . . there may be a tendency for some professionals to uncritically accept alternative explanations given by caregivers and to minimise indicators of suspicion.' (Ibid.: 121).

FATAL CHILD ASSAULT AND NEGLECT IN THE USA

We now turn our attention to the report of the US Advisory Board on Child Abuse and Neglect (USABCAN 1995) entitled *A Nation's Shame*. The report, which is based on a two-year study of child fatalities, is divided into four chapters and we will briefly summarise the discussion that is relevant to our study.

The first chapter attempts to define the scope and nature of the problem of fatal assault and neglect. The report draws attention to the apparent lack of interest in the problem, contrasting responses to the research efforts made to understand child deaths by gunshots, polio, car accident and measles, and the subsequent prevention efforts. Early in this first chapter, it is stressed that men cause the majority of physical assault fatalities. The child's birth father, step-father or mother's boyfriend are said to be the most common perpetrators of fatal assault and/or neglect. The report states that mothers are most commonly held responsible for child deaths by neglect but urges caution in the interpretation of such findings:

> '. . . the supposition that the female is generally responsible can lead to unfair assignment of blame when a mother is held accountable even when the father was the parent in charge of the child. Clearly these findings demonstrate a serious need for rethinking the design of prevention and treatment strategies that now focus primarily on females.' (Ibid.: 13–14)

The report states that there has been no clear indication of a set of personality factors that identify parents who are extremely abusive or neglectful but refers to professionals who state:

> '. . . that many parents involved in fatal abuse and neglect are substance abusers with histories of child or spousal abuse or other violence.' (Ibid.: 14)

According to the report, the fact that there is little solid data on these issues is a feature of the lack of breadth in recording that is undertaken in these areas.

The need for research into serious non-fatal assault and/or neglect can be drawn from the emphasis the report places on evidence that death caused by assault is often 'a matter of chance' (ibid.: 15).

> 'One of the most alarming outcomes of life-threatening abuse and neglect by parents is the legacy of damaged and disabled children alive today who survived medical emergencies that would have killed other children.' (Ibid.: 16–17)

The report draws the conclusion that 'luck plays a major role' in deciding which children survive and which children die (ibid.: 17).

Deaths by assault and neglect are said to be 'drastically underreported' because of poor investigative procedures and inadequate sharing of information between agencies and investigators (ibid.: 19). The information available on the subject in the USA is said to be incomplete, with data collection flawed. Strategies for improving the collection of data, including expanded research efforts are outlined in the report.

Chapter 2 in the USABCAN report sets out to address issues of shared responsibility, stressing that in many cases there is a lack of accountability. The practices of mandated reporters are examined, and cases are quoted where professionals are described as seeking to protect those who have fatally assaulted a child (ibid.: 41). Much of this chapter is devoted to identifying weaknesses in training in many of the disciplines involved, and the possibility that cases of fatal assault and neglect may be categorised as SIDS deaths is also raised. Obstacles to prosecution in cases of child homicide are also examined, with the suggestion that some of the basic procedures used for the prosecution of sex crimes against children are not utilised in child deaths caused by familial assault. Recommendations include expanded training for all workers (including doctors), joint criminal investigations, multidisciplinary teams in hospitals, mandatory autopsies in unexpected child deaths and better evidence gathering.

The third chapter in the report focuses on the need for a nationwide system of teams that review child deaths. Child death review teams are seen as an important source for understanding contributory factors in child assault and neglect deaths, including better profiles of individual perpetrators. Increased prosecution rates for child homicides have also been reported as a result of the establishment of teams that subject such deaths to closer scrutiny. The report describes some of these teams, including what is called 'state of the art' teams that have been proved to function effectively (ibid.: 87–90). Strategies for overcoming obstacles are discussed and the importance of helping surviving siblings and other relatives is stressed.

Chapter 4 in the US report comes closest to identifying the issues at the heart of our research. Early in the chapter, the inadequacy of services and decision-making is emphasised. It is asserted that close to one in three families where assault, abuse or neglect is substantiated receive no help (ibid.: 110). Controversial issues surrounding family preservation programmes, including the aim of saving money on foster care and inappropriate and indiscriminate use of family preservation services, are also reviewed. Questionable placements of children who have been maltreated, with extended family members, are also challenged.

The section on preventing fatalities is especially relevant. The report asks 'who is at fault' when a child dies:

> '. . . the unfortunate answer must be: usually, no one person or agency is at fault. The difficult truth is that, except in obvious cases of imminent danger, no individual has the understanding or scientific tools needed to foresee serious abuse or neglect that causes the death of a child.' (Ibid.: 121)

The report emphasises that deaths caused by assault and neglect are a 'low base-rate' phenomenon with about 2000 deaths out of some 1.9 million reports in the USA (ibid.: 121–122). It is possible, however, to examine the serious cases of assault and neglect because these do not comprise such a 'low base-rate' occurrence. The report states that more than 140 000 children are severely injured with 18 000 being permanently damaged.

The report repeats the assertion that no consistent set of personality characteristics has been discovered that will predict who will cause severe injury or death. Many parents, however, are said to:

'. . . stand out because of behavioral, emotional, and cognitive difficulties; histories of other violence; involvement in substance abuse; and highly negative views of themselves and their children.' (Ibid.: 123)

The connections between domestic violence and fatal assault of children is examined:

'. . . some experts argue that domestic violence is the *single major precursor* to child abuse and neglect fatalities . . . Child protection professionals rarely identify, report, or intervene to stop or prevent domestic violence.' (Ibid.: 124; emphasis in original)

The report quotes verbal testimony that stresses that almost half of the mothers of assaulted children are themselves subject to violence:

'Children not only become covictims, but . . . they mimic abusive behavior. . . . Many women may be discouraged from reporting spousal abuse or related risks to their children for fear that they could lose custody of the children.' (Ibid.: 124)

The result, the report suggests, may be that:

'. . . many prevention programs are directed to single mothers who, in fact, do not play the dominant role in child abuse and neglect fatalities, and may themselves be victimized by the males in their lives.' (Ibid.: 124)

The report acknowledges that there is 'no easy way to reach fathers, male companions, or stepfathers' (ibid.: 134).

In the concluding section of this chapter, one of the recommendations addresses possible prevention programmes that specifically address men. Specific strategies are necessary, the report suggests, in order to overcome the deficits caused by the focus of programmes on women. These must not only involve men but 'alert women to the potential role of men in abuse', and programmes should address all forms of family violence (ibid.: 142). These strategies can include (ibid.: 142–143):

- parent 'mentoring' that involves fathers at baby's birth;
- hospital-based education of new fathers . . .;

- preventive education programs for prison-based males . . .;
- domestic violence programs that recognise that adults who abuse a spouse or partner are also at high risk of abusing a child; and,
- school programs . . . to educate children about male roles in parenting.

Other factors and proposals are, of course, discussed in this US report, and many of these are very important, including expedited termination of parental rights, broad public prevention campaigns, and a broader array of primary prevention programmes. We have drawn attention to those that bear on our research. The US report at least draws attention to the coexistence of child abuse and domestic violence and, to a far lesser extent, the possible coexistence of child assault and other forms of violence. While the report also emphasises the various ways of minimising assault and/or neglect, and even the fact that child deaths caused by assault and neglect may be misdiagnosed or excused, the major contribution of violence in all its forms to the failure of child protection systems is not recognised. The US report is not alone in this significant failure.

CHILD DEATHS IN THE UK: BEYOND BLAME

Reder, Duncan and Gray (1993) undertook a review of 35 child death inquiry reports, published in the UK between 1973 and 1989. The cases were reappraised using systems theory in order to discover any new lessons that could be learned from the children's deaths. Reder and colleagues (1993: 33) state that, using a systems approach, these:

> '. . . events are most usefully understood in terms of their participation within a network of inter-related events. In practice, attempts are made to understand how historical and contextual factors influence an individual's current relationships and behaviour.'

Reder and his colleagues assert that this re-examination of child deaths was undertaken from a 'non-blaming perspective'. Their work is widely cited in reviews of child deaths (for example, in the Australian child deaths reports examined above) and for this reason alone an analysis of their work is essential.

In the final chapter of their book they consider the practice implications of their work and divide their recommendations into six sections.

The Work Setting

Reder and his fellow authors start by stressing that child protection workers carry out their jobs in a 'complex, fluctuating, emotive and stressful' environment (ibid.: 122). Resources are subject to political pressure and little value is openly placed on child protection work. Protective workers are 'readily criticised but rarely praised', with much practice described as 'defensive' (ibid.: 122). The authors argue that much could be learned from the business world where investment in staff is seen as paying dividends. Child protection workers are seen as needing greater support and the implementation of practices and systems that reduce stress, continuing education, regular supervision and the opportunity to reflect upon practice and case issues are seen as some of the essential features of such a system.

Assessment

Reder and colleagues divide the lessons for assessment into three subsections. The first, the assessment of immediate risk, commences with Greenland's (1987) high-risk checklist. They critically analyse such checklists, arguing that the advantages include assistance in organising protective workers' assessments, but also suggest that the disadvantages include those of constraining thinking and their routine or thoughtless application. They propose that an 'interactional model' of assessing immediate risk is more useful, with factors needing to be assessed 'within and between families and networks' (Reder et al. 1993: 125).

Reder and colleagues highlight a number of issues that can increase the risk to the child. These include a crisis in the caregivers' relationship, the child being regarded as property, excessive workloads for key workers, and 'closure' in the child protection-family relationship:

> 'This was manifested as withdrawal from contact with outsiders, recurrent flight or disguised compliance. Furthermore, in the face of such closure, renewed efforts by professionals to take a controlling stance had the potential to escalate further the risk to the child.' (Ibid.: 33)

(The term 'disguised compliance' is potentially confusing. The caregivers are, in fact, disguising their *lack* of compliance in such cases.)

Reder and his colleagues suggest that warning signals of 'impending crisis and fatal assault' could be perceived in some cases, 'although the association only became clear in retrospect' (ibid.: 126). Referring to the work of Greenland (1987) and Korbin (1989), they suggest that acknowledgement on the part of caregivers that the child has been injured, or that relationships are troublesome, should not be viewed positively as lessened risk because of openness, but as warning signs that the situation is deteriorating.

The paragraphs on assessing parenting draw on the interactional factors outlined in Reder and Lucey (1991). This framework emphasises the relationship with the child, how the parents view their roles as parents, as well as influences in the family and the world external to the family. Reder and colleagues' reappraisal of child deaths suggests the need to assess care issues, for example, pre- and post-natal care, the failure to attend appointments, and unresolved dependency needs.

Working Together

The importance of communication and liaison with other professionals is the focus of this part of the concluding chapter. Reder and colleagues stress that the relationship factors are as crucial as the organisational procedures that are set in place. They focus on case conferences as the example of the functioning of the networks, again underlining that it is the group dynamics of such meetings that may impede effectiveness. The role of the person chairing the conference is seen as crucial, as is preparation on the part of participants.

Intervention

Reder and his colleagues see intervention as building upon the preceding phases of assessment and case conference. Again, while practical support is seen as important, intervention must address the relationship problems that underpin the assault and/or neglect of the child. Protective workers must assume control in their relationships with the parents, on occasions introducing an 'authoritative and controlling posture' (Reder et al. 1993: 131). Their review of the fatal cases suggests that assault of the child can be accompanied by a withdrawal or 'closure' on the part of parents, with the child killed in a number of cases where an 'episode of closure' was occurring (ibid.: 131).

Reder and colleagues, however, acknowledge the problem of prediction, and admit that no clues were found to assist in predicting whether closure was likely to be fatal:

'. . . if there is a history of previous abuse within a household, professionals should assume that the child's life may be in danger once that family begins to close off from the network.' (Ibid.: 131)

If access to the home is denied, or if the child is withdrawn from nursery placement or school, the child should be assumed to be at risk and other workers involved in the case should be contacted. The full complexity of the task of child protection is revealed in the following paragraphs. Reder and colleagues describe 'another perplexing theme':

'Not only was it impossible to predict which episode of closure might end in the child's death but it was not possible to anticipate how the family would react to mounting control from outside.' (Ibid.: 131)

Any intervention must be 'authoritative and decisive', for taking 'a little control may be more dangerous than none at all.' The relationship between worker and client is touched upon here. The shift to a 'confronting stance' from a relationship of 'partnership', it is acknowledged, may pose dilemmas for the protective worker (ibid.: 132).

Education and Research

The heading for this part of the final chapter is entitled 'Implications for training and research'. (We are on record as stressing the need for education rather than 'training' in the field of child protection, given the complex nature of the work (Goddard & Carew 1989).) Reder and colleagues stress that interdisciplinary education is potentially as full of conflict as interdisciplinary practice. The relationship facets of child protection work are again emphasised, as is the use of personal authority. The importance of supervision, case conferences and research are also stressed. The chapter closes with a sixth section, an examination of the implications of the study for future inquiries.

Missing Violence

Violence apart from child assault and/or neglect is not entirely missing from the recommendations outlined in this concluding chapter. Indeed, 'escalating violence' in the parental relationship (Reder et al. 1993: 125) and 'repeated violence to partners' (ibid.: 127) are mentioned in passing under the sections dealing with assessment of immediate risk and assessment of parenting. The subject of violent relationships is addressed, but again only briefly, earlier in the chapter on families and it is worth examining Reder's work in some detail (ibid.: 43–45).

The discussion follows on from a slightly lengthier section on unmet dependency needs. This section on violent relationships occupies a mere four paragraphs and comprises little more than a listing of the caregivers' 'proneness to violence' (ibid.: 43). Even so, the violence identified is quite extraordinary in its extent and seriousness and merits close examination. The four paragraphs deal with previous physical assault and/or neglect of other children, violence between caregivers, attempts to punish those seen as a threat, and episodes of rage due to frustration. We have combined these to provide a summary (Table 3.1).

There are a number of important observations on this material. Firstly, these high levels of violence reported by Reder and his colleagues (1993: 43–45) are barely noted in the concluding chapter. This is of great significance since much of the focus of that chapter is on the need to be 'authoritative and decisive' and to take a 'confronting stance' (ibid.: 132). This section on taking control of 'potentially fatal' circumstances neglects to mention that the violence towards others, recorded earlier by the authors, may be a significant obstacle to this way of working.

Secondly, the brief summary of violence presented by Reder and his colleagues (1993: 43–45) minimises the violence present in these families. The magnitude of family violence is, to some extent, noted in the brief pen portraits or case summaries that make up the appendix to the book (ibid.: 138–176). The case of Graham Bagnall serves as an example. This child is not mentioned in the section on violent relationships (see Table 3.1), even though in the case summary (ibid.: 142–143) Graham's father is described as having 'a history of violence and psychiatric hospital admissions'.

Thirdly, and even more importantly, there is considerable evidence that the violence that was occurring in some families – violence that is described in the original child death inquiry reports – is also significantly reduced in the book. The case of Susan Auckland highlights this surprising finding. In the section on violent relationships, Reder and his colleagues (1993: 44) provide the following information on violence in the Auckland family:

> 'Susan Aukland's [sic] father had been imprisoned for killing his first daughter aged 9 weeks and he scalded his next child so badly that he required two months hospitalisation'.

The section on assessment process includes more detail on the case, although it is used as an illustration of the failure to connect the information

Table 3.1 Violence in the families where fatal child assault occurred (drawn from Reder, Duncan & Gray 1993: 43–45)

Susan Auckland's father	Imprisoned for killing his first daughter, aged 9 weeks and scalded severely his next child, resulting in two month's hospitalisation.
Doreen Aston's mother	Admitted to smothering her first baby.
Tyra Henry's father	Charged with serious assault on the couple's first child, resulting in intellectual disability and blindness; convicted of actual bodily harm to adults; and, violent to Tyra's mother.
Stephen Menheniott's father	Imprisoned for neglect of first two children; imprisoned for ill-treating his next two children; described as an 'aggressive psychopath' and had beaten up a number of his sons, and daughter's boyfriends.
Gemma Hartwell's father	Imprisoned for assaulting his 3-week-old daughter; imprisoned for assault on his second wife's daughter (aged 2½ years) from a previous marriage.
Maria Mehmedagi's father	Convicted of actual bodily harm to Maria.
Lester Chapman's mother	Previously had a miscarriage after she was assaulted by a male friend; and assaulted by Lester's father after revealing that she had commenced divorce proceedings.
Lucie Gate's mother	Beaten up by her boyfriend whom she was hoping to marry.
Kimberley Carlile's mother	She had two previous marriages with violent men.
Richard Clark's mother	Her first husband was killed in a brawl. She stabbed Richard's father and was charged with attempted murder.
Richard Fraser's father	He was twice gaoled for violence, once for assaulting a woman police officer who returned Richard to hospital after he and the child's step-mother forcibly removed him; and, for assaulting the step-mother when she threatened to leave him. The social worker undertook 'low profile' visits because she feared violence.
Anonymous mother	A history of violence and assault on a social worker.
David Naseby's father	Assaulted nursing staff.
Carly Taylor's mother	Assaulted staff in hostel.
Darryn Clarke's step-father	Assaulted a police officer.
Jason Caesar's mother	Assaulted a police officer.
Maria Colwell's step-father	Threatened violence to a visiting educational welfare officer.
Heidi Koseda's step-father	Had a violent outburst in hospital when he banged his head against a wall.
Shirley Woodcock's father	Created a disturbance on the post-natal ward when he discovered that his wife had discharged herself.
Charlene Salt's father	Insisted on taking the mother and baby home hours after the birth and later refused to allow mother to visit Charlene in hospital alone.
Simon Peacock's father	Angrily demanded mother's and baby's discharge from hospital.

available to the past history of the family, not as an examination of violence. This material refers to the father as an 'irresponsible psychopath'. It notes that mother left home because of 'her husband's cruelty', and the shift of blame from father to mother for the first child's death (ibid.: 85–86). The killing of this earlier child by father is also referred to in a section on 'dependency conflicts' (ibid: 54).

The case summary provided in the Appendix is as follows:

> 'John Aukland [sic] was chronically ill throughout his life, often off work, and described as having a nervous disposition. He was prone to drink excessively and be violent, whilst his wife, Barbara Aukland, was seen by others as incompetent. Their marriage was characterised by frequent arguments, separations and reconciliations. John killed their first child, Marianne, and was found guilty of manslaughter with diminished responsibility and imprisoned for eighteen months. Social services were first involved to help with John Roy who was a low-birth-weight baby but later because of family violence. When Barbara finally left John she took Susan with her but was persuaded to let Susan eventually return to her father's care. Once settled in London, Barbara made efforts to get her children back but after a night of drinking John Aukland fatally assaulted Susan. He was sentenced to five years' imprisonment for her manslaughter.' (Reder et al. 1993: 141–142).

As Reder and colleagues note, it is interesting that the report of the inquiry into Susan Auckland's death is entitled *Report of the committee of inquiry into the provision and co-ordination of services to the family of John George Auckland* (HMSO 1975). The violence that is recorded in this report is extensive. John Auckland, Susan's father who killed Susan and another child, is described as 'inclined to be violent especially after drink', and displaying 'no evidence of remorse or grief or responsibility' for the two killings (HMSO 1975: 13). Barbara Auckland, Susan's mother, was 'beaten' and 'intimidated' by her husband (ibid.: 13).

John Auckland also assaulted his own parents, according to this Inquiry report (ibid.: 14). He is described as 'becoming violent' when his wife 'displeased him' (ibid.: 20), involved 'in a fight within his family' (ibid.: 19), and when he killed his first daughter he also assaulted his wife (ibid.: 22). He is described as admitting 'vindictive outbursts for at least the last 18 months of their marriage' and as having an 'aggressive–sadistic trait in his personality' (ibid.: 22). In 1970, he criminally assaulted his father, mother and sister (ibid.: 32, 39) and is described as blaming his wife for the killing of the first child (Ibid.: 34). In 1971, he is described as in an 'extremely poor state' after being involved in a fight in town (ibid.: 35). It is also very interesting to note that the child care officer visited the family but never saw the father.

In 1971, a psychiatrist described the father as a 'plausible hysterical psychopathic personality' and 'calm, composed, off-hand and indifferent in the manner of an irresponsible psychopath'. The death of the first child is now described as due to a 'blackout' when he dropped her (ibid.: 48). By 1972 the first child's death is described as '? battered baby' (ibid.: 52). Later in the year, the police were called when he 'turned his wife, his parents, and his sisters out into the street'. The next day, Barbara Auckland was seen with 'some marks on her face' which were attributed to her 'having fallen against an ironing board during the scuffle' (ibid.: 54). In 1974, Barbara Auckland left home with Susan because 'her husband was drinking heavily and beating her' and asked for her address to be kept secret as 'she was afraid of her husband' (ibid.: 63–64). Social workers returned Susan to her father, who later killed her.

This pervasive atmosphere of violence, created by a man described in the Report as a 'psychopathic personality', is ignored in the recommendations of the Inquiry, although there is a paragraph devoted to 'Funds for training wives' (ibid.: 92). The totality of violence is also largely ignored in the book by Reder and colleagues (1993), even though it is clear that the recommendations that refer to taking control of cases, referred to above, might be difficult in a case where such violence is so prevalent. It also needs to be stressed that the violence outlined in some detail in the Inquiry Report merely summarises the information that was available to the Inquiry, information gleaned from reports and witnesses. Other violence, it is safe to assume, may not have come to the attention of those involved in the child's welfare.

Closer examination of other child death inquiry reports reveals a similar reluctance on the part of those reviewing child deaths to confront violence. One further example will suffice. Darryn Clarke's mother reported that she was beaten by Charles Courtney, Darryn's step-father (*The report of the committee of inquiry into the actions of the authorities and agenices relating to Darryn James Clarke* (HMSO 1979: 5)). It was also reported that Charles Courtney threatened 'to pull her teeth out with a pair of pliers' (HMSO 1979: 23). This violence is completely ignored in Reder and colleagues' summary of violent relationships (1993: 43–45). Reder and colleagues (1993: 44) report that Charles Courtney assaulted a police officer, but according to the Inquiry Report, the conviction is described as resulting from 'running over a police officer' (HMSO 1979: 16).

BEYOND BLAME AND BEYOND EXPLANATION

We noted in the introduction to this chapter that this was not an exhaustive study of child deaths. What we have attempted to do is provide a detailed analysis of some of the material available in three countries, Australia, the UK and the USA and to review the explanations given for the fatalities.

There are other reviews of child deaths from familial assault and neglect in which the findings are remarkably similar. A recent study commissioned by the Welsh Office in the UK has generally arrived at similar conclusions. Sanders, Colton and Roberts (1999: 261) identify seven themes in professional intervention: assessment; inter-agency communication; the numbers of professionals involved; responsibility; the role of doctors; training for medical staff; and parental choice. It is this last theme that concerns the authors; the section is brief (four lines) and entitled 'Parents Given Too Much "Choice"?':

> '. . . there is evidence that the rejection of certain elements of support packages by a number of parents, and their subsequent withdrawal, undoubtedly led to an increased level of risk for their children. This begs the question as to whether or not some parents were afforded too much "choice" with regard to accepting or declining support . . .' (Sanders et al. 1999: 263)

This theme is also given a paragraph in the discussion at the end of the paper where the authors reflect on the balance of 'partnership' and 'closure'. The issue of partnership and attempting to find intervention methods that are less 'intrusive' is also reviewed (Sanders et al. 1999: 266). The work of Reder and colleagues (1993) and the concept of 'terminal closure' is cited. The conclusions drawn from such discussions give us cause for concern. Sanders and colleagues (1999: 266) state that: '. . . the interagency procedures seem to be appropriate and the problem now is to find ways to ensure that staff adhere to them'.

Many other assumptions are made in these retrospective views of child deaths. As Lyon and de Cruz (1993: 29) suggest, in their critique of the Jasmine Beckford report (LBB 1985), there are repeated assumptions that the child protection worker is only working on the case examined and that she is well resourced. Lyon and de Cruz (1993: 29) propose that the inevitable conclusion is that there is a 'simple' answer to most of the problems that protective workers face.

It is our contention that there are two fundamental flaws in the material available to these child death inquiries. Firstly, by their very nature, such exercises are methodologically flawed. Much of the material they have analysed was drawn from records that were produced for very different purposes. This problem can only be overcome, as the US report states, by a greater devotion to research into serious abuse. The second problem with the material, we suggest, is that in general the studies from all three countries have not closely examined the connection between the assault, abuse and/or neglect of children and other family and broader violence. Even where such connections have been noted, as in the US report, no attempt has been made to examine the possible effects of such violence on the relationship between the protective worker and the family. Until these factors are closely scrutinised, some child deaths will remain beyond explanation.

The following chapter examines further aspects of the failure to protect children after protective service intervention.

4

THE FAILURE TO PROTECT: REPEATED ABUSE

INTRODUCTION

A major deficit in child protection research has been the dearth of studies that examine what happens to children who are referred to protective services. Farmer and Owen (1995: 21) make the point in the introduction to their research:

> 'Research and practice developments in child protection . . . have, tended to concentrate on "entry" processes, such as the identification and investigation of children at risk. Little attention has been paid to the crucial question of what makes subsequent professional action effective.'

While there is a quite extensive literature on child deaths (as we have seen in Chapter 3), there has been surprisingly little research into the effectiveness of child protection intervention. One clear measure of success is whether assault, abuse or neglect ceases after child protection intervention. Protection of the child from further harm must feature largely in any assessment of effectiveness.

Rates of repeat assault, abuse and/or neglect vary widely in the research literature. An early British study found that 60% of children known to a protection agency were further harmed (Skinner & Castle 1969) while an American study placed the rate at 66.8% (Herrenkohl, Herrenkohl, Egolf & Seech 1979). It is likely that these early studies examined a more severely assaulted population of children than would be found in an all-inclusive study of abuse today.

MESSAGES FROM RESEARCH

Recent British research – *Child protection: Messages from research* (HMSO 1995) – investigated the issue of further assault, abuse and neglect and summarised some of the findings, suggesting that between a quarter and a third of children were 're-abused' after the child protection intervention (ibid.: 42). The caution noted above, that studies may approach the same problem from different perspectives, is relevant here:

> 'Each research study set its own parameters and considered particular outcomes for particular people, which were measured in particular ways. These peculiarities need to be borne in mind when considering the evidence.' (Ibid.: 41)

Child protection: Messages from research provides the following summary. Cleaver and Freeman's study found that 26% of children were re-abused in the two years following contact with protective services. Farmer and Owen (1995: 280) found that 25% of children had been re-abused or subject to further neglect, while other children had been left 'without any safeguards'; in total, 30% of children had not been protected by intervention. Thoburn and colleagues found that 20% of children had been abused or were suspected of having been re-abused within six months (cited in HMSO 1995).

Where children were registered as being physically abused, Gibbons and colleagues found that, after 10 years, 20% had been physically re-abused and 5% had been sexually assaulted, with much of the abuse occurring within two years of registration (HMSO 1995: 43). A study by a team at the University of Oxford by Sharland and colleagues, however, found that 43% of sexual abuse cases were still 'unsafe' after nine months (ibid.: 43).

Child protection: Messages from research argues that the extent to which children are protected is but one of three outcome measures that are important, the other two being the effects of the abuse on the children, and the effects of child protection intervention on the families (ibid.: 41–44). The effects of the abuse on the children will be clearly linked in major ways to whether or not the children were protected from re-abuse. We have some concerns about the comments on the re-abuse of children in this summary report. While the report (ibid.: 44) states that:

> 'The conclusion that between a quarter and a third of the children studied were re-abused is disquieting but concern is tempered somewhat by the low incidence of severe maltreatment.'

the definition of serious abuse is, we suggest, a cause for disquiet:

> 'Some comfort can be gained from the fact that rates for serious abuse were
> very much lower. None of the cases in the Cleaver and Freeman study (and
> just 2% in Thoburn and colleagues') required medical treatment.' (Ibid.: 43)

This appears to us to be a very narrow definition of serious abuse upon
which to base a judgement of effectiveness. Nevertheless, the concluding
sentences are particularly relevant to our research:

> '. . . those risks that did occur were varied and not necessarily a repetition of
> previous experience. Children who had been physically abused were some-
> times abused sexually or emotionally and vice versa, or else, another child
> in the family could become a victim or a new perpetrator could emerge.'
> (Ibid.: 43)

We present our findings on this issue towards the end of this chapter.

Child Protection Failings Revisited

Leaving aside the question of what constitutes serious re-abuse and serious
further neglect, it is clear that there is cause for concern about many children
after they have been referred to child protection. Many of the suggested
causes for these failings have been referred to in the previous chapter and
need not be 'revisited' here. There are, however, other analyses.

Nearly 20 years ago, for example, Dingwall, Eekelaar and Murray (1983)
suggested that social workers function under a 'rule of optimism'. The
most favourable interpretation is put on parental behaviour and anything
that may conflict with this is discounted or redefined. Workers believe
that parents love and care for their children unless there is substantial
evidence to the contrary. There is:

> '. . . an injunction to front line workers to interpret the available "facts" as
> evidence that parents are honest, competent and caring, unless an ex-
> haustive inquiry into their motivation renders this impossible. If parental
> failure is established these same facts can be read in a quite different
> fashion.' (Dingwall et al. 1983: 78)

How can Protection be Provided? More Messages

Child protection: Messages from research suggests that in spite of the
'peculiarities' of the research reports, all of the studies 'identified five

pre-conditions of effective practice to protect children' (HMSO 1995: 45). It is
said that if these pre-conditions 'prevail' outcomes for the children who have
been abused will be better. The pre-conditions are said to be (ibid.: 43):

'– sensitive and informed professional/client relationships
– an appropriate balance of power between participants
– a wide perspective on child protection
– effective supervision and training of social workers
– services which enhance children's general quality of life.'

The social worker–client relationship is the subject of our next chapter
and supervision is reviewed in Chapter 10. It is important, however, to
note that it is possible to draw other messages from the UK research.
Taking Farmer and Owen's study as an example, they provide three
dimensions of outcome. They place, correctly in our view, protection
from harm as the first dimension, enhancement of the child's welfare as
the second, and meeting the needs of the *parents* (our emphasis) as the
third. They indicate, therefore, that the parents' needs are not necessarily
synonymous with those of the family.

Farmer and Owen (1995: 281) ask how protection of the children in their
study was achieved. They assert that 70% (31 children) had been protected. However, this was achieved for 14 children (nearly half) by the
child being placed elsewhere or the perpetrator being removed from the
home for the whole follow-up period. Furthermore, another nine children
had been separated for at least part of the time:

'It is interesting to note that only eight out of the 31 children who were
protected had remained safe while living with the abusing parent for the
entire follow-up period.' (Farmer & Owen 1995: 281)

Four of those eight children who had been 'protected' were described as
subject to neglect or emotional abuse.

While a detailed analysis of all the research evidence in Farmer and
Owen's study is not possible here, on the second dimension, enhancement of the children's welfare, 68% (30 children) had made gains in the
follow-up period. Once again, 16 of these children 'had moved to a more
beneficial family environment' (ibid.: 282). While not all these children
were separated from their parents (for example, two families were moved
into residential family services) and some placements were not satisfac-
tory, it is clear that one message from Farmer and Owen's research is that,
in a significant number of cases, separation of the child from the abusive
setting led to protection.

THE FAILURE TO PROTECT: FINDINGS FROM THE VICTORIAN STUDY

The authors' Victorian study examined the protection files of a random sample of 50 children who were on, or had been on, a legal protection order. Thus, by implication, these children had been subjected to severe assault, abuse and/or neglect. Additional information about this research can be found in the Appendix.

Abuse Experienced by the Children before and after Referral to Protective Services

The case files were used to compare abuse occurring before and after the first referral to protective services. Abuse was deemed present where the file recorded that an abusive event had occurred or where the worker had a strongly held belief that the event had occurred. The events were categorised into the widely accepted categories of abuse: physical assault, sexual abuse, psychological abuse and neglect.

The extent of abuse experienced by each child

The files recorded that most of the children (44 of the 50 children) had experienced more than one category of abuse before referral to protective services. Five children had experienced all four categories of abuse, 20 children had experienced three categories of abuse and 19 children two categories of abuse (Table 4.1).

Subsequent to the first referral to protective services, 43 children were recorded as being subject to more than one category of abuse: 12 children

Table 4.1 Recorded categories of abuse experienced by the children in the Victorian study, before and after referral to protective services (N = 50)

Number of categories of abuse*	No. of children experiencing abuse	
	Prior to referral	After referral
4	5	12
3	20	20
2	19	11
1	6	5
Nil	0	2

* The categories of abuse are: physical assault, sexual abuse, psychological abuse and neglect.

had experienced all four categories of abuse, 20 children three categories of abuse and 11 children two categories. Five children were recorded as being subjected to psychological abuse only. For two children, no abuse was recorded after referral.

When interpreting this data, the following information needs to be kept in mind. Firstly, the information is as recorded in the child's protection file. Thus, it may be an underestimation of the true levels of assault, abuse and/ or neglect to which the child had been subjected. Secondly, the findings presented above only reveal that at least one event within the category of abuse was recorded after referral. No consideration here is given to the frequency of occurrence or the severity of abuse. It is possible that although the child was re-assaulted, re-abused and/or neglected again after referral, this behaviour may have subsequently stopped and contact with protective services may have prevented further harm. It is also possible that some abuse may not have been detected until after referral.

The frequency of occurrence of each category of abuse

The following categories of abuse were recorded *before referral* to protective services (Figure 4.1):

- 48 children had experienced psychological abuse;
- 38 children had experienced physical assault;

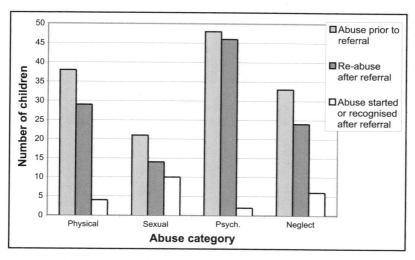

Figure 4.1 Number of children in the Victorian study, who experienced each category of abuse prior to referral, who experienced re-abuse after referral, and for whom the abuse started or was recognised after referral ($N = 50$).

- 33 children had experienced neglect; and
- 21 children had experienced sexual abuse.

The following categories of abuse were recorded *after referral* to protective services (Figure 4.1):

- 46 children experienced a repeat of psychological abuse;
- 29 children experienced a repeat of physical assault;
- 24 children experienced a repeat of neglect; and
- 14 children experienced a repeat of sexual abuse.

In addition, the case files of some children recorded the following categories of abuse commencing, or being recognised, *after referral*:

- 2 children had a new record of psychological abuse;
- 4 children had a new record of physical assault;
- 6 children had a new record of neglect; and
- 10 children had a new record of sexual abuse.

Interpretation of this information must take account of the qualifications given above.

The frequency of repeat episodes within each of the categories

The findings presented above reveal only that the child experienced at least one abusive event before and/or after referral. There is no indication of frequency. However, the files record that over half of those children who experienced a repeat episode of abuse after referral experienced this on two or more occasions. Neglect proved to be the most intractable.

- Of the 24 children who were recorded as experiencing neglect after referral, 21 experienced at least two episodes, and 11 experienced four or more episodes.
- 16 (of 29) children were recorded as being subjected to at least two episodes of repeated physical assault after referral to protective services.
- Of the 14 children who experienced a repeat episode of sexual abuse, 8 experienced at least two repeat episodes.
- 27 of the 46 children who experienced psychological abuse after referral were recorded as being subjected to at least two episodes of psychological abuse after referral to protective services.

Again, this information needs to be viewed with extreme caution as a number of possibly abusive events were excluded due to a lack of recorded detail. Moreover, information was missing in some files. Thus, these figures are likely to be an underestimation of the true levels of repeated abuse experienced by the children.

The severity of repeat episodes of abuse within each category

Given that many children apparently continued to experience assault, abuse and/or neglect after the involvement of protective services, the authors sought to ascertain whether there was any change in the severity of child abuse after the involvement of protective services.

The authors documented the exact type of the assault, abuse and/or neglect that was recorded in the files. This was subsequently grouped into like events. Table 4.2 illustrates this in relation to the types of physical assault. For example, before the first referral 15 children were recorded as having experienced 'hitting, punching or kicking (except at the child's head)' and after referral 15 children experienced this form of assault. The Pearson's coefficient of correlation was used to test whether there was any statistical difference between the types of abuse before, and after, involvement of protective services, for the group of children as a whole,

Table 4.2 Physical assault recorded in 50 case files as occurring at least once, before referral to protective services (N = 38 children)[*] and after referral to protective services (N = 33 children)[*]

Type of physical assault	Before referral	After referral
Hitting, punching, kicking, except at head, using a hand or object	15	15
Throwing things at child, pushing, shoving, grabbing	12	12
Hitting the child's head	8	13
Inappropriate administration of medicine or failure to seek medical treatment	7	6
Shaking or being thrown	5	1
Burning, biting, sticking pins in child	3	3
Suffocation, strangulation, attempted drowning	2	2
Being tied-up or physically confined	1	3
Use of knife or other weapon	1	2
Other	5	2
Type not specified in file	1	2

[*] More than one type of physical assault may have been recorded for each child

but no statistical difference was found, and any differences were due to chance variations. Thus, the authors conclude that it would appear that the types of abuse experienced by the children before, and after, referral, were equally severe.

CONCLUSIONS FROM THE STUDY

Given the above case file data, it is apparent that the protection afforded to the more severely abused children was inadequate. These children were not protected from re-abuse. Indeed, many children were re-abused on more than one occasion. Further, the severity of abuse suffered by these children did not appear to be diminished.

It is important to attempt to place these findings in context. As we have noted, direct comparison with other studies is not possible but the rates of re-abuse are higher than those found in *Messages from Research* (HMSO 1995). This may in part be due to the fact that the population of children examined was different, the Victorian study examining more severely abused children. All the children in our study were, or had been, on a legal protection order. This also means that it is likely that the cases were more serious than those studied in *The Last Resort* (Hunt, Macleod & Thomas 1999), where a number of the children who were brought before the courts were not made subject to an order.

The differing results may also be due, in part, to methodological differences. Farmer and Owen (1995) examined outcomes for children after a period of 20 months, whereas in our research some children had had contact with child protection services for a much longer period, the range being from 3 months to 15 years (see Appendix).

A more fundamental difference concerns placement of the child. A significant number of the children in Farmer and Owen's study were separated from the perpetrator for the whole of the follow-up period:

> 'The most important element in protection was *physical separation*. Where children were effectively protected, this result was achieved by total separation from the abuser in 45% of cases.' (Farmer & Owen 1995: 311; emphasis in original)

This total separation did not occur for *any* of the children in the Victorian study.

In the next chapter we begin to explore some of the reasons why child protection failure occurs.

5

THE SOCIAL WORKER–CLIENT RELATIONSHIP: FROM LOVE TO VIOLENCE AND BEYOND

INTRODUCTION

In the preceding chapter we noted that *Child protection: Messages from research* suggested that the first 'pre-condition' of 'effective practice' in child protection (HMSO 1995: 45) was 'sensitive and informed professional/client relationships' (ibid.: 43). At the end of the chapter we provided a summary of the abuse and neglect experienced by the children in our Victorian study. It is clear that many of the children in our study were not protected from further abuse and neglect. In this chapter we review the social worker–client relationship, a key element in all social work practice.

We briefly review the origins of social work before examining some descriptions of social worker–client interaction in the 1950s through to the 1970s. Our objective is to contextualise some of the child abuse inquiry findings described in Chapter 3. Some of the early work in child protection is briefly analysed and efforts are made to locate the violence that is missing from much of the writing. The issues of partnership, power, stress and violence are reviewed.

THE HISTORICAL FOUNDATIONS

Social work is a relatively recent activity and, perhaps because of its infancy, its historical development is rarely acknowledged. This is unfortunate, as a historical perspective can assist us in understanding what

Hindmarsh (1992) describes as the 'tensions and dichotomies' that all social workers experience in their day-to-day practice.

There are dangers in a historical approach, however, as Timms and Timms (1977) point out. History in social work writing tends to be used to 'vindicate the present':

> '. . . article after article in the social work journals truncates history by referring briefly to a past in which we rather foolishly did *x*, where as now we (more wisely) do *y*.' (Timms & Timms 1977: 43; emphases in original)

Timms and Timms also suggest another danger: certain interpretations of history 'gain a mastery which is hard to shake' (ibid.: 43), a warning relevant to the analyses of child deaths (see above).

Timms (1962) recognises the importance of reflecting on the history of casework in child care. He writes that there are several reasons for taking into account a historical view. Firstly, it makes 'economic' sense, because many of the problems workers face have been experienced by workers previously. Secondly, from a generic perspective, it is important to recognise the traditions that are common across specialised settings. Finally, the perspective of history teaches us that social work:

> '. . . has in the main developed from the continual confrontation of social workers with people in need of help.' (Timms 1962: 2)

The beginnings of social work practice are usually traced back to the establishment of community organisation societies (COS). These roots, it is suggested, still influence practice today. The fundamental philosophy was that:

> '. . . significant social problems could be modified by changing individuals who experienced those problems.' (Connaway & Gentry 1988: 11)

While some of the earlier religious beliefs have been lost, other assumptions remain:

> 'It was assumed clients would change when helped by a concerned, interested person with whom they could establish a fairly long-term relationship . . . It was assumed the visitor's encouragement, advice and role modeling would result in clients' finding work and solving other problems.' (Connaway & Gentry 1988: 12)

Other writers have also identified COS as providing the foundations of current social work (see, for example, Midwinter 1994). Leat (1975: 21) gives COS a 'central role' in the development of social work and describes the practices of the time as closely related to the prevailing economic and social philosophies. Leat, however, claims that much of the historical analysis is rather oversimplified. There have certainly been increasing attempts to understand the 'ambiguities' and 'tensions' (Clarke 1993: 19) that were present even at that time; and the dilemma posed by balancing care and control was identifiable:

> 'Compassion drove the efforts to provide help and assistance to the "unfortunate". Fear prescribed the limits and conditions to such assistance.' (Clarke 1993: 19)

The methodology of COS was 'built on paradox'. COS claimed that (Humphreys 1995: 173):

> '. . . their representative, after rudimentary training in scientific investigation, would naturally conjure an ambience of cheery kindness while delving unreservedly into the most personal circumstances of the poor.'

The reality was very different, according to Humphreys. There was little time for compassion, the masses of volunteers never materialised, and paid workers were required. A picture of 'caring friendship' was painted over the 'abject deference' that was required from applicants (ibid.: 173).

Other features of these charitable origins of social work also resonate through history. Clarke identifies what he describes as significant features of this early work. These, we suggest are relevant to our work today: the activities took place around the margins of major institutions; these activities were largely carried out by women; and, the work was dominated by middle-class assumptions (Clarke 1993: 9). Leonard (1966) has also described how the work of COS held to views of personal inadequacy. The problem of poverty was defined as 'essentially a problem of character not of circumstance' and there was little stress on the contribution of structural conditions (Leat 1975: 23).

According to Levine and Levine (1992), there were two rival schools of thought in American social work at the end of the nineteenth century. On the one hand, the settlement house movement was working towards social change through a community organisation approach. On the other, the charity organisation society had grown out of the tradition of giving alms. Investigation was seen as necessary to ensure that such charitable donations were not wasted and that those helped were worthy (Levine & Levine 1992: 155).

Another element can be traced in this history of the origins of social work that is also relevant today: the influences that British social work had on the work in the USA and vice versa. Leonard (1966), for example, argues that Americans were quicker to examine the environmental influences on the problems with which they dealt. He also notes the sociological orientation of Richmond (1917) and draws attention to Richmond's stress on the interaction between the family and the environment.

Mary Richmond and Risk Assessment

Richmond (1917: 30) also traces the beginnings of social work back to the London Charity Organisation Society and acknowledges the early struggle between a 'comprehensive method of inquiry and of treatment' and a purely economic one. 'Social reinstatement' was the aim, and the human being was seen as separate from his or her economic circumstances, and thus above the need to regulate relief. The chapter headings of Richmond's text are in themselves a measure of how far social work language has travelled; for example, there are chapters on 'The homeless man – the inebriate' and 'The insane – the feeble-minded'.

Many years before the current emphasis on risk assessment, she provides a chapter on 'The neglected child' which comprises a questionnaire (or checklist) to aid the social caseworker. This was prepared by Brannick for the book and comprises more than 100 questions. Neglect is defined in this questionnaire as: desertion; neglect of medical care; lack of control; exploitation; cruelty, physical injury or abuse; moral neglect; and, chronic dependence (Richmond 1917: 408–410). While some of the terms, as noted above, appear dated, there are many questions that are still relevant to a child protection worker many years later. The section on 'cruelty, physical injury, or abuse', for example, asks:

> '72. Is parental discipline rigid to the point of cruelty? . . . 73. Are the older children permitted to punish or abuse the younger? 74. Do the children show evidence of such abuse or punishments?' (Ibid.: 410)

Careful scrutiny of the questionnaire demonstrates that there are many other concerns that are still with us:

> '94. Is the father so nearly wholly responsible for the neglect that action against him would be more just than the general charge of neglect, which involves the mother?' (Ibid.: 411)

Perhaps views of, and concerns about, children have not changed so dramatically either:

'63. Are the children constantly on the streets and late at night? . . .' (Ibid.: 409)

Much of the philosophy of the text still holds true:

'. . . it should be said with emphasis that there can be no good case work without clear thinking . . .'. (Ibid.: 99)

There is other advice that has been reflected in child death inquiries. She states that it is a serious omission on the part of many agencies that they do not 'individualise each child in the families' (ibid.: 153–154). Richmond particularly stresses the importance of the social worker's relationship with clients, stating that they are more important than the social workers' relationships with other agencies (ibid.: 294).

The Social Worker and the Client

There is another important reason for visiting social work's history and one that is rarely, if ever, remarked upon. A historical view can provide an all-important context for the material to which we commonly refer. The death of Maria Colwell, for example, is included in Reder and colleague's systemic analysis of child deaths (1993). An analysis of that child's death is likely to be deeply flawed if the full context of what was occurring at that time is not explored. An essential part of such an exploration should consider the views that were then held on the social worker–client relationship.

We recognise that there are risks in undertaking a brief historical review of the social worker–client relationship. As we noted above, Timms and Timms (1977: 43) suggest that histories can be written to 'vindicate the present' and that certain interpretations gain an unchallengeable 'mastery' (ibid.: 43). The result, they suggest, can be merely 'bland generalisations' (ibid.: 44). We undertake the following analysis, however, because we believe that there were 'bland generalisations' about the social worker–client relationship at the time of many of the child deaths analysed, and that a fuller understanding may help us to understand the past and the present more clearly.

Having noted in Chapter 3 many of the deficits in child death inquiries in the USA, the UK and Australia, it is necessary to analyse in a little more detail the context of social work practice at the time. One relatively straightforward way of doing this is to examine some of the social work texts that were then in use.

Biestek's book, *The casework relationship*, for example, was very influential in social work schools in the late 1960s and early 1970s. The social worker–client relationship is described as 'the channel of the entire casework process' (Biestek 1957: 4). Although the social workers' relationships with their clients are just 'one species' of all interpersonal relationships, they are described as central. Through the social workers' relationship with the client:

> '. . . flow the mobilization of the capacities of the individual and the mobilization of community resources; through it also flow the skills in interviewing, study, diagnosis, and treatment.' (Biestek 1957: 4)

Biestek traces the development of attempts to describe the client relationship and recognises the analogies:

> 'The casework relationship has been compared to an atmosphere, to flesh and blood, to a bridge, and to an open table. The essence of the relationship has been called an interplay, a mutual emotional exchange, an attitude, a dynamic interaction, a medium, a connection between two persons, a professional meeting, and a mutual process.' (Biestek 1957: 11)

Biestek (1957: 15) at least recognised the 'dynamic interaction of feelings and attitudes' and that they were operating both from client to worker and from worker to client. The response of the worker, however, was seen as 'principally internal'; the worker:

> '. . . wordlessly through his attitude says to the client: "knowing your problem, your strengths and weaknesses, I continue to respect you as a person. I have no interest in judging you innocent or guilty; I want to help you make your own choices and decisions".' (Biestek 1957: 16)

This casework relationship is founded on Biestek's seven principles: individualisation; purposeful expression of feelings; controlled emotional involvement; acceptance; a non-judgemental attitude; client self-determination; and confidentiality. All the principles are seen as interconnected and inseparable. Some conflicts are expressed – for example, those regarding confidentiality – but none is seen as insurmountable. The caseworker, described throughout as male, is expected to balance realism and idealism:

> 'He is expected to be both a firm-footed realist and a clear-eyed idealist . . . As an idealist he sees each client as a precious child of the heavenly Father. As a realist he sees the client as he really is, with attitudes and behavior which perhaps are quite unlike to God's . . . The caseworker hopes that he is, in some small way, an instrument of Divine Providence.' (Biestek 1957: 136–137)

Briar and Miller (1971), another influential work of this time, write of the 'views of man in social work practice' and the 'scientific method'. It is also interesting to note that the index of some eight pages does not mention children. There is, however, a short chapter entitled, 'Who is the client?'. This chapter concludes with an examination of the role of the caseworker who may have, among others, the role of the therapist, enabler and advocate. Among these is the 'aggressive caseworker' who is described as reaching out 'to persons who do not seek his help' (Briar & Miller 1971: 118).

Briar and Miller's book does, however, contain a major critique of the foundations of much casework theory. They argue that the casework literature of the time was flawed, based as it was on the average client as an individual, coming to an agency voluntarily, asking for help with psychological problems (and not for material aid), and undertaking counselling sessions for some period of time (Briar & Miller 1971: 93). This was seen, at least in its American context, as quite revolutionary.

Children do rate a brief mention in Compton and Galaway (1984). The third edition of this book, first published in 1975, acknowledges, for example, that '. . . dependent children, developmentally disabled persons, and aged persons may be victimized and harm themselves . . .' and that self-determination may have to be limited in order to provide protection for such clients (Compton & Galaway 1984: 80). Violence, child abuse, and sexual abuse do not appear in the index.

The chapter on relationships in social work practice provides a brief review of the literature, before examining purpose as an element of relationship, and the development of a relationship. The elements of a social worker–client relationship are said to include concern for the other, commitment and obligation, acceptance and expectation, empathy, authority and power, and genuineness and congruence (ibid.: 228–243). Some attention is also paid to the rational and irrational aspects of helping relationships. Irrational elements of the relationship are described as those elements that carried over into the current relationship from earlier experiences (ibid.: 243). The chapter concludes with an examination of the helping person and his or her qualities: the capacity to be self-aware, creativity, the desire to help, and sensitivity (ibid.: 243–248). Courage is also required and the possibility of threats of violence is briefly acknowledged. Workers must be prepared to face a number of risks:

> '. . . of failing to help, of becoming involved in difficult, emotionally-charged situations that they do not know how to handle, of having their comfortable world and ways of operating upset, of being blamed and

abused, of being constantly involved in the unpredictable, and perhaps of being physically threatened.' (Ibid.: 248)

In her influential work *Social casework: A problem-solving process*, Perlman (1957) identified the components of what she termed the 'casework situation': the person, the problem, the place, the process, the caseworker–client relationship, and the problem-solving work. While the work might be viewed very differently nearly 50 years later, the framework proposed by Perlman is still a useful tool for analysis. The fundamental proposition is still seen as true: the process 'must use relationship as its basic means' (Perlman 1957: 65).

The language, as one might expect, appears dated but the challenges outlined by Perlman are remarkably similar to those faced by the child protection worker today: the relationship between worker and client must be controlled or managed (ibid.: 79). Perlman acknowledges that the worker must manage the feelings that the relationship may cause in the worker (ibid.: 81). From the client's side, however, difficulties are described as being caused by ambivalence, resistance and reluctance. In later work, Perlman revisited the 'helping relationship' in some detail and acknowledged more clearly the difficulties of working with clients that she described as the 'unlikeables' (ibid.: 99). The chapter entitled 'But can you love everybody?' identified some of these less than 'ideal' clients, including 'the surly man who has beaten his baby into unconsciousness' (ibid.: 99). The problems are identified as 'denial', 'projection' and 'distancing'. The 'angry or indignant' client is also identified as using 'antagonism' as a defence:

> 'Antagonism may be expressed by openly hostile words and acts or by stony silence and looks that speak louder than words.' (Ibid.: 115)

This brief review of these texts suggests that there was a slowly developing understanding in the literature of the complexities of the social worker–client relationship.

Child Abuse and Child Protection Intervention: Early Work

In the editorial in the first edition of the *British Journal of Social Work*, Stevenson writes of social work being 'in ferment' (1971: 1) and describes the content of the new journal as being a balance of three kinds of writing: research; description; and reflection and argument. Stevenson draws attention to the address given by Drake to the last UK Children's Officers Conference, published in the journal, as an example of this reflection.

The title 'On change' is prescient. Social workers, Drake writes, are often called upon to intervene on behalf of society against the wishes of parents, to use court orders to remove children, or to refuse parents' applications to return children in care:

> 'Thus he comes into direct conflict with the client, and unable to form any kind of relationship which might be helpful . . . There is an inherent conflict here which the profession has not, as yet, fully faced and certainly not fully worked out . . .' (Drake 1971: 66)

Drake describes these tasks and expectations as placing a heavy burden on social workers who struggle with the same problems as some of their clients, although perhaps to a lesser extent:

> 'All of us have learnt what we know of affection, love, caring and acceptance from our parents, as we have also learned discipline and control. All of us have ambivalent feelings about this.' (Drake 1971: 67)

Drake describes how most clients (by this term she refers to parents) have more significant problems with authority and affection although social workers themselves are not immune. The social workers, as a result, may be 'at odds' either with themselves or with part of society. Social workers will find themselves 'castigated for being too firm, or condemned for being too lenient' (Drake 1971: 67).

Three years later, in her last editorial for the *British Journal of Social Work*, Stevenson (1974), after spending eight weeks reviewing the life and death of Maria Colwell, reflected upon the role of social workers. Stevenson's editorial could not, at the time, reveal much of the case itself but it led her to examine the ambivalence felt by society towards social workers who deal 'in shades of grey where the public looks for black and white' and who are 'brothers in lesser evils' (Stevenson 1974: 2).

Among articles on agoraphobia, school phobia and systems theory, there was little in the *British Journal of Social Work* to assist the social worker working with children who had been subjected to assault, abuse or neglect. A paper by Prins (1975: 297) was an exception. It examined offenders and patients defined as potentially or actually dangerous, and 'an apparent reluctance' to work with them. Although some of the case examples included child murder, the perpetrators had been identified as dangerous, mentally disturbed offenders, and the paper examined the issues from a mental health perspective.

A review of *Australian Social Work* (formerly the *Australian Journal of Social Work*) reveals a similar dearth of papers on child assault, abuse and neglect. Brazier and Carter's article (1969) examines the coordination of services for children in Western Australia. Brazier and Carter state that the mass media have examined the problem of child abuse in some detail, although 'sometimes in a rather sensational climate' (1969: 15). Their paper stresses the importance of the coordination of services while stressing that 'child protection and therapeutic help for the parents are not necessarily incompatible' (Brazier & Carter 1969: 21).

Dawe's paper (1975) some years later, was the next contribution by *Australian Social Work* to the literature on the assault, abuse and neglect of children. Dawe, like Brazier, a senior social worker in a paediatric hospital, draws on the Maria Colwell inquiry in the UK to set the scene for her research. She records a total of 518 cases of 'suspected maltreatment' at the Royal Children's Hospital (Melbourne, Australia) in the years 1967–1974. She cautions that not all cases were identified, while others were not referred but 28 of the children died. Dawe takes a broad approach to the resources needed, including specialist services in the community. She also examines the role of the social worker, stating that she regards counselling and casework as central forms of help required. She suggests that assisting children who have been assaulted, abused and neglected, and their families, requires enormous 'skill, imagination and therapeutic caring' and that no other area of work offers a greater challenge to the social worker (Dawe 1975: 23).

In the USA, where much of the early work on the assault, abuse and neglect of children was undertaken, there was more material for social workers to consult. It is interesting to note, however, that the papers were not always written by social workers. The authors of the early paper on agency cooperation in *Social Casework* were psychiatrists and a researcher (Silver, Dublin & Lourie 1971). The only other paper to deal with the assault, abuse and neglect of children in *Social Casework* published in the early 1970s was also concerned with the multidisciplinary treatment of child abuse and was written by a director of social work, a paediatrician, and a psychiatrist (Barnes, Chabon & Hertzberg 1974).

Surveys of other journals show similar patterns: child abuse and child protection are rarely referred to in the early 1970s. In the USA, the journal *Social Work*, for example, even ran a special issue in 1974 on the future of social work, but the problems associated with protecting children from assault, abuse and neglect were confined to a few paragraphs in over 100 pages (Brieland 1974).

Conclusion: Missing Violence

There was, as we have shown in this review, little to guide the social worker in the 1970s working with the assault, abuse and neglect of children, at a time when inquiries into child deaths were gaining widespread media coverage. There was even less to guide the social worker working with families where threatened and actual violence to the worker occurred. The reality is that, even today, the majority of social work texts make only passing reference to threatened and actual violence to workers.

The relationship with the client is still seen as being 'at the heart of all personal helping', even with those who have serious mental health problems (Vaughan & Badger 1995). Assessment of risk in a few books may now include not only the risk to others, but also the risk to workers. The risk is not always realistically assessed, however. Vaughan and Badger (1995: 95), for example, rather optimistically stress that there should never be:

'. . . a situation when a worker need go alone into a potentially dangerous situation or otherwise knowingly expose themselves to risk.'

The reality of violence, and its impact, is largely missing. Lishman's work on communication, for example, acknowledges that threats of violence have been responsible for changes in reception areas in social services offices, and that home visits may not always be appropriate:

'Violence to social workers is increasing and, if we have any indication that a client is potentially violent, making a home visit alone may be dangerous.' (Lishman 1994: 59)

In contrast to these few sentences, however, empathy, sensitivity, warmth and other qualities identified elsewhere receive detailed consideration.

Text after text places such a burden on those who are expected to create helping relationships. Tossell and Webb (1986: 243–249) claim that their list of the qualities required is not exhaustive. Even so, empathy, love, sensitivity, respectfulness, politeness, the ability to listen, liking people, warmth, naturalness, practical ability, acceptance, tolerance, non-judgemental attitudes, and self-awareness are some of the elements required. It is hardly surprising that Irvine (1979: 155) said, in a slightly different context, that 'this is asking too much of a single human being'.

SOME RECENT WRITING ON CHILD PROTECTION

There has been increased acknowledgement of the difficulties in child protection work in some recent research and writing, particularly in the UK. Farmer and Owen, for example, write of the focus of child protection intervention in their study shifting from the father figure to the mother. They state that, as the attention shifts to the mother, the risks to the child can become obscured; this change of focus 'often also allowed men's violence to their wives or partners to disappear from sight' (Farmer & Owen 1995: 223). In their study, they discovered:

> '. . . that the men who physically abused their children were frequently also violent to their wives, yet it was rare for incidents of domestic violence to be accorded much significance in the management of cases.' (Ibid.: 223)

Farmer and Owen also note that there was concurrent violence in more than half of the physical assault cases:

> 'This was usually a man's violence to a woman, except that in two cases parents were violent to each other, in one case the woman was violent to the man, and in another there was violence amongst the older children and between them and their mother.' (Ibid.: 224)

Farmer and Owen observe that practice appeared to fail to recognise the links between domestic violence and the assault, abuse and neglect of children, in spite of increasing research evidence of the links. They make reference to earlier work at Monash University, Australia and to the links between child abuse and domestic violence.

Farmer and Owen ask why the focus of professional attention was so often deflected away from the abusive father figure and onto the mother. They describe as 'fairly typical' the scenario where, although the father was abusive to the child, emotional support was offered to the mother (ibid.: 225). There is a hint of the difficulties faced by social workers:

> 'In some cases this deflection was assisted by father figures who made sure that they were out during social work visits or who refused to engage in discussions with the worker about the child. In addition, since these father figures were known to be violent men, they could be intimidating to professionals.' (Ibid.: 225)

Farmer and Owen give case examples to bolster their arguments about the shift in focus, but while the violence of the males is emphasised, there is still no analysis of the impact of the violence on the workers. We cite in full one of the cases:

'In another case where the father had physically abused his nine-year-old daughter, Beverley, it was partly the male social worker's strong identification with the father which influenced his perspective. The worker joined the father in viewing the girl as difficult and disobedient and he offered general support to the parents by means of financial and material help, whilst relying on the mother to "protect" the child. Work was not directed at the father's abuse (interpreted as discipline, albeit excessive), nor on child management issues. The worker knew about the father's violence to his wife and that the children witnessed these scenes and were distressed by them. He also took no action when the father later assaulted his son. No protective action was taken until Beverley finally disclosed sexual abuse by her father. She took this step in order to protect her mother from further violence after her mother's arm had been broken by her husband.' (Ibid.: 225)

Given our findings (discussed in Chapter 6) the following paragraph is also of interest:

'In all of these cases the work was directed at the mother, but in the background there was severe and prolonged domestic violence from the men in the families towards the mothers. Since in all the families it was the father figure who presented the risks to the children, the impact of the work with mothers was limited. Two of the mothers attempted suicide during the course of the study, one of them on two occasions.' (Ibid.: 303)

To their credit, Farmer and Owen repeatedly stress the need to examine more closely the links between domestic violence and child abuse, and emphasise that this will lead to more effective interventions (see, for example, Farmer and Owen 1995: 319).

This shift of focus has also been identified in work in Canada by Swift (1995), who suggests that it is part of a process of 'manufacturing bad mothers'. She argues, in a critical analysis of child neglect, that little or no account is taken of the violence that is so often such an important factor in child neglect cases:

'The reality beneath the surface of many of these mothers, however, is that in addition to long-term poverty and resource deprivation, their lives are filled with violence perpetrated by fathers, husbands, and lovers . . .' (Swift 1995: 120)

According to Swift, workers regard such violence as a 'normal feature' of many of their clients' lives (ibid.: 121). This is seen not solely as the mother's problem but rather as an indictment of her ability to care for her child, and she may thus be seen as 'failing to protect' (ibid.: 175).

Child protection: Messages from research (HMSO 1995), a report summarising the Department of Health research in the UK, includes summaries of the research we have analysed above. It is interesting, once again, to note that although the links between assault, abuse and neglect of children and domestic violence were a recurring theme of the Farmer and Owen (1995) study, the issue is barely referred to in the *Messages from research* document. There is, however, as we noted in Chapter 4, considerable focus on the quality of the relationship between the child protection worker and the family. The report states that 'sensitive and informed professional/ client relations' are what is required for 'success' (HMSO 1995: 45). *Messages from research* reviews the terms used ('alliance, empowerment, support and information') and identifies what is required:

> 'An alliance is needed which involves parents and, if possible, children, actively in the investigation, which takes account of their views and incorporates their goals into plans. Failure to achieve this level of co-operation helps to explain why some children remain safe when others do not.' (HMSO 1995: 45)

The burden of establishing this partnership is once again presented as one-sided; 'honesty', 'reliability' and 'clearly presented information' are seen as the keys to achieving 'the right balance of power' (HMSO 1995: 46–47). Yet once again, there is no analysis of how violence might make such an alliance impossible and/or ill-advised.

More Missing Men, and the Missing Effects of Violence

Other writers have identified missing men as a problem in child protection work. O'Hagan (1997) has analysed what he calls 'the problem of engaging men in child protection work'. He proposes that the avoidance of men is not influenced by gender:

> '. . . the majority of front line staff involved in child protection were women, but their male colleagues were no more inclined than they were to meet, engage and assess men encountered during the child protection process.' (O'Hagan 1997: 26)

O'Hagan suggests that both child protection practice and research focus on mothers and tends to ignore the significant men in the households. This avoidance of men has its origins, according to O'Hagan (1997: 33–35), in four main factors.

Firstly, the public and professional perceptions of the roles of men and women have given men only a minor role in child care and development, in spite of their prominence in child abuse statistics and inquiries. Secondly, there is some feminist writing that emphasises hostility towards, and distrust of, men. Thirdly, O'Hagan draws attention to the lack of preparation and 'training' that child protection workers receive about engaging men. Dealing with angry men is one of the areas in which the 'training' of child protection workers is lacking. Finally, O'Hagan (1997: 34) identifies fear of men as a significant factor:

'Social workers avoid men because of anticipated violence or intimidation. Their fears may be based on actual experience, or on the experience of colleagues, or upon an acute awareness of the growing level of violence directed against professional people generally, and child protection professionals in particular.'

O'Hagan suggests that male workers may even be more vulnerable than females because of assumptions that male workers will be less likely to be intimidated. Such assumptions, O'Hagan argues, may compel male workers to conceal their fears.

O'Hagan makes the important point that fear and avoidance of men has been acknowledged in some child abuse inquiry reports. He goes on to claim that no violence was recorded as perpetrated against child protection workers in the reports. As we note in Chapter 9, threatened violence may be as powerful as actual violence in influencing behaviour.

The avoidance of men is also a theme in the work of other authors. The avoidance of men is described by O'Hagan and Dillenburger (1995: 178) as 'a potent and prevalent form of the abuse of women.' They argue that both in order to avoid men and as a consequence of such avoidance, workers:

'. . . invest in the mother a child-protective power and authority which they hope she will be able to exercise over her male partner.' (Ibid.: 143)

Violence against workers is acknowledged. Workers, it is argued, 'rightly . . . believe their work is dangerous' and child protection work 'fuel[s] the anxiety of workers' (ibid.: 145):

'Violent men consistently dominate the 35 inquiry reports produced since 1974, and have, with very few exceptions, been responsible for the deaths of the children in those reports. Many of the mothers of these children were frequently battered by the men.'

O'Hagan and Dillenburger (1995: 145) argue that violent men can induce a 'paralysing effect' on the workers:

'Men who appear cold, arrogant, loud-mouthed, distant, resentful, or who have been convicted for offences of violence . . . are perceived as threatening and dangerous by many childcare workers.'

In spite of these apparently overwhelming obstacles, the child protection worker is still urged by O'Hagan and Dillenburger to practise with real parental participation, or partnership, in mind. The policy of parental participation should be real, without rhetoric, and a principle that should 'pervade the whole process of child protection . . .' (ibid.: 180). Again, the effect of violence on child protection workers appears to be minimised or overlooked. This oversight is the more extraordinary given that the authors list serious attacks on colleagues and report on men murdering their social workers.

Partnership

The issue of partnership between families and child protection workers can be viewed as merely approaching the dilemma of care and control through the use of different language. Indeed, this is tacitly accepted in some of the research. Thoburn and Lewis, for example, in their work on partnership with parents of children who are in need of protection, openly state that it is not possible in all cases to work with parents as partners:

'. . . it may be harmful or even dangerous to the child even to keep an alleged abuser fully informed in the very early stages of an inquiry.' (Thoburn & Lewis 1992: 56)

Thoburn and Lewis's analysis is redolent of the earlier work on the social worker–client relationship that we have cited above:

'. . . if the parents welcome social work help, accept that there is a problem, agree with the social worker about the nature of abuse and degree of harm, and about the way to proceed to improve the situation, it would be difficult for the worker *not* to engage in participatory practice.' (Ibid.: 57; emphasis in original)

Unfortunately, as Goddard and Tucci (1991) note, not all cases are as straightforward. Problems arise for the child protection worker when the situation is more complex, as Thoburn and Lewis (1992: 57) all-too-briefly describe:

'. . . a worker striving very hard to achieve parental involvement may not succeed if parents deny that abuse or neglect has taken place, if parents and social workers disagree about the degree of harm and ways of helping, if parents reject social work involvement (particularly if they have behaved violently towards social workers in the past).'

Thoburn and Lewis identify what we suggest is a major obstacle in child protection work but then, as so many others have done, move on. More than a quarter of the cases in their study were identified as falling into this 'worst scenario' category and yet little advice is offered to the child protection worker. Thoburn and Lewis (1992: 57) pose the question as to whether certain 'types of abuse' make partnerships with the parents harder to achieve. They acknowledge that they have not arrived at an answer, perhaps because they have not examined the context of violence more broadly.

Fleeting glimpses of 'domestic violence' (as violence between caregivers is generally labelled) can be gained in some of the UK research (see, for example, Gibbons, Conroy & Bell 1995). Even where the existence of domestic violence is reported to affect outcome, however, discussion of the association is scant, as in the study by Gibbons and colleagues (1995). There are one or two notable exceptions. The work of Farmer and Owen, for example, identifies domestic violence as 'the missing link' (1995: 223).

The Question of Power

One of the problems in O'Hagan and Dillenburger's (1995) work is the overall acceptance of a virtually unidirectional imbalance of power in spite of much evidence to the contrary. O'Hagan and Dillenburger reflect on the power imbalances in child protection work but, although they recognise that workers themselves may be subject to a range of abusive power relationships (for example, sexual harassment), the power is generally said to reside in the worker:

'Often, the worker has control and the client is being controlled . . . the worker usually has the power to control her, tell her what to do, and decide on the consequences of her behaviour.' (O'Hagan & Dillenburger 1995: 96)

Healy (1998) approaches the problem from a somewhat different perspective. Child protection work involves the use of statutory powers and yet many workers are unprepared for this; they are 'so aware' of the dangers inherent in such power 'that they are paralysed from using this power in a productive way' (ibid.: 906). In addition, workers have such difficulty in 'making negative judgements about the families with whom they work' that they can tend to minimise the extent of assault, abuse and neglect (ibid.: 906). Healy's work is particularly useful in rejecting the view that power is 'singular or unilateral' (ibid.: 907). Drawing on the work of Foucault, Healy (1998: 907)

> '. . . warns against a divide between workers as powerful and service users as powerless and alerts us to the multiple relations of power that may exist within the practice context.'

Healy (1998: 911) argues forcefully that participation in child protection does not require:

> '. . . a retreat from assessment and judgement but, rather, clarity and openness about one's judgements and the processes by which they were reached.'

There is a wide literature for social workers to refer to when they want to empower people and work in partnership with those in need (see, for example, Smale, Tuson, Biehal & Marsh 1993). Wilding (1982), in his review of power in the social welfare arena, also calls for partnership between professionals, their clients and society. There are, however, insightful exceptions. Braye and Preston-Shoot (1995) acknowledge both the complexity of social service provision and the need for the empowerment of front-line workers and management if quality services are to be delivered.

Other writers identify absence of power or powerlessness as a major stress factor (see below) in front-line workers. Edelwich and Brodsky, in their 1980 study of burn-out in the helping professions, emphasise that burn-out is caused by a sense of powerlessness in workers. Such descriptions of front-line workers experiencing feelings of powerlessness do not entirely sit comfortably with the more usual analyses. Baldwin and Harrison (1994), for example, in a critique of calls for partnership, refer to the view that social workers are extremely powerful while families and children are powerless.

None of this should be read as an attempt to deny that social workers have a great deal of power. As Hugman (1991) describes, those in the caring professions have a number of powers, which include the power to define the client and the power to control the client. Power, according to Hugman (1991: 1), is an 'integral aspect' of the working lives of social workers and others in the helping professions. In some circumstances, however, that power may not be enough to protect the child who has been abused.

Stress

There are also an increasing number of texts devoted to stress in social work practice. Some of these books tend to pay a little more attention to violence. Thompson, Murphy and Stradling (1994), for example, deal with violence and aggression as part of the social work task. They argue that such violence against social workers can be seen as reflecting the stress to which clients are subjected, which in turn is related to broader social issues such as male power, racial oppression and class exploitation. Social work services are delivered mainly by women, and while Thompson and colleagues acknowledge research that tends to suggest that male workers may be more vulnerable, their own research suggests that women reported a greater impact from threats of violence. At the end of the day, they emphasise that 'the reasons underlying the act of violence may make little difference to how the practitioner experiences the assault' (ibid.: 98).

Thompson and colleagues report that dealing with physically violent and verbally abusive clients were the tasks that ranked first and second in terms of potential stress in a series of 29 social work tasks. They cite the Jones, Fletcher and Ibbetson (1991) study, which proposes that the more a worker suffers threats of violence, the more he or she will perceive the threat of assault as a major stress factor:

> 'This would appear to contradict the common assumption that working in an area of high violence is likely to give some degree of immunity from the stress of such incidents. On the contrary . . . exposure to threats of violence diminishes our ability to ignore the problem.' (Thompson et al. 1994: 99)

It is interesting to note that the study by Jones et al. found that more than 1 in 10 social workers had been assaulted in the preceding two years. Thompson and his colleagues also propose that, regardless of whether violence is becoming more common or is simply increasingly seen as a problem, the stress that is caused remains high. An increased awareness of the problem, on the other hand, does not necessarily mean that there is greater awareness of the impact on workers. Thompson and colleagues quote Hopkins:

> 'There is little reference in the current 'violence training' to the impact of threatening behaviour. It focuses on the management of violence. The fact that another human being may hate you so much that they want to kill you, is something that you are expected to accept and live with.' (Hopkins 1987 cited in Thompson et al. 1994: 101)

Not all the literature on stress in social work directly addresses the issue of violence, however. Gibson, McGrath and Reid (1989), for example, in an examination, conducted by postal survey, of stressors in social work practice, found that the emotional demands of clients and imposing controls on clients were the fourth and fifth most stressful aspects of social workers' practice. Direct contact with social work clients ranked eighth in 13 sources of stress identified. All three of these stressors could be masking some of the impact of violence, which apparently was not addressed directly.

Davies, in the introduction to his edited volume *Stress in Social Work*, captures some of the core elements of the problem:

> 'Social work deals in chaos, poverty, hatred, child abuse, violence, criminality, delinquency, depression, debilitation, incompetence, vulnerability, deprivation and mental ill-health. Many of its clients will have experienced and internalised a sense of being dehumanised through being treated as "inanimate" objects of violence or sexual abuse.' (Davies 1998: 17)

As a consequence of attempting to respond as a professional, the worker 'is open to be traumatised to some degree on a daily basis' (Davies 1998: 17). Both workers and organisations seek to defend themselves, according to Davies. The workers often feel that they should be able to cope, and be able to prevent the cases with which they deal having any impact on them. As a result they too can become 'dehumanised'. The organisations also 'create structures for protecting themselves' (Davies 1998: 17) against the demands placed on them by society and, in turn, by politicians, as we described in Chapter 2.

Managers also have to meet financial restrictions and Davies suggests that many organisations, in an attempt to give at least an impression of being in control, repeatedly reorganise themselves (ibid.: 18) – another recurrent theme in child death inquiries. Davies also draws attention to the way in which many social work organisations are structured to place much of the day-to-day responsibility (or, we would add, the blame for anything that goes wrong) onto the most junior, front-line workers (ibid.: 18). All these factors, Davies contends, add to the stresses of an extremely difficult job:

> '. . . a social worker who having listened to the disclosure of a child's horrendous abuse by a parent has to "allow" the abuse to continue while he or she contends with the [legislation] (which leans towards the rights of the parents), attempts to gather watertight evidence for a court and experience [sic] the frustration of the child who withdraws the "disclosure" because . . . it seems safer to do so.' (Ibid.: 12)

Davies also acknowledges some of the effects on workers who have to handle several complex cases at once. Workers find that the only way to cope in such circumstances is to distance themselves from the anxieties that are unavoidable:

> 'The anxiety that is intolerable to the conscious mind, in becoming unconscious, takes with it the capacity to think properly, the capacity to "remember" what once might have felt engraved on the mind. "Mistakes" may be made, a tragedy may occur, enquiries and press coverage enhance an already paranoid situation.' (Ibid.: 12–13)

Inflexible guidelines, and supervision that is concerned with complying with procedures, confirm for workers that this is a 'mechanistic' means of escape from intolerable pressures (ibid.: 13).

While Davies' book highlights many of the factors we believe are important in examining the failure of child protection services to protect children who had been assaulted, abused and neglected, there are few references to violence. Wilmot, in his chapter 'Public pressure: private stress', includes a brief section on hostility and violence. Wilmot argues that it is not surprising that there is 'reluctance' on the part of some parents and caregivers to work with the child protection worker who represents the statutory power of child protection services. Wilmot (1998: 24) suggests that this 'reluctance will sometimes develop into hostility directed to the worker'. Parents and caregivers can gather a group of supporters, including politicians, and this can make the child protection worker feel 'under siege' (Wilmot 1998: 24). Such hostility may in turn develop into threatened or actual violence. Wilmot cites the study on support by Balloch and colleagues (1995). In another chapter, Kutek (1998) also draws on this study. Even in this major and insightful text on stress in social work there is only passing reference to the potential for violence in the relationships between social workers and their clients.

Violence

The literature on violence against social workers, and violence against other health, education and welfare workers, has also developed in recent years. In this section we review some of the significant texts. Brown, Bute and Ford (1986) chose the title *Social Workers at Risk* for their book. They begin by attempting to identify the size of the problem and report on the 1979 Wessex study. This study used mail questionnaires to 560 staff working in personal services, and the results (there were 338 responses) are divided into violence experienced by workers in day centres, residential settings and fieldwork. In short, 50% of day centre, 45% of residential and 22% of fieldwork staff reported that they had been assaulted in the previous three years in their current posts. Brown and colleagues note that this measurement may have been influenced by the fact that 35% of field workers had been in their current positions for less than a year. The levels of threatened violence (43% of fieldworkers, 45% residential workers and 39% of day care workers) were similar, as was the response indicating those who had had possessions damaged by clients (12% of fieldworkers compared to 13% of all respondents) (Brown et al. 1986: 4).

The authors analysed the data for possible precipitating factors and conclude that the 'deprivation of personal liberty', involving the removal of children, and the compulsory admission to hospital of clients with psychiatric problems, were the two groups to most commonly feature in worker assaults. They recommend that further research be undertaken in these particular areas of work (Brown et al. 1986: 22).

Brown and colleague's book contains chapters on understanding violence, recognising potential violence, preventing violence, what to do if violence occurs, and what support workers should expect. The concluding chapters deal with reducing risk and the training implications of their findings. They suggest that fear and guilt are common responses to violence or threats of violence.

In her foreword to Bowie's (1989) Australian text on violence in the human services, Raphael emphasises the importance of violence against workers in helping professions. She states that violence:

> '. . . is often denied in its significance to human service workers and organisations, as indeed it has been in the past for most of those who have been victims of violence.' (Bowie 1989: ix)

Bowie (1989: 15) examines some of the possible reasons for what he terms 'increasing violence' against human service workers; these include: difficult economic circumstances and unemployment; the increasingly investigatory roles of some workers; the deinstitutionalisation of people with significant problems; and increasingly problematic children and young people in residential care.

Bowie also examines theoretical approaches to the causes of violence and attempts to predict violence. He identifies fear, frustration, manipulation and intimidation as the major motives for violent behaviour. There is a chapter devoted to communication strategies and a lengthy chapter on the principles of physical intervention. This latter chapter is extensively illustrated with photographs demonstrating how to defend against bear hugs, choking attacks, grabs and holds (see Bowie, 1989: 51–83).

A further chapter, entitled 'The hurting helper', examines the effects of violence on human service workers by reviewing the literature on responses to such trauma among the general population. He seeks to explain responses to trauma by drawing on Post Traumatic Stress Disorder, and reviews immediate, short-term and long-term reactions to violence (see Bowie 1989: 107–121). Bowie devotes a chapter to depression, one possible response to victimisation, and suggests that further work needs to be undertaken on the links between stress, depression and burn-out in workers. The final major chapter in the book (pp. 135–147) deals with agency responses to and responsibilities for workers who have been traumatised by violence.

There are also recent books that include violence against social workers which take a broad view on violence in families and in society. Lupton and Gillespie (1994), for example, include a chapter on violence against social services staff (Hester 1994). Hester's work is relevant to ours in that she identifies the context:

> '. . . violence to social services staff who, as professionals, may be in a position of relative power over their clients, but who, especially as female workers, may also be in a less powerful position in relation to colleagues and possibly male clients.' (Hester 1994: 154)

Rowett's (1986) UK study is one of the most extensive studies examining violence against social workers. He undertook a three-stage approach: a national postal survey; a questionnaire sent to all of the social workers in one social services department; and structured interviews with 120 social workers – 60 assaulted workers matched with 60 who had apparently not been assaulted. Rowett's (1986) study defined violence narrowly. He states that it 'refers only to physical (including sexual) violence' (ibid.: 30). Threats, for example, and any other type of psychological violence were excluded.

All three stages of the study provide rich data. Two-thirds of the social services departments did not respond to stage one, the national survey:

> 'It would not seem unreasonable to construe this as a general indication that physical assault on social work staff is not viewed by senior management as an area of particular concern . . ..' (Rowett 1986: 47)

Residential social workers were more likely to be assaulted than their colleagues in the field (this finding was confirmed in the second stage).

Senior managers in the survey considered that the level of violence was 'acceptably low' (ibid.: 43).

The second stage found a far higher rate of assault than would have been predicted from stage one. While most social workers are women, most of those assaulted were men. The structured interviews carried out in the third stage revealed yet more violence:

> 'From the interviews with the 60 assaulted . . . it was apparent that the incidence rate for assault indicated by the scanning survey and the national survey represented only a small proportion of the actual number of assaults . . .' (Ibid.: 125)

Hester (1994), from a gender perspective, criticises the narrow definition of violence in Rowett's study, suggesting that violence against women workers may be obscured. We would like briefly to draw attention to the language used in the study. The degree of physical harm described by the social workers was classified as minor, moderate and severe. Minor assault was said to comprise 'bruising, cuts, lacerations, sprains, etc.' (Rowett 1986: 59), a description we would suggest shows remarkable tolerance towards the violence described.

In common with most research on violence against social workers, there is little consideration of the effects of violence on social work practice:

> '. . . substantial numbers . . . reported that the incident had changed their approach to practice and/or left them feeling less confident in their ability to do their job . . . assaulted [social workers] tended to spend less time with clients . . . held fewer child care cases, and were more inclined to take precautions with clients who they thought might be violent.' (Rowett 1986: 130)

There is a great deal in this one brief paragraph to suggest that violence may have major implications for practice, although Rowett does not elaborate. Another finding of particular relevance, both to our study and to theoretical approaches to violence, concerns the backgrounds of the clients who attacked the social workers. Almost one-half had a least one conviction, with one-quarter having a conviction for violence. In addition, more than one-third had had at least one admission to a psychiatric hospital (Rowett 1986).

Saunders' (1987) study of violence in Surrey in the UK was notable for using a much broader definition of violence: physical assault; physical abuse; sexual assault; sexual abuse; threats; property theft or damage; and other forms of assault or abuse. The research also surveyed a broader range of staff. The study comprised a scanning questionnaire sent to 4,055 staff, a second questionnaire to the 263 who indicated they were willing to answer more questions, and a personal interview with a small sample of 20 staff selected to cover different types of violence and work situations.

Saunders (1987) also found that residential workers are more likely to experience violence and that men are more likely to experience violence in any setting. The inclusion of sexual abuse and sexual violence found that the risks to men and women in the categories were equal.

The Nova study also briefly examined how the violence or threats of violence against social workers had affected their practice (Norris 1990). Some reported that violence had 'de-skilled' them while some had become more analytical of their styles of practice. Further analysis provided by Norris (1990: 45) includes:

'One reply indicated that a person had made a conscious decision to avoid risks by retreating into a more administrative role. Others decided to be less confrontational with their clients, although a much smaller number believed they had in consequence adopted a new tough and direct style.'

Other changes include not visiting dangerous clients alone, or at all, more checking of clients' previous histories, and recording all incidents of violence no matter how small.

Norris's study comprised the 38 replies to 100 questionnaires sent out to residential staff and field social workers. No definition of violence was used in the questionnaire although Norris did specifically state in the accompanying letter that sexual assault should be considered as an act of violence. Of those responding, 23 had been attacked and all 38 had been threatened. When asked about frequency, the responses averaged 2.6 successful or attempted attacks and 2.6 threats of harm per worker in the preceding year.

One of the fundamental questions asked by a number of authors is whether the incidence of violence against social workers is increasing (see, for example, Norris 1990). If there has been a substantial increase, it might account for the dearth of literature on the subject until recently. In his book examining violence against health care professionals, including social workers, Wykes (1994) suggests that, apart from increasing violence in the community, there have been changes in the way services are provided that may have increased both the likelihood that assaults will occur, and the severity of those assaults. There are more people working in the community, visiting people in their homes. There are more people with more legal powers over their clients' actions, including the powers to remove children or to admit people to a psychiatric hospital. Wykes also suggests that many of those working in the caring professions are stressed. Stress, he argues, might reduce the workers' perception and communication skills in threatening situations.

Parton and Small (1989) locate concern about violence towards social workers in a broader dynamic of dangerousness in child abuse. They review some of the research and describe three features that they describe as particularly important. The first, they suggest, is that violence against social workers is generally seen as 'a hidden phenomenon, one that has been newly *discovered*' (1989: 129, emphasis in original) as opposed to a new phenomenon. The second shows that certain situations involve a greater risk. The third, and more speculative, is that workers find it difficult to take effective action to avoid attack. Parton and Small link this both to management failure and to confusion around care and control issues.

Parton and Small (1989: 135) claim that the reason why violence against social workers has become an issue:

> '. . . is not because their clients are inherently more dangerous or that social workers are less able to cope, but because the number of potentially violent situations they face has increased.'

Unfortunately, their recommendations about voluntary admissions to care and participatory work with parents merely repeat the obvious:

> 'Working through a mutually agreed relationship where both parties – client and social worker – can negotiate the nature of the problems and what to do about them is also the way most social workers prefer to go about their task.' (Ibid.: 137)

The vital questions remain unanswered. Should we expect a female social worker, for example, to form a 'mutually agreed relationship' with a man who is violent towards his partner and his child, and others?

CONCLUSION

This review of the social worker–client relationship demonstrates a number of shortcomings in the available literature, including the child protection literature. It also reveals, we suggest, a failure to make important connections or to resolve certain contradictions. While some studies may cite the importance of domestic violence, others acknowledge the failure to engage men. The need for partnership is proposed in spite of violence, and there is still a tendency to view all or most power residing with the social worker. In short, the child protection literature has still to incorporate messages from other research that front-line workers are subject to a great deal of violence and stress. The following chapter presents some of the findings from our Victorian child protection study.

6

PROTECTIVE WORKERS IN THE FIRING LINE: THE TRUE EXTENT OF VIOLENCE AND ISOLATION

INTRODUCTION

In this chapter we present some of the findings from the Victorian child protection study that describe some of the obstacles faced by child protection workers. We begin by describing the intimidation and violence experienced by the workers in our sample. We also examine other violence in addition to child abuse occurring concurrently. Information was also collected on violence and other criminal activity in the community. Factors contributing to possible isolation of the child protection workers are also described.

Before presenting these findings, it is interesting to observe that some early research into child abuse and neglect examined some of these issues. The characteristics of parents who abused or neglected their children were examined in an attempt to differentiate them from parents who did not abuse or neglect. While many of these studies suffered from definitional and sampling problems, they proposed that there were personality problems in parents who abused or neglected their children (see, for example, Birrell & Birrell 1968, Kempe & Kempe 1978, Smith, Honigsberger & Smith 1973, Young 1964). Although many of these studies were conducted prior to the general recognition of various forms of family violence, they often examined criminal activity outside the home. This issue has since received little attention. The studies suggest a strong association between parental assault, abuse and/or neglect, and criminal activity outside the home. The figures again vary widely. For example, Smith, Hanson and Noble (1973) found that 29% of fathers who assaulted a child were also involved in criminal activity outside the home, while 65% of fathers who murdered their child were so involved (Scott 1973). The first section deals with violence directed at child protection workers. Other criminal activity perpetrated on non-family members is examined later in this chapter.

VIOLENCE TO PROTECTIVE WORKERS IN THE VICTORIAN CHILD PROTECTION STUDY

The 50 randomly selected protective workers were asked how often they had experienced a range of intimidating and violent acts *in the six-month period prior to the research interview*:

- 23 workers had received at least one death threat;
- 9 workers had been assaulted by a person;
- 4 workers had been assaulted by a person using an object;
- 7 workers had been subject to attempted assault;
- 3 workers had been threatened with a knife or other sharp object;
- 5 workers had been threatened with a gun;
- 22 workers had been threatened with assault;
- 13 workers had been threatened with an implement;
- 32 workers had received intimidating phone calls;
- 28 workers reported that complaints had been made about them to supervisors, the media or politicians;
- 18 workers had received threats to their families, friends or colleagues;
- 5 workers had been threatened with sexual assault; and
- 14 workers described other major intimidation, including blocking exits, grabbing car keys, etc.

The full findings can be seen in Table 6.1.

The assaults on workers included pushing and shoving, punching, hair pulling, hitting with a chair, coffee table and ash-tray, and an attempted strangulation. The attempted assaults included one incident where the assailant had attempted to hit the interviewed worker with an object, but missed, instead hitting and injuring a co-worker. In total, the workers reported 68 episodes of threatened assault. Reported death threats often related to bomb threats, or statements like, 'I'll have you shot and you'll never be seen again.'

Table 6.1 Intimidation and/or violence the workers reported experiencing in the six months prior to the time of the Victorian study (*N* = 49)*

Type of intimidation/violence	Frequency			
	Once	Some-times	Often or always	Total
Complaints				
Threatened with suing†	11	14	4	29
Threat of complaint to superiors/ politicians/press	12	18	12	42
Complained to superiors/politicians/ press	13	15	0	28
Verbal abuse				
Called names/sworn at for a short time	3	19	21	43
Yelled/screamed at for a short time	8	22	17	47
Extensive verbal aggression	10	17	11	38
Minor intimidation				
Intimidating phone calls	11	17	4	32
Obscene phone calls	3	1	1	5
Mockery/humiliation/sarcasm/ 'put-downs'	6	22	6	34
Glaring/threatening looks	3	25	15	43
Major intimidation				
Threats to worker's property	7	2	0	9
Behaviour such as blocking exits, grabbing car keys, following	7	6	1	14
Threats to worker's family/friends/ colleagues	9	8	1	18
Sexual threats to worker	3	2	0	5
Threat of physical assault				
Threatened with being assaulted	8	14	0	22
Threatened with an implement (other than with a sharp object or gun)	5	8	0	13
Attempted physical assault	6	1	0	7
Physical assault				
Assaulted by a person	5	4‡	0	9
Assaulted by a person using an implement	3‡	0	0	3
Sexual assault	0	0	0	0
A potential life-threatening situation				
Threatened with a knife or sharp object	2	1	0	3
Threatened with a gun	3	2	0	5
Death threat	9	14	0	23

* One worker was not seeing clients due to stress.
† One worker was taken to court.
‡ In one incident a worker was assaulted by a person using both his hands and an object.

The workers spoke of other forms of intimidating and violent acts which had occurred in the same six months but which were not adequately covered in the research questionnaire. Examples of these included:

- the use of dogs to intimidate;
- car passengers travelling with the worker who grabbed and turned the steering wheel in an attempt to hit other cars;
- a person informed the worker that he knew the registration number of the worker's car;
- a worker had to run from a house to avoid an incident;
- workers' cars in the office car-park were scratched and damaged, radios stolen and rubbish thrown around;
- a worker felt intimidated when she was shown a collection of toy guns;
- some workers were fearful about the safety of their own children; two were told that the person knew where their children went to school; and
- some workers were concerned that a vexatious protection notification would be made on their own children.

Violence and/or intimidation were sometimes directed at child protection workers in general. For example, one large child protection office received multiple bomb threats. One of the authors was present when one of these threats was made and the office evacuated.

The following case illustrates how one person may engage in different forms of intimidation, which may also be extended to other professionals and community members.

'The case file records a warning given by a relative of the child to protective services. The relative alleged that the father was dangerous to workers, the child and his family. He said that the father had 72 pages of documentation on various people and had intimated that court action and media disclosure was his intention. The father claimed he was "going to get" certain protective workers. He also named specific workers, demanding that they be stood down and have psychiatric evaluations. The father claimed a particular worker had "acted improperly", "made false allegations", "refused to discuss information with him" and was "a sexual pervert". The father was alleged to have said that if the child is removed from his care, he will "fix up" protective services. The relative reported that the father had also made threats against local people, police and the child's teachers.'

Some workers were keen to talk about incidents which occurred *prior* to the six months covered in the questionnaire. Some examples of these are:

'The worker spoke of how she had been locked in a house with a drunk person who threw a coffee table and other objects at her, and was also "lunging" at her. The worker had to call the police to come and let her out.' (Worker 2160)

'The worker was threatened with a knife and metal pole on one occasion and physically pushed in front of traffic outside a court on another occasion.' (Worker 2260)

'The worker spoke of an incident that had occurred four years ago, when children in her caseload were held at knifepoint and the perpetrator wanted to swap the children for the worker.' (Worker 3310)

'The worker spoke of the time she and a colleague ran out of a house when a psychiatrically ill person was going to hit them. The worker told of how her bag got caught in the door as she ran.' (Worker 6190)

'The worker said that a person with a history of physical assault of police "lost-it" and threatened to hit the worker when she was on a home visit, about 12 months prior to the interview.' (Worker 2440)

'The worker said she was threatened two years ago (when removing children) by a woman who said that her partner had a gun and would use it. A gun was found by police when the partner's accommodation was raided in relation to a drug dealing matter.' (Worker 2450)

'The worker said she had a "gun turned on me once".' (Worker 6220)

'The worker told how a person holding bamboo skewers had threatened her with assault.' (Worker 6620)

'The worker said that a man, who had previously made a number of death threats, had held a knife to a foster mother's throat and said he was going to "get the worker". This person was subsequently seen hovering around the protective services office. The worker said that on one of these occasions the security doors were undergoing maintenance and the repairer kept propping the doors open, not understanding the situation. The worker said she was scared. She called the police who escorted her from the office to her car. She was taken off the case, but subsequently became a supervisor for the next worker responsible for the case.' (Worker 8210)

Concurrent Violence in the Families

While information about violence towards family members, other than the subject child, did not appear to be routinely recorded in the protection files, the Victorian child protection study collated the information that was available. For the study, the term 'family' was defined as those who formed the primary child-raising household for the subject child, including those extended relatives who appeared to be significant to the child. Table 6.2 summarises the number of families where at least one incident of each particular category of family violence, apart from assault and/or neglect to the child, was recorded in the case files. The table does not show frequency of the event, only that the violence type occurred at least once, perpetrated by at least one family member. Table 6.2 shows that at least half of the families had at least one incident of each of four types of family violence recorded. Verbal aggression between adults significant to the child was the most common form of violence (41 or 82% of the families), with personal violence also common (39 or 78% of the families). At least half the families had experienced an incident of physical and psychological violence between adults significant to the child (31 or 62% and 25 or 50% respectively). Sixteen children perpetrated at least one incident of intimidation or violence to a carer.

Table 6.2 Family violence/intimidation (where at least one event is) recorded in the case files examined for the Victorian study ($N = 50$)

Type of violence	No. of families
Verbal aggression between adults significant to the child	41
Violence to self such as suicide threat or attempt, or severe drug abuse	39
Physical aggression between adults significant to the child	31
Psychological aggression between adults significant to the child such as intimidation or exploitation	25
Violence between siblings or children in the household	21
Violence by the child towards a significant adult (verbal, physical, psychological or sexual)	16
Sexual aggression between adults significant to the child	5

There was also a record, in 13 files, of police attending the household on at least one occasion because of domestic violence. This information on violence in the family is likely to be an underestimation of the true situation, as violence, other than assault and/or neglect of the child, tended not to be investigated by the child protection worker and was not necessarily recorded in the casefile. In addition, a number of children, particularly adolescents, had left home and their files contained few details about their families.

Table 6.3 shows the specific forms of intimidation and violence, other than assault and/or neglect of the child, recorded in the files. Again, frequency is not shown, just the recording of at least one incident of the event. The files recorded a wide range of family violence. Physical assault was the most common (39 or 78% of families), followed by verbal aggression (36 or 72% of families), and drunken or drugged behaviour (in 22 or 44% of families). Of the more severe forms of violence, sexual violence

Table 6.3 Types of family violence/intimidation (where at least one event is) recorded in the case files examined for the Victorian study (*N* = 50)

Type of violence	No. of families
Throwing, hitting, pushing, shoving, punching, kicking, biting	39
Loud verbal arguments, yelling, insults	36
Offensive drunken or drugged behaviour	22
Threat of suicide	19
Suicide attempt	17
Sexual violence	17
Threatening with a weapon or sharp object (other than terror tactics)	13
Violent threats or terror tactics	13
Damage to shared living environment	11
Violence against self (other than suicide threats and attempts)	11
Threats to kill	9
Aggression, of a type not specified in the file	9
Intimidation such as sending letters, warnings, stares or following	8
Domestic violence, of a type not specified in file	5
Damaging manipulation	4
Attempt to kill	4
Successful suicide	4
Psychological violence not specified elsewhere	3
Kidnap	1
Arson	1

was present in a third of the families (17), threatening with a weapon in over a quarter of families (13) and attempted murder in four families.

The natural mother was recorded as the most frequent perpetrator of at least one incident of family violence, other than assault and/or neglect of the child. However, she was also the most likely to remain in the child's household and was often the most common family member seen by the worker. Although many males in a parental role did not remain in the household, they appeared to be the perpetrators of a disproportionate level of violence. The natural father was recorded as the perpetrator in 27 families, the first male partner (who was not the child's father) in 23 families, a second male partner in 7 families and subsequent male partners in 3 families.

The subject child was implicated in a lot of violence in the household, as he or she was the perpetrator of at least one recorded incident of violence in 22 families. At times, this made the removal of the children very difficult. One case file reported the following:

> ' "The transport of the children turned out to be more problematic than anticipated. Police acted gently and quietly and were able to get the children

away from mother and into the back of the car. The children were by now screaming hysterically. We left immediately hoping that once out of sight of home and mother, the children would quieten. Alas, after two kilometres they were beginning to demolish the car and throwing bits of the car out of the window. With both workers in the front and one driving this was difficult to control. When stopped for traffic, one child wound down the window and opened the door and fled. We immediately turned off the main road and stopped and held the other child who was screaming abuse hysterically." '

Only one family had no members recorded as being involved in intimidation or violence, apart from assault and/or neglect of the child. The average number of members of each family who had a record of at least one incidence of family violence, was just under five (4.86). Examples of recorded family violence can be seen as follows:

'A case file recorded the following violence between family members: verbal and physical aggression, intimidation, threats to kill and burn down the house, sexual aggression and destruction of possessions.'

'A case file recorded that a male partner had assaulted and threatened to kill the female caregiver.'

'Multiple instances of sexual abuse between family members over three generations were recorded in another case file.'

'In a case file the worker reported that during a home visit the subject child, a 15-year-old male, threatened to kill an uncle with a large knife.'

The extent of intimidation, violence and criminal activity by members of the abusive family towards the community

It was also possible that a worker may have been traumatised by knowledge of violent and criminal activities in the community. Table 6.4 shows the number of families from the case file sample which were recorded as being involved in at least one episode of the listed criminal activities, outside the family. The event was noted where the family member was either the perpetrator or the victim of the crime, the latter occurring on only five occasions.

Many families were recorded as being involved in a range of criminal activities, including petty crime such as street crime (18 families) and associating with criminals (14 families), property crime such as burglary (24 families) and drug offences such as trafficking (10 families). Many families had at least one incident of what would appear to be a serious personal crime, such as assault (20 families) and sexual assault (18 families).

Table 6.4 Criminal activities outside the family (where at least one event is) recorded in the case files examined for the Victorian study ($N = 50$)

Type of intimidation, violence, or criminal activity	No. of families
Burglary or theft	24
Assault (other than sexual assault)	20
Risk-taking, delinquency, street crime	18
Sexual assault	18
Associating with criminals	14
Intimidation	12
Drug possession	11
Drug trafficking	10
Serious driving offence	10
Personal crime with a weapon	10
Possession of a weapon	9
Drug offence, type not known	9
Petty crime other than categorised, such as shoplifting	7
Non-assaultive sex-related crime, such as exposure	7
Threats to use a weapon	5
Violence associated with drunken behaviour	5
Prostitution	5
Handling stolen goods	4
Fraud or perjury	4
Threats of bodily harm	4
Death threats	4
Alcohol offence	4
Physical violence (type not specified)	3
Arson	3
Aggravated cruelty	1
Nature of offence not recorded but a jail term was served	15

The family members involved in these activities reflected a similar pattern to that found with violence within the family. The natural mother was recorded as being involved in criminal activity in the community in 22 families. However, males as a group were involved in criminal activity more often: the first recorded partner, 16 families; the natural father, 12 families; and a second partner, six families. Thirty-five families (70%) had a male in a current or part parental role who was involved in at least one criminal activity where the police were involved.

The large number of subject children recorded as being involved in criminal activity (22) was not anticipated by the researchers and was an area not specifically pursued in the interview with the workers. The finding may, in part, reflect the fact that the worker would be more likely to know about the activities of the subject child. Thus, the subject child may be a source of concern in relation to the worker's safety. Recorded examples are:

'In one case the subject child, when 15, was selling drugs, shoplifting, and stole goods and a car.'

'In another case the subject child at 12 years of age, had been charged with over 30 offences, and at 13, the offences included escape from custody, theft, theft of a car, reckless conduct endangering others, criminal damage, drug possession, unlicensed driving and assault.'

When the number of people involved in crime and/or violence outside the family was examined, only eight abusive families had no member involved. The average number of people involved in at least one incident of community crime and/or violence in each case was over two (2.5), or just under three (2.9) if the families with no involvement were excluded.

Other disturbed and/or unpredictable behaviour in the families

In addition to the events already noted, some families had at least one member with a number of other conditions (current or past) recorded that could lead to difficult, threatening and/or unpredictable behaviour, which may be intimidating or cause some stress or anxiety in the worker. Close to half of the families had, at some stage, at least one member with a psychiatric problem (24 families), a drinking problem (23), a drug abuse problem (23), or an intellectual disability (9).

As an example, one case file recorded three generations of intellectually disabled people living in the household, some of whom also had a psychiatric illness, and the subject child's father was a drug user who displayed violent behaviour. The file noted a visit by a worker where five intellectually disabled adults were present, all in 'a highly agitated state'. Comments made by the workers demonstrate the type of problems people with these behaviours may cause. For example:

' "Recently I had to call the police. A mother was extremely threatening to me and was mentally ill. It was personally directed and so intimidating . . .".' (Worker 3220)

' "A solicitor had a pay-phone wrenched off the wall and thrown at him. We are operating in a level of fear all the time . . . [people are] unpredictable because of psychiatric and drug problems, some have very violent backgrounds. There is nothing like taking someone's child to make them angry." ' (Worker 6410)

THE WORKERS' EXPERIENCE OF ISOLATION

The following case example illustrates how protective workers may sometimes need to handle difficult and dangerous situations by themselves.

'Protective services had worked with the family for three years. There was a record in the case file of one visit where the protective worker was in the house for five hours. She had attended with two volunteers from another agency. The father was found to be ". . . in an extremely aggressive and hostile state", "tipsy", drinking alcohol, he had been using "speed", and he was threatening his wife with physical violence. The protective worker wrote in the file that during her visit the situation deteriorated to such an extent that she became fearful for the safety of the wife, children and other family members present. The protective worker suggested that the volunteers take the family away from the house, and the protective worker stayed with the father. The file noted that "after much reasoning" father "slowly calmed down". Following this event, a "safety alert form" was placed in the file. The alert noted that father "is well known to police and is extremely violent. He should never be approached without police escort." The file recorded a subsequent visit by protective workers. Police were contacted but were not available to accompany the workers on the visit. Police from another station were approached who said the man was well known to the police and that they would be available. However, the visit was made with two protection workers only. The police were apparently unavailable to attend.'

Little attention has been paid in the literature to the issue of whether protective workers feel supported or isolated in their work. The connections between trauma and isolation are noted in the traumatic stress literature. Herman (1992), for example, suggests that those already disempowered or disconnected from others are most at risk of traumatic stress. In addition, a supportive response from other people may mitigate the impact of a traumatic event, while a hostile or negative response may compound the damage and aggravate the traumatic stress: 'It cannot be reiterated too often: *no one can face trauma alone*' (Herman 1992: 153; emphasis in original). When isolation is referred to in the trauma literature it is almost exclusively viewed in a context of post-traumatic recovery. Whittington and Wykes (1989) have documented the importance of social support in reducing the negative effects of exposure to violence in the work place. However, both the quantity and the type of support has been found to be important in leading to a positive impact on the victim (Pratt & Barling 1988).

The recent interest in the experience of trauma by emergency personnel sees social support as an important mediator between the exposure to a traumatic event and the nature and intensity of the experience of traumatic symptoms (Solomon 1986). The trauma literature suggests that an isolated trauma victim is likely to experience more intense symptoms and experience slower recovery (Paton & Smith 1996). Paton and Stephens (1996: 187) see emotional support as 'central' to the recovery process.

For a protective worker to escape a sense of isolation, support may be sought from a range of sources: from supervision; from management and the organisation; from colleagues; from family; from the wider community; and, from a strong theoretical basis to the work. Supervision and further findings are examined in detail in Chapter 10.

A Lack of Organisational Support

Little research has been undertaken into the role of organisational support in protective services. Some findings are presented in this section and the subject is further discussed in Chapter 10. Discussion in the social work literature largely centres on the alienating effects of the bureaucratisation of social work and of the structure of protection organisations. Arches (1991) argues that rule-governed and codified behaviour and separation of services, limits peer consultation and informal interactions, and results in an increase in feelings of isolation. The worker becomes de-skilled, feels a lack of power and control within the organisation, feels she is perceived only as a means to an end, and feels alienated (Form 1975, Israel 1971, Seeman 1972). If the organisation functions as a closed system, it is not only characterised by conformity to guidelines and procedures, but it closes down communication with staff and clients (Preston-Shoot & Agass 1990). As reported in Chapter 10, communication was seen to be a problem by many workers:

'A worker reported that she had been wanting to consult with Head Office for the last four months. An appointment was cancelled four or five times. She was told there was no facility to speak directly and to go back to her own office.' (Worker 1170)

'A worker said that a field workers' meeting was regularly held at lunchtime. The meeting had to be conducted in the workers' time as "management doesn't approve" of protective workers meeting.' (Worker 6140)

' "The bureaucracy bogs you down so much".' (Worker 9130)

' "They say they leave the door open but they don't listen".' (Worker 5150)

' "Head Office is faceless and irrelevant".' (Worker 6130)

Indeed, seven workers spoke about the fact that you had to be careful about what you said within the organisation, for example:

> ' "We need to tread carefully if we have any major complaints".' (Worker 1130)

The organisation may become less effective as it produces passive practitioners, who are stuck and demoralised, and ultimately collude with organisational practices (Preston-Shoot 1989). A sense of helplessness was repeatedly expressed by many of the workers interviewed in the authors' study:

> 'Protective workers are ". . . at the bottom of the heap" and ". . . in a no-win situation".' (Worker 4130)

> ' "Child protection is all about negatives really. You don't come into it to be loved. You are dealing with dysfunctional families. Families don't have a sense of hope themselves. . . . you end up feeling futile ...".' (Worker 2220)

> ' "In this department there is not much point about doing anything about anything . . . [You] can talk to seniors who would listen and do nothing further . . . very disempowering, you can't do anything, you feel anger and frustration." ' (Worker 2340)

> 'The interviewed worker did not appear to share the other workers' concerns about the lack of resources and was asked about this by the researcher. The worker responded that you get used to the lack of resources, saying, "there is no control over anything. Nothing you do will change it, so it is not worth mentioning. All the striking you can do will not change anything." ' (Worker 2180)

As a result of this loss of control in a bureaucracy, the worker may find that some professional concepts are undermined and therefore face additional ethical dilemmas over which he or she has little control (Rhodes 1986). Two examples from the authors' study illustrate this:

> 'The worker told of how, although she believed that cutting a mother's access to her child was the correct action to be taken for the child's welfare, her "opinion" was insufficient. The worker said "games" had to be played, where you had to offer all sorts of options to the mother and have the mother refuse, before you could go back to the court to stop her access to the child.' (Worker 6410)

> 'A worker spoke about how sometimes information had to be "altered" for a court hearing. For example, the severity of the abuse had to be reduced to make it more acceptable to the court, as the reality of what happened in some families was, at times, not believed. Unless this action was taken, there was a risk that the whole case may be "thrown out" and the child be left with no protection against further abuse.' (Worker 4110)

In our study, 70% of workers believed they would get automatic support from their supervisor following a stressful incident, and 58% believed they would get this from the manager of their office. However, this support was not felt to be available outside the office: 72% of the workers were unsure as to whether support would be given, or believed it would not be there, from the Regional Director, and 79% were unsure about the support, or believed it would not be there, at the Head Office level. While one worker expressed the view that issues of safety and stress were 'blown up out of proportion' and exaggerated, some workers expressed the view that management at office level was very mindful of safety issues (remarking on locks on office doors and alarms in interviewing rooms). However, other workers expressed the view that management failed to acknowledge the size and extent of some workers' concerns about safety and stress. For example:

'One worker said she believed management's view was that risk and stress are ". . . just part of the job and have to be put up with".' (Worker 1180)

'A worker said a past senior manager would "put you down" verbally if you were frightened.' (Worker 8120)

'A worker said that "I don't think the department really cares about workers ultimately". She gave an example of how she made a "serious incident report" about a death threat and the response was that they would "monitor the situation".' (Worker 6350)

'A worker told the researcher about two workers who had a car accident in the duty car on the way to a home visit. The workers received only minor injuries, but the car was written-off. The worker was shocked that the response by a senior management person was to ask whether they were still going to do the visit.' (Worker 6410)

A Lack of Support from Other Agencies and Other Professionals

A common theme expressed by many workers in the Victorian study related to inadequate support, and even hostility, they sometimes received from other agencies:

'The worker spoke of the battle to get other agencies to provide a service. "They have got the attitude that the department [protective services] doesn't know what they are doing." ' (Worker 2130)

Some workers reported a lack of support from the police, for example:

'The worker spoke of how she went to the police to report death threats being made to her. The police convinced her to drop charges as they believed it would be a waste of time.' (Worker 3220)

The following case example illustrates how a lack of support from other professionals may compound the sense of isolation in a worker and create additional barriers to protecting the child.

'The child, aged two years, was found to have many injuries: bruising above both eyes, a black eye and other head injuries; bruising over his body, including finger print bruising; bruises and bite marks on his penis; two healing fractures; and, evidence of past injuries. The child's mother and her partner claimed that the injuries were self-inflicted, caused by the child hitting himself on a coffee table during a temper tantrum and sticking objects in his eyes. It was suspected that mother's partner had perpetrated the injuries. Protective services hoped to make a protective application to the Children's Court. However, the police were reported as being largely unco-operative. They refused to wait and see departmental workers at the time of the initial investigation and would not allow workers to view a police statement taken from mother's partner, during which he was said to have made a "partial admission". Protective services also obtained little support from two medical practitioners. For example, a paediatrician felt that the child was ". . . playing on the mother's insecurities". The doctor said to the worker during a telephone call, "you're not protective services or anything disgusting like that?" On learning that the worker was from protective services, the paediatrician said there was nothing further she wished to say.'

A final illustration is given, where even other professionals within protective services do not always provide support. A file recorded documentation from a protective services' legal representative to a protective worker:

' "At the Pre Hearing Conference you will be expected to negotiate with the other parties' lawyers in order to settle the matter. . . . You should be aware that the contents of any discussion may be used by other parties in later court proceedings, to the tactical advantage of their own client, including trying to have discussions entered into evidence in the contested hearings. . . . If these discussions fail, it is uncertain at this stage as to whether the department will be represented by a barrister at the Court hearing." '

It can be seen that the worker was expected to step into the role of a lawyer and conduct difficult negotiations with other lawyers. Should she fail, she may disadvantage her client (the child who had been maltreated) and may still not receive legal support at a subsequent court hearing.

Barriers to Support from the Worker's Own Family

In the Victorian study, 39 workers (85% of the 46 who responded) revealed that they censored information they told their families about their own safety, and 36 workers stated that they did this in order to prevent their family from worrying. Two other workers had partners who worked in a similar field, so they discussed issues as a way of debriefing. One worker had been advised by a counsellor to discuss everything with her partner. Many comments were made along similar lines to the following:

' "I tell very rarely and I don't discuss in detail. I don't tell if I feel it might worry them and they may make more of it than it is. I only really tell colleagues. I would be more worried if I had children." ' (Worker 6450)

' "I don't tell my family or partner when I've been threatened. They would worry, so I don't tell . . .." ' (Worker 6130)

' "I tell my fiance everything but deliberately choose to downplay, minimise." ' (Worker 9140)

' "I avoid telling my parents the 'nitty-gritty' because they would be concerned about my safety." ' (Worker 6640)

' "My husband hasn't expressed concern. I have told him of some dangers, not everything. Some he couldn't handle. It's not part of his framework." ' (Worker 4210)

What the Workers said about Public Support for Child Protection

Almost without exception, the workers reported believing that the general public had a low opinion of the standard of child protection work. Of 47 workers who responded, 22 said that they believed that the public perceived child protection work to be 'very poor', and 19 said 'poor'. Some 36 workers commented specifically about the causes, all but two remarking that such poor public perceptions were due to adverse media coverage. Comments included:

' "People believe we are incompetent and lazy, don't follow procedures and don't get around to do the right things ...." ' (Worker 6450)

' "Every reaction you get from the public is bad. It used to make me feel bad, now I feel uncomfortable. Nobody likes these issues." ' (Worker 8470)

' "The public would understand if they knew the constraints workers were working under. . . . Not having enough time is very stressful, most appalling stress." ' (Worker 2220)

' "Being a protective worker you are dammed if you do and dammed if you don't. The press picks up on bad stuff. The public doesn't understand that you have to act according to the Act. Professionals also don't understand our role . . .." ' (Worker 5280)

'People "believe we have something personally invested in removing their children or interfering with their lives, that we enjoy hassling people and wrecking families".' (Worker 2160)

The Educational Background of the Protective Workers and the Theoretical Basis for their Work

Child protection workers in Victoria have a variety of educational backgrounds; 27 (54%) of the protective workers in our Victorian child protection study were qualified social workers. A significant minority (22%) had been educated in welfare studies, while 44% had more than one degree. Staff development was offered by the organisation and half of the workers were satisfied with this, although there were concerns about finding time to attend.

Just over two-thirds of the workers (34) had come to protective services as a new graduate, with only two workers having had experience in relevant child protection work before their current job in protective services. The workers thus had little experience to draw upon in the face of the violence that they had to confront. The quality and quantity of supervision varied (this is discussed in detail in Chapter 10). Twenty workers reported that they received less than between one and two hours' supervision a fortnight. There are many risks associated with these factors of varied educational backgrounds, inexperience and limited supervision, and some workers may have to rely almost entirely on procedures to guide them.

Our study also found that workers reported varying responses to the usefulness of theoretical approaches to child abuse and child protection. While over half (58%) often or always found theory to be useful in guiding their practice, a quarter reported theory to be 'sometimes' useful, and 16% reported that they seldom used theory. While the varied educational backgrounds of the workers may have had made a significant contribution to these findings, there is another major factor that requires scrutiny.

A broader view of violence, within families and in the community, raises further contradictory pressures for the child protection worker. The clearest indicator of this philosophical divide is provided by an examination of the coexistence of child abuse and domestic violence. In recent years, the general separation of research into the abuse of a child and research into family violence has led to equally separate programmes and policies (see, for example, Stanley & Goddard 1993a, 1993b). A full analysis of these developments is beyond the scope of this text, but it is important to recognise these differences.

The fuller understanding of the extent of domestic violence has led to major criminal justice innovations in the UK, the USA, Australia, New Zealand and Canada, at least (see, for example, Dobash, Dobash & Noaks 1995). In short, there has been a growing understanding that criminal justice responses 'need to improve' and this is done 'by supporting the victim and arresting the offender' (Dobash, Dobash, Cavanagh & Lewis 1995: 359). While Dobash and colleagues assert that arrest and prosecution remains a relatively infrequent result of police involvement, there is an apparent fundamental philosophical difference: the arrest of perpetrators of domestic violence appears to be more favourably viewed than the arrest of perpetrators of violence against children.

Walklate (1995: 108) summarises what she describes as 'a remarkable change of direction in policing policy . . .'. She reviews the perceptions of police that domestic violence was not real policing and that arrests, even when the women were in favour of prosecution, were rarely carried out. (Walklate places inverted commas around the word 'domestic' in order to underline its problematic labelling (1995: 87), a view with which we concur, as we noted earlier). Many writers, however it is named, now more readily regard domestic violence as a criminal act.

Writing about the male perpetrator of violence against his partner, Ford and Regoli sum up their approach in another short sentence: 'What matters is that he face prosecution' (1993: 157). In this view, counselling of perpetrators of domestic violence is seen as just one possible approach which is 'unlikely to have any greater preventive effect than other alternatives' (ibid.: 158). The criminal justice system is seen as an integral part of any response to domestic violence:

> 'One of the fundamental principles inherent in a community response is that domestic violence is illegal and that there should be criminal justice consequences for wife assault.' (Stordeur & Stille 1989: 65)

The role of prosecutors is seen as 'absolutely critical' (Johann 1994: 97) and as a consequence many texts on domestic violence devote chapters to the prosecution of perpetrators (see, for example, Schornstein 1997). It is also interesting to note that in the title of Johann's (1994) book, perpetrators are called 'terrorists'.

The philosophical differences between many approaches to domestic violence and approaches to the assault and/or neglect of children should not be underestimated. The gulf that still exists in the two major intervention programmes, child protection and domestic violence programmes, is highlighted in an issue of the journal of the American Humane Association. Dykstra (1995: 3) points out that protective organisations have a legal mandate to demonstrate that 'reasonable efforts' were made to preserve families before an assaulted child is removed. The current trend is to work in 'partnership' with the abuser, or often in practice, the partner of the person who assaults the child (Turnell & Edwards 1999). The child is often left at home in the '. . . hope that by working together things can be made safer for the family's children' and the social worker–client relationship can be used to 'build cooperative relationships' (Turnell & Edwards 1999: 32, 33). In stark contrast, the organisations which aid women who have been assaulted have as their primary goal:

> '. . . empowering and enabling battered women to separate from their abusers . . . and seek the surest and safest path away from continued violence.' (Dykstra 1995: 3)

Another author in the journal of the American Humane Association sums up this dichotomy:

> 'Unfortunately, leaders in child welfare and in battered women's organizations have had little opportunity to discuss this key sticking point between the fields: the relative optimism of the child welfare system and the extreme pessimism of the battered women's groups about work with perpetrators.' (Schecter & Edleson 1995: 9)

CONCLUSION

Our study has revealed an extraordinary amount of actual and threatened violence against child protection workers. Serious incidents were common and psychological violence appeared to be all-pervasive in everyday practice. The levels of concurrent violence within the families and in the community were also extremely high.

In Chapter 4 we addressed the issue of comparing these findings with those in previous studies. Hunt and colleagues suggest that the child protection referrals who 'end up in the court system' have a 'more problematic profile' (1999: 18). It is evident from our research that those who are subject to a resultant court order may have an even greater array of serious problems, with higher levels of domestic violence (defined as physical aggression) in our study, 62%, compared to 51% in Hunt and colleague's court sample. As we stated in Chapter 4, methodological differences between the studies may also contribute to the variations in levels of violence. The purpose of our research was to check rigorously for each form of violence recorded in the protection files, leading to what, we suggest, is a far fuller record of such information.

Our research further found that workers often felt that they lacked the support of the organisation and other agencies when facing such extensive violence. Workers came from a variety of educational backgrounds and some struggled to relate theory to practice. These findings, we suggest, serve to illustrate the urgent need to integrate theoretical perspectives from a range of fields and, in turn, to develop realistic expectations of what is achievable in practice. The following chapter provides an outline of hostage theory.

7

HOSTAGE THEORY

INTRODUCTION

This chapter outlines hostage theory. We contend that hostage theory at least partially explains why some children, who are under the care of protective services, are not adequately protected and continue to experience abuse. The theory suggests that protection failure may be due to a particular form of relationship which occurs between the child protection worker and members of the child's family. The theory draws on aspects of this relationship and some of the external factors which impinge upon and shape it. It is important to note at the outset that the hostage theory does not place any blame on individual child protection workers but merely describes behaviour which may occur on some occasions and the consequences that may result from that behaviour.

AN OVERVIEW OF RELATED FIELDS

Hostage theory draws heavily from the field of political terrorism and hostage-taking. The scientific community has taken an interest in terrorism and hostage-taking since the 1970s. This interest developed from a need to counter terrorism and develop a theoretical approach to secure the safe release of hostages, without prejudicing the capture of the terrorists (Flynn 1987, Wardlaw 1982). In the early 1970s broad public attention was also drawn to the possibility of unexpected, and even bizarre, behaviour by hostages. A kidnapped victim, Patricia Hearst, was filmed on a bank security monitor taking part in an armed robbery (Hearst 1982). Hearst explains her behaviour as due to 'brainwashing', using an analogy to behaviour adopted by some prisoners of war and concentration camp victims (Hearst 1982). A more systematic examination of the behaviour of hostages was undertaken following the kidnapping of victims who were held for four days in a bank vault in Stockholm in 1974. The victims again displayed unexpected behaviour, negotiating on behalf of their captors, trying to protect their captors from the police and, in a subsequent court hearing, refusing to testify against the terrorists (Wardlaw 1982).

In unrelated developments, the 1970s saw the beginning of a new field of study, defined as Post Traumatic Stress Disorder (PTSD). In 1980, this condition was included in the third edition of the *Diagnostic and Statistical Manual of Mental Disorders* (APA 1980). While the 'shell shock' of soldiers had been described following the First World War, it was only after the reluctant recognition of continuing disturbances associated with the American veterans of the Vietnam War, that PTSD was seriously studied (Frederick 1994). It is largely from this background that there is a growing interest in addressing the stress of emergency service personnel (Paton & Violanti 1996). A large literature on Critical Incident Stress Management (CISM) has developed (see, for example, Mitchell & Everly 1997).

In the 1970s Walker (1979) described the unexpected behaviour of some victims of abuse and assault in the home, which she called 'the battered wife syndrome'. The theory describes how some women, controlled by fear perpetrated by a violent male, are unable to take protective action against psychological and physical violence (Barnett & LaViolette 1993). In 1974, Burgess and Holmstrom looked at the psychological effects of rape and proposed the term 'rape trauma syndrome'. Similarly, Symonds (1982) has pointed out that the behaviour of people subjected to violent crime is akin to that of political hostages. He called the behaviour 'patho-logical transference' (1982: 99). Summit's 'accommodation syndrome', which describes how children who have been sexually abused adapt to abuse, was reported in 1983.

The media sometimes graphically report the apparently inexplicable be-haviour of some victims. For example, a woman who was assaulted, choked and stabbed a day after she gave birth, and two days after her 2-year-old child had been attacked by her husband, was reported as being 'reconciled' with him (Adams 1996: 3). Examples of similar behaviour have also been reported in fictionalised biographical literature, such as *Perfect Victim* (McGuire & Norton 1992), *Murder in the Heart* (Artley 1993) and *What Lisa Knew* (Johnson 1991), and also in Sara Hamilton-Byrne's (1995) account of her upbringing in the sect, 'The Family'.

In 1980, Goddard published an article which explored the safety at home of a child who had been abused. He noted that in some situations the child protection worker has unfounded optimism, over-identifies with the abusive parent and accepts the parent's denials of abuse, thus the worker has '. . . completely lost sight of the priorities so vital to effective child protection work' (Goddard 1980: 5). Hostage theory, as such, was first presented at a conference in Melbourne (Goddard 1988b). As well as examining particular relationships which may form between child protection workers and adults significant to the child, hostage theory contributes to understanding the nature of some relationships between the child and the abusive adult (see Chapter 9). It also aids understanding of the impact of other systems, such as organisational structure and broader environmental settings, on statutory protection failure (see Goddard & Carew 1988, Goddard & Stanley 1994, Goddard & Tucci 1991, Stanley & Goddard 1993a, 1993b, 1995, 1997).

Many of these theoretical developments, as outlined above, have advanced in parallel, with little cross-fertilisation and without an overarching perspective. Such a position has been described as a 'silo model', where there are independent, free-standing lines of thought, with little communication between these positions. The issue of trauma in itself has now developed into a distinct and growing field of interest. Brown and Fromm (1986: 269) have identified what they call 'complicated PTSD' in people chronically exposed to trauma, and similarly, Herman (1992: 377) describes 'complex PTSD'. However, neither of these conditions has been described in detail.

In addition to political terrorism and military literature, hostage theory uses social work theory, psychoanalytic theory, PTSD theory, psychological theories on defences, helplessness, intrusive imagery and avoidance, and the more recent upsurge of theory exploring the personal impact of trauma. Although many of these theories have specific situational characteristics, the authors believe that hostage theory offers important connections between the 'silos'.

THE STOCKHOLM SYNDROME

The term 'Stockholm Syndrome' is used in the political hostage literature to describe a particular pattern of behaviour commonly found in political hostages. As a result of severe trauma, where the person is unable to muster the physical and mental resources:

> '. . . feelings of impotence shatter the self-image, dissolve the self-confidence and set in motion sequelae of complex and interrelated social-psychological and physiological response mechanisms. Some of these involve conscious efforts on the part of the victim, others are deeply submerged in the subconscious.' (Flynn 1987: 342)

Strentz (1982) describes the syndrome as an automatic and often unconscious response to the trauma of becoming a victim. This response involves hostages becoming psychologically pressured '. . . to understand, co-operate or even love their captors in order to save themselves', and this cooperation with the terrorist does reduce the violence (Wardlaw 1982: 155). The Stockholm Syndrome may develop under certain conditions, namely:

> '. . . in a social context that exacerbates stress through denial of institutional supports and prolonged threat to life, bodily integrity, and identity presented in a circumstance of powerlessness, helplessness, and unpredictability to victims . . ..' (Fields 1982: 147)

To summarise, the elements critical to the development of hostage-like behaviour are severe ongoing trauma involving threat or fear, an ongoing interaction between the terrorist and hostage, time for an interaction to take place, and isolation of the hostage from normal supports. To cope with the severe ensuing stress and to enable adaptation to the situation, the person's perception of reality may change and ego defences may be employed.

Although the Stockholm Syndrome has been repeatedly observed in over half of the hostage situations reviewed by Soskis and Ochberg (1982), it is still far from being completely understood. It is known, however, to affect all ages, sexes and cultures and to occur in different environments, with different motivational issues and in previously psychologically healthy people. The extent to which people are subject to the Stockholm Syndrome may vary. Victims may suffer serious and long-lasting damage to their physical, mental and emotional health (Flynn 1987). The Stockholm Syndrome can commence within hours of capture and can continue for years after the hostage is released (Eitinger 1982). An investigation of a number of people who had been held as hostages found that they all had trauma symptoms in the first month after being released, 75% still being symptomatic six months to one year after release, and 46% still had some effects six to nine years later (van de Ploerd & Kleijn 1989). It is suggested that the longer the hostages had been in captivity, the more symptoms they displayed and the slower they were to recover.

The symptoms of many released hostages appear to be profound and lasting (Flynn 1987: 344). Attitudinal and behavioural changes include a range of anxiety symptoms, depression and:

> '. . . insomnia, startle reactions, nightmares and nightsweats, inability to concentrate, memory lapses, sexual problems and interpersonal difficulties with spouses or significant others. Obsessive reviews of the terroristic incident lead to much self-recrimination, self-blame and circular spells of anger, apathy, depression, hostility, rage, reclusiveness, resentment and resignation.' (Flynn 1987: 350–351)

Physical illness such as hypertension and the suppression of the body's immune system may occur.

The Stockholm Syndrome occurs to varying degrees in different people. For example, Patty Hearst was reported to have strongly experienced the Stockholm Syndrome because of her young age (18 years). Ochberg (1982) presents a detailed case example of Gerard Vaders who was on a train that was hijacked by seven gunmen in 1975. He was held hostage for 12 days and witnessed the random shooting by the terrorists of four other hostages. Vaders was described as having a mild case of the Stockholm Syndrome, but still displayed positive feelings towards the terrorists during the incident. More than a year later he stated that:

'You had to fight a certain feeling of compassion for the Moluccans [terrorists]. I know this is not natural, but in some way they come over as human. They gave us cigarettes. They gave us blankets. But we also realised that they were killers. You try to suppress that in your consciousness. And I knew I was suppressing that. I also knew that they were victims, too. In the long run they would be as much victims as we. Even more. You saw their morale crumbling. You experienced the disintegration of their personalities. The growing of despair. Things dripping through their fingers. You couldn't help but feel a certain pity.' (Vaders cited in Ochberg 1982: 25–26)

As Soskis and Ochberg note, this is a valuable, eloquently written passage, open to various analyses. It is suggested that the ability to see the terrorist as victim is 'crucial', an extremely pertinent observation for our research (1982: 123). Vaders' account also offers clear insights into a complex relationship:

'Valders realized that he was experiencing simultaneously contradictory cognitions and emotional responses and also that he was suppressing much of what he thought and felt in the interests of survival.' (Soskis & Ochberg 1982: 123)

The purpose of the capture of hostages is for the terrorist to achieve his or her aims. The hostage is a tool to this end. The 'purpose' of the Stockholm Syndrome is to maximise the chances of survival for the hostage. The practical outcome of the Stockholm Syndrome is that the hostage becomes less helpless, accepts his or her subjugation, and cooperates with the terrorist, at times to the point of actively promoting the terrorist's objectives (Soskis & Ochberg 1982, Strentz 1982). Where the Stockholm Syndrome has developed, physical abuse of the hostages is reduced and the chance of hostage survival is enhanced (Strentz 1982).

Essential Features of the Stockholm Syndrome

While there is some variation between authors about the relative significance of the components of the Stockholm Syndrome, important and consistent findings are repeated throughout much of the political terrorism literature. These are now outlined.

Severe ongoing trauma

Terrorism is described as:

> '. . . the deliberate use of violence or threat of violence to evoke a state of fear (or terror) in a particular victim or audience. The terror evoked is the vehicle by which allegiance or compliance is maintained or weakened.' (Crelinsten 1987: 6)

The aim is for the captor to create a hostile, totally dominating environment, so that the victim feels isolated, powerless and helpless (Symonds 1982). In this state, the victim, and often a wider audience, can be manipulated (Flynn 1987). The violence or dramatic threats of violence:

> '. . . induce extreme fright or terror in victims so that they will be rendered helpless, powerless, and totally submissive.' (Symonds 1982: 97)

To maximise this condition occurring, the captor aims to achieve a continuous, high level of anxiety (Wardlaw 1982). Thus threats are often vague, unpredictable and incomprehensible, leaving the victim not even sure what he or she fears and unable to construct a meaningful framework from his or her own resources. Fear is also created by the terrorist's violent acts and compounded by the loss of control experienced by the victim (Bandura 1990). The most important result for the terrorist is not the physical and mental damage to the hostage or victim but the effect this has on someone else (Bandura 1990, Freedman 1983).

Time and ongoing contact between terrorist and hostage

The nature of the relationship between the hostage and the terrorist is complex. While there has to be time for a certain amount of interaction between the terrorist and the hostage, factors in addition to time compound the behavioural outcomes of the relationship. Strentz (1982) found that the Stockholm Syndrome does not develop where the hostage and terrorist have little or no contact with each other. It also tends not to form where the hostage is physically injured by the terrorist (Miller 1980). The mere threat of physical assault may be all that is necessary.

The Stockholm Syndrome is most likely to form where there is some form of positive contact between the terrorist and the hostage. It could be that the terrorist shows some 'lenience' or 'kindness' to the hostage such as offering a cigarette, or it may be that the terrorist does not severely harm the hostage.

> 'As time went on and my re-education continued, the SLA comrades became more and more friendly and amenable. The trick was to agree with everything they said, to feign an interest in every one of their concerns – to be a model prisoner: subservient, obedient, grateful, and eager to learn. They talked with me more and more all day long. That meant that my closet door would remain open and I could breathe relatively fresh air and also that I was not left alone with my own thoughts and misery.' (Hearst 1982: 92)

The positive contact can also take the form of the hostage being able to identify with the human quality of the terrorists, as can be seen in the passage written by Vaders, reproduced above. Understanding may be generated because terrorists often come from a situation of exploitation and poverty (Bandura 1990). As noted above, some authors believe that the terrorist being viewed as a victim may be crucial for understanding the Stockholm Syndrome (Soskis & Ochberg 1982). Irrespective of how it is generated, increased understanding may be accompanied by increased compliance by the hostage which, in turn, may leave the victim feeling negative towards the police or authorities. Often, although not always, the terrorist may begin to develop positive feelings towards the victim (Soskis & Ochberg 1982).

Isolation or anomie

While there is little discussion about the notion of isolation in the political terrorism literature, the concept is not simple. It appears to be a combination of physical and psychological isolation, and thus isolation from information. Most hostage events at least start with some degree of physical isolation. Patty Hearst spent about eight weeks in a closet, at times moving in and out. After this she was increasingly allowed physical freedom, but preferred to stay in the house occupied by her captors (Hearst 1982). The woman described in *Perfect Victim* (McGuire & Norton 1992) spent three years in and out of a coffin-like box, often being confined for extended times. Even when she had contact with the outside world, contact with neighbours and eventual employment in the local community, she remained a hostage.

Isolating the victim separates the person from supports, both social and institutional. It also has the effect of cutting the person off from his or her usual sources of understanding, explanation and meaning. In the absence of other information the victim of terrorism may turn to the terrorist for explanation. Indeed, in his or her role as controller or manipulator of information, the terrorist may have a more profound impact on the victim than through any physical abuse (Soskis & Ochberg 1982). Hearst (1982: 194) wrote:

> 'My only source of information or news analysis all this time was Cinque and the others in the SLA. We lived in a world of our own, never going outside our safehouse in Hunters Point. Reality for them was different from all that I had known before, and their reality by this time had become my reality.'

Once released, the hostage victim is in need of reassurance, comfort and support:

> 'If victims are met with indifference, detachment, emotional insulation so characteristic of professionals, their silent expectations will go unmet. Their feelings of helplessness and rejection will be reinforced and a "second injury" will have been inflicted by the system,' (Flynn 1987: 353)

Defence mechanisms

Where a hostage has developed characteristics of the Stockholm Syndrome, this behavioural change is usually explained through reference to an unconscious operation of defence mechanisms. A list of defences and their definitions can be found in a paper by Horowitz, Markman, Stinson, Fridhandler and Ghannam (1990). Denial is usually the first defence used, as it enables the person to reduce the shock to a manageable level, thus giving the victim a little time to evaluate the situation and allowing gradual assimilation of the event (Strentz 1982).

However, as more of 'reality' impinges on the individual, anxiety increases and other defences also have to be used (Tinklenberg 1982). Common defences include identification with the aggressor, introjection, and reversal or reaction formation. The use of these can be seen where, to avoid the wrath and potential anger of the aggressor, the now admired values of the terrorist or captor are adopted, even if they are contrary to the hostage's previous view (Strentz 1982).

> 'By this time, I entertained no doubts whatever about my future. I thought of myself as a soldier in the SLA. I had joined and agreed to their recruitment and thereby had given up all of my past life. Thoughts of my family, friends, and acquaintances of my past life almost never entered my mind, and when they did I criticized myself for such bourgeois thoughts as

mercilessly as Teko or Yolanda would have. I did not ever want to think of them anymore. The SLA was my whole life. . . . There was no other reality for me.' (Hearst 1982: 260)

Flynn (1987) also refers to conversion syndrome, repression, rationalisation and sublimation. The more mature defences of intellectualisation, creative elaboration and humour are also utilised (Tinklenberg 1982: 65).

Factors that influence adaptation to the threat

Tinklenberg (1982), in particular, provides a discussion on how the hostage adapts, or accommodates, to the trauma of terrorism, in addition to the use of mechanisms of defence. He believes that the repertoire of adaptive behaviours is extensive, varies among individuals and is often similar to those used by people in any situation of stress. What is used depends on the nature of the event, the duration and severity of the threat, and the motives, goals and actions of the terrorists; and the prior life experiences of the hostage, including training, and their personality factors. One conscious act of coping is the hostage deciding that he or she must relinquish control to the terrorist. This reduces the need of the terrorist to resort to more severe acts to gain control. Other coping activities may be engaged in over a longer period, such as gathering information, establishing positive bonds with the terrorist and establishing group affiliation with other victims. The feeling of common adversity is stress reducing and found repeatedly to be of great value to the hostage (Tinklenberg 1982).

Characteristics of the terrorist

A common finding is that terrorists appear normal, usually not displaying any of the traditional psychiatric conditions. They tend, however, to be people with particular personality traits who show narcissistic and borderline personality disturbances (Post 1987). Post found that they characteristically come from a troubled family background, with one-quarter having suffered early parental loss and one-third convicted in a juvenile court. Many of their personality characteristics resemble those found in some victims of severe child abuse. These include a fragmented self-concept with a failure to fully integrate between the good and bad parts of the self, exaggerated self-absorption and low self-esteem (Post 1990). The terrorist feels a loss of personal power, frustrated and helpless (Wardlaw 1982). He or she needs an outside enemy to blame and on which to focus his or her narcissistic rage in an attempt to re-establish self-esteem (Crayton 1983, Post 1990).

The cognitive functions of logic, rational thinking and judgement have also been found to be impaired (Crayton 1983). Such a person misrepresents the injurious consequences of his or her actions by blaming or dehumanising the victims, or reconstructing or distorting their conduct and its consequences (Bandura 1990). The individual's destructive conduct is perceived to be socially acceptable by justifying it as being undertaken for moral reasons (Bandura 1990).

Ideology

In a state of helplessness, the hostage's continued existence is dependent on the behaviour of the captors. A common response is for the hostage to turn to the captor who gives the appearance of wisdom and is able to interpret and control events (Wardlaw 1982). The terrorist uses compelling rhetoric which is 'absolutist, idealising and de-valuing', polarising 'us versus them' and 'good versus evil' (Post 1987: 310). Information and moral positions are greatly and crudely oversimplified (Hacker 1983). This pattern is common to all terrorists despite the diversity of their causes (Post 1990). The seven criminals who captured Hearst believed they were the Symbionese Liberation Army engaged in a class war against the enemies of the people and were obliged to fight to the death for the cause (Hearst 1982).

Group identification and detachment from the outside world

In situations where a group of terrorists work together, each member strongly identifies with group norms because:

> '. . . joining the terrorist group represents an attempt to consolidate a fragmented and incomplete psychosocial identity, and, most importantly, is an expression of an extremely strong need to belong.' (Post 1987: 309)

The survival of the group is all-important (Post 1987). There is a need to maintain the terror to consolidate group identification or bring the other terrorist members under control (Miller 1980). The terrorists 'crave' the support and approval of affiliation or belonging and it is this which may give them identity and meaning (Miron & Goldstein 1978: 80).

Contributory behaviour from the victim and the wider setting

The terrorism literature contains the notion that hostages have usually in some way contributed to their plight by their behaviour (Bandura 1990). This factor is used by terrorists to achieve self-exoneration, by viewing their destructive conduct as forced by circumstances. It is also used by observers who witness the victim's suffering, who may derogate the victim, seeing him or her as partially responsible for the events. The devaluation and indignation aroused by the ascribed culpability, in turn provides moral justification for even greater maltreatment by the terrorist.

Few nations assume any responsibility for their citizens who become the unwitting victims of terrorism (Miller 1980). Miller believes there is a lack of concern by government and a bureaucratic insensitivity to the victim's plight, as the presence of a hostage is a reminder to others of everyone's vulnerability to terrorism. In addition, after release, the person often finds his or her career cut short.

Bandura (1990) highlights the dilemma faced by democracies of how to morally justify countermeasures that will stop terrorists' atrocities without violating societies' own fundamental principles and standards of civilised conduct. He also makes the interesting comment that:

> 'States sponsor terrorist operations through disguised, roundabout routes that make it difficult to pin the blame on them. Moreover, the intended purpose of sanctioned destructiveness is usually linguistically disguised so that neither issuers nor perpetrators regard the activity as censurable. When culpable practices gain public attention, they are officially dismissed as only isolated incidents arising through misunderstanding of what, in fact, had been authorized. Efforts are made to limit the blame to subordinates, who are portrayed as misguided or overzealous.' (Bandura 1990: 174)

HOSTAGE THEORY

Overview

In Chapter 5, we drew attention to some shortcomings of the traditional view of the social worker–client relationship. Hostage theory, we suggest, provides significant links between many unresolved and inadequately explained complexities of practice and a failure of the protection system to protect some children from further harm. Hostage theory draws on the political hostage-taking literature to describe the reality of what may happen in certain situations between the child protection worker and the child's family. In some cases, and in some situations, the child protection worker acts like a political hostage and the child abuser acts like a terrorist (Goddard & Carew 1988).

Hostage theory can be summarised as follows. Protective workers are placed in an extraordinarily difficult position.

'Social workers . . . are the only workers (with authority to remove children) who are expected regularly to visit the homes of violent people.' (Goddard 1989: 14)

When a worker is explicitly, or implicitly, threatened with violence, he or she may unconsciously act as a hostage. Previously learned behaviour may be lost because of a sense of isolation and powerlessness in a hostile environment. The victim or worker may develop characteristics of the Stockholm Syndrome, and adopt defences in response to the need for self-preservation and relief from severe stress. These defences may include:

- denial of the threat;
- rationalisation;
- intellectualisation of the situation;
- identification with the aggressor or adopting the aggressor's viewpoint;
- reaction formation, or adopting a viewpoint opposite to what the person truly believes;
- creative elaboration; and
- black humour.

A Model of Hostage Theory

Figure 7.1 shows a summary model of hostage theory. Where the protective worker is subjected to both trauma and isolation, there is a risk that she will develop hostage-like behaviour and the child may be left

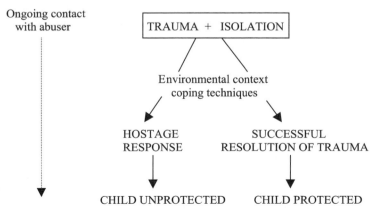

Figure 7.1 Summary model of hostage theory.

unprotected. This response is influenced by the environmental context. Environmental factors may include contact with abusers, the personality and background of the worker, the child protection organisation and procedures, the judicial system, and other involved professionals, agencies and the political climate. The techniques used to cope with stress will also influence the worker's vulnerability to developing a hostage response.

Once the hostage relationship has become established, it tends to become circular and self-reinforcing. Compliance with the abuser reduces the threat and stress to the worker, which in turn reinforces the positive attributes of the abuser, who had the ability to harm the worker but did not do so. This attitude further increases any alliance or positive regard between the worker and the abuser. Thus the terrorist or abuser has gained some control over the relationship.

Differences between Terrorist–Hostage and Child Protection Situations

One major difference between the political hostage and the situation of the child protection worker is that the worker is responsible for the welfare and safety of another person. Thus, while the hostage-like behaviour may be adaptive in the short term in aiding the safety of the worker (Wykes & Whittington 1991), it may not be so adaptive in ensuring the safety of those for whom the worker is responsible.

A central task of the child protection worker is to make ongoing decisions leading to actions to ensure the safety and welfare of the children under the protection of the statutory authority. The possible actions range from a position where no change is made to the child's existing situation, to permanent removal of the child from the family. Many options lie in-between, such as provision of resources, removal of the abuser from the household, supervision of the welfare of the child at home, and parental counselling. It is recognised that many of these decisions are made in consultation with one or more other people, such as supervisors or through a court process.

It is usually assumed that the worker is able to make an unbiased and rational judgement in deciding action. However, if the worker is distorting the facts to protect herself (the hostage effect), the 'correct facts' on which to base judgements about the safety of the child may not be available to the worker. If the worker is minimising the violence and risk to herself, it is likely that she will also be minimising the violence and risk to the child, and the child may be inadequately protected from further harm. Hostage theory is certainly not viewed as the only reason for the occurrence of re-abuse. The circumstances around protection failure are extremely complex and many factors may interrelate to contribute to failure.

A second major difference between the political hostage model and that proposed in the field of child protection is that in many situations the political hostage is far more isolated and the hostage experience is likely to be more dominating than would be the case with the child protection worker. The political hostage is usually, although not always, a hostage 24 hours a day, while the child protection worker returns home after a day's work. On the other hand, the worker may be subject to a greater number of traumatising experiences than political hostages. A worker may have to interact with many different people who threaten her, and her exposure to traumatic events may last for many years. She may be a witness to violence between family members, which demonstrates the power of the aggressor. In particular, she is dealing daily with children who have been severely harmed.

Where the worker is showing some hostage behaviour, it is difficult to predict the permanency and depth of the behaviour. It may be that the worker moves in and out of hostage behaviour, it may be 'switched on' when the worker arrives at work or when the worker is involved with a particular family or situation. The outcome will depend on many factors that are unique to each individual worker. The fact that the political hostage may retain hostage-like behaviour for years after release suggests that, for some, the behaviour has become strongly entrenched and may override other influences.

Expanding Hostage Theory

The nature of trauma

The definition of a traumatic event in the literature is somewhat circular, in that any external event that causes a traumatic response in a person can be defined as a traumatic event. This includes natural disasters, such as cyclones and fires, and man-made events, such as airline crashes, terrorism and assault, through to 'secondary traumatisation' of people working with trauma victims (Lee 1995). *The Diagnostic and Statistical Manual of Mental Disorders*, when speaking particularly about PTSD, defines trauma as an:

> '. . . event or events that involve actual or threatened death or serious injury, or a threat to the physical integrity of self or others.' (APA 1994: 427)

Thus, it is both a person's response to an external event, as well as the event itself, that defines a traumatic event. This was understood by Freud (1926: 166), who wrote:

> 'The essence and meaning [of the traumatic situation is] . . . the subject's . . . admission of helplessness in the face of it . . . It is the subjective experience of helplessness which determines that a situation is traumatic as distinguished from one of danger.'

The concept is one where the event is not only extremely distressing to the person, but the nature of the event is such that the person is partly disabled by the event. The person is unable to draw on the customary ways of organising herself and the outside world (Horowitz 1997). While there is little disagreement about these general statements, the details of the impact are variously described by different authors. Krystal (1971: 91) describes the person as experiencing a '. . . paralyzed, overwhelmed state, with immobilization, withdrawal, [and] . . . regression'. Kardiner and Spiegel (1947: 186) write:

> '. . . the whole apparatus for concerted, coordinated and purposeful activity is smashed. The perceptions become inaccurate and pervaded with terror, the coordinative functions of judgement and discrimination fail . . .'

Traumatic events may alter personality functioning in both pathological and non-pathological ways (Wilson 1989). Herman (1992) believes that the most powerful determinant of trauma on a person is the character of the traumatic event itself. However, as the response of the person is part of the definition of trauma, by implication other factors may form an integral part of the traumatic experience. Thus, a person's response will depend on the nature of the event, the person's previous experiences, personality, emotional conflicts, adaptive style, other people's responses, and any mitigating conditions that may be present (Herman 1992, Wilson 1989). Herman notes that those who are already disempowered or disconnected from others, and particularly those who are already troubled, are most at risk when traumatised.

Trauma has a specific impact. People develop defences against the trauma which numb or restrict the experience, but other life events may weaken defences causing intrusions of the trauma. Thus, traumatised people may alternate between feeling numb, and reliving the event. If the trauma is not integrated or resolved, secondary problems may emerge such as depression, anxiety and damage to intimacy and trust (Herman 1992). Pease (1992) draws attention to Conte's (1985) view that a single trauma may have multiple impacts, as a second-order trauma may be created by the psychological processing of the first trauma.

The concept of transference and counter-transference in child protection

Social work has passed through a number of ideological stances that dominated professional thinking. In the 1950s and early 1960s, importance was placed on the social worker's understanding of the concepts of transference and counter-transference, as both a diagnostic and therapeutic tool within the social worker–client relationship (Germain 1970). However, social work generally failed to adopt the subsequent theoretical developments. The concept fell out of favour, although there has been a small recent revival of interest (Preston-Shoot & Agass 1990).

Transference is seen as the unconscious projection onto the counsellor of the client's attitudes towards an important person in his or her childhood (Garrett 1958). Depending on the theorist, counter-transference refers either to the social worker's response (grounded in his or her childhood conflicts) to the client's transference or, more broadly defined, as all the social worker's responses to the client (Teitelbaum 1991). The social work relationship is the medium through which all communication takes place. Preston-Shoot and Agass (1990) argue for a social work approach which understands and absorbs both the psychoanalytic approach, with its understanding of transference issues, and the more recent systems models.

The social worker who is not aware of these issues may miss a lot of the communication in the social worker–client relationship (Preston-Shoot & Agass 1990). The worker, in fact, needs to consider the origin and impact of communication along two dimensions, past/present and conscious/unconscious. Given the difficulties with which some families may present (for example, violent behaviour and personality disorders), even the seemingly most straightforward present-based conscious communication can be complex in child protection work.

Psychological defences

The hostage uses defence mechanisms in response to overwhelming fear and anxiety where he or she is unable to use other coping behaviour (Goddard 1988b). A person is likely to be using a defence when he or she simultaneously holds two contradictory beliefs, only one of these beliefs being subject to conscious awareness (Sackeim 1983). The concept of defences has evolved over time and is increasingly being associated with normal behaviour. Sackeim (1983) uses the term 'self-deception' as an alternative term to defences. One area of development is the use of defences in association with theoretical approaches to trauma (Horowitz et al. 1990).

Defences do not avoid conflict, but disguise them by transforming them into a more acceptable form, thereby achieving partial expression and/ or discharge of the underlying conflict (Blatt 1990). Persistent use of particular defences, or a group of related defences, may result in specific personality characteristics or cognitive style (Blatt 1990, Singer 1990). For example, a person who has suffered severe childhood sexual abuse develops a pattern of defences that operate in the person's adult life (Polkowski 1993). Singer (1990) proposes that people develop a megastrategy or an automatic style of responding and reducing or filtering the complexity of inputs, choosing which stimuli enter consciousness.

There has also been a move away from associating defences only with pathological behaviour. Some defences may be adaptive, particularly humour (Horowitz et al. 1990). Individuals may employ self-deception not only to avoid displeasure but also to achieve gain, such as to enhance self-esteem or give wishes expression (Sackeim 1983). In fact, it may be 'normal' to use particular distorting strategies and it may be at times pathological not to use defences. Such normal distortions may be 'self-serving biases', 'unrealistic optimism', 'egocentric attributions' and 'illusions of control' (Sackeim 1983: 140). Sackeim concludes that some self-deception is useful in maintaining psychological well-being.

Coping behaviour and helplessness

Other theoretical approaches may contribute to a fuller understanding of hostage-like responses on the part of the child protection workers. Seligman and his colleagues first wrote on the concept of helplessness in 1967 (Overmaier & Seligman 1967, Seligman & Maier 1967). Since then, the subject has been extensively researched experimentally in animal and human subjects, largely under the title 'learned helplessness' (Mikulincer 1994). Once a failure has been experienced a person will initiate coping and adaptation responses to try to address the mismatch between the actual course of events and what is desired (Lazarus 1991). Learned helplessness results from a realisation that outcomes are uncontrollable (Mikulincer 1994). It carries cognitive, motivational and emotional implications for the person.

Mikulincer (1994) proposes four categories of coping strategies: problem-solving, reorganisation, reappraisal and avoidance. Problem-solving uses cognitive strategies to overcome obstacles. In reorganisation, the person rearranges their goals and adopts a more realistic viewpoint. Rather than address the person/environment mismatch, reappraisal attempts to reduce stress by making the mismatch less threatening. It can involve reality distortion, such as selective attention to positive information, making excuses for the person's own bad performance, and biasing memory to positive aspects of the person's performance.

While avoidance involves a wide range of strategies, cognitive processes, designed to prevent the intrusion of threat-related thoughts and affects into consciousness, are commonly used. Whereas reappraisal entails a partial denial of threatening aspects of the problem situation, avoidance strategies involve a total denial of a person/environment mismatch, cognitive disengagement with the problem, and the use of ego defences (Mikulincer 1994). Cognitive avoidance may also take place through effort withdrawal or passivity, alcohol and drug consumption, ideational processing, as well as selective attention (Horowitz 1997).

The problem with coping strategies is that they are carried out at the expense of task performance and may have some dysfunctional side-effects (Mikulincer 1994). Helplessness leads to appraisal of the cost of failure and leads to emotional arousal such as fear, anxiety and anger. It is this arousal which initiates and maintains the coping strategies and defences (Mikulincer 1994). Thus, the higher the cost of failure, the higher the arousal and the stronger the coping strategies. Repeated failure leads to an abandonment of problem-solving behaviour, adoption of other strategies and a belief by victims that they will have the same lack of control in the future (Mikulincer 1994). The particular emotion experienced depends on the person's expectation of control. A high expectation of control initiates anger while a low expectation of control evokes anxiety and depression (Lazarus 1991).

Relating this to hostage theory, the hostage learns that he or she is helpless and unable to take action against severe trauma. Appraisal of the possible severe consequences of an inability to control leads to high motivational arousal and a realisation that the:

> '. . . world is a dangerous place in which unpredictable and uncontrollable events may endanger one's well-being, that one is unable to attain what one wants, and that one's conceptions of the self and the world are incorrect.' (Mikulincer 1994: 240)

Depending on the nature of the initiating event, the extent of isolation and other factors in the person and the environment, the protective worker, unlike the political hostage, may be able to engage in a range of coping behaviours. Some of these may be successful in establishing control. Some strategies will not be successful and the worker may turn to other strategies for coping, such as avoidance. This may be physical avoidance, such as the protective worker avoiding the abusive male, or cognitive avoidance with the accompanying use of other defence mechanisms.

Intrusive imagery and avoidance

When using the avoidance coping style, cyclical phases of intrusion of experience and denial is a common pattern in traumatised people (Horowitz 1997). Intrusion includes behaviours such as 'hypervigilance', preoccupation with 'event-related themes', 'intrusive-repetitive thoughts, images, emotions and behaviours', 'sleep and dream disturbances' and 'flight readiness' (Horowitz 1997: 25). Where a person is subject to re-peated intrusion from stressful thoughts, he or she may feel over-whelmed. As a consequence, the person may be fatigued, and have excessive arousal and anxiety leading to preparation for the next episode of re-experiencing the trauma (Wilson 1989). Part of this behaviour may manifest itself in startle reactions and excessive alertness. The behaviour leaves little time to think and thus also serves as a means of avoidance. Denial or avoidance includes 'selective inattention', 'amnesia', 'disavowal of meanings of stimuli', 'a sense of numbness or unreality', 'frantic over-activity' and 'constriction and inflexibility of thought' (Horowitz 1997: 26).

This pattern of the coexistence of intrusion and denial may be adaptive in resolving stress (Horowitz 1997). After experiencing trauma, a person may be flooded with unwanted images, ideas and intense emotion. De-nial and regulation of these emotions may allow the person to gradually work through the trauma so that emotional intensity can be maintained within tolerable limits. Ideas and feelings can be regulated in a number of ways. For example, a person can develop selective recall of the traumatic event. A maladaptive outcome may be to deny the threat or the urgency of the threat, to become obsessed with work, or to subdue emotions. The worst scenario of disintegration could be a chaotic intrusion of stress, panic or exhaustion. The avoidance stress response can be measured using the Impact of Event Scale (Horowitz, Wilner & Alvarez 1979, Horowitz 1997). Content analysis of conversation may be used as another measure of avoidance stress responses.

THE BROADER IMPACT ON WORK EFFECTIVENESS O
HOSTAGE-LIKE BEHAVIOUR

It is likely that those workers who show some hostage-like behaviour will have their general work functioning affected. Traumatic experiences disrupt a person's physiological and psychological equilibrium and ability to concentrate at work (Barling 1996, Wilson & Walker 1989). For some people in some circumstances,

> '. . . there may be relatively permanent changes in nervous system functioning that result in chronic hyperarousal and a cognitive information-processing style that functions in trauma-associated ways in nearly all situations.' (Wilson & Walker 1989: 22)

Some workers, fearful that they may be reminded of a traumatic event, may become emotionally detached or emotionally restricted in an attempt to control intrusion of the events (Barling 1996). Alternatively, a person may respond to apparently relatively minor threats in a highly intense manner. Thus the person may become sensitised to apparently minor events (Wilson & Walker 1989). Due to the very nature of their work, and the intimidation to which they are subjected, protective workers are likely to be particularly vulnerable to reminders of traumatic events. In addition, workers who may be physically and emotionally exhausted, and distracted by events which create high levels of anxiety, are likely not to be in an optimal state to make critical judgements about the welfare of children.

CONCLUSIONS

Hostage theory, based on the Stockholm Syndrome, describes a complex form of association which may take place between the child protection worker and a child's family. This hostage-like behaviour may occur where the worker is exposed to trauma in addition to isolation, the outcome mediated by environmental and personality factors. The worker may display behaviour suggestive of helplessness and/or high arousal, and may engage in defensive practice and reality distortion. This behaviour may shield the worker against high levels of stress, but the cost may be borne by the child, whose safety may not be accurately evaluated.

8

CHILD PROTECTION
WORKERS AS HOSTAGES

INTRODUCTION

The previous chapter provided a theoretical outline of hostage theory. Figure 7.1 summarised the essential components of the theory. It shows that where a protective worker experiences trauma and isolation, she may display a hostage response. This hostage response may result in a failure to protect children from further harm. Contextual factors may impact on the development of hostage-like behaviour. This chapter examines the major findings from our Victorian child protection study. While many details of the study findings are given throughout the book, this chapter presents the core findings in relation to the protective worker showing hostage-like behaviour. Information on the workers' experiences of trauma and isolation is summarised and the association between trauma and isolation, and hostage-like behaviour is examined. Links are made to protection failure.

A HOSTAGE RESPONSE IN PROTECTIVE WORKERS

A major problem presented to the authors when designing this research was that hostage-like behaviour is largely unconscious. Information therefore had to be obtained by reviewing other forms of evidence. The authors examined whether some of the features of a hostage relationship were present in the characteristics and behaviour of the workers involved in protecting children known to have been severely assaulted, abused and/or neglected. The research results include findings suggesting that some workers are experiencing trauma, some appear to be engaging in reality distortion, and some of the behaviour of protective workers and perpetrators appears to be suggestive of hostage and terrorist interaction.

A Traumatic Response by the Workers

As we described in Chapter 6, workers had been exposed to extreme levels of violence. In Chapter 7 we reported how Horowitz (1997) believes that people who are subject to a traumatic reaction, experience a pattern of repeated intrusion of the traumatic event into their thoughts, along with behaviour which promotes a denial or avoidance of the event. Such behaviour can be measured using the Impact of Event Scale (IES; Horowitz et al. 1979). The IES comprises two sub-scales, defined as follows by Horowitz and colleagues (1979), and Zilbert, Weiss and Horowitz (1982):

- *the Intrusion sub-scale* measures intrusively experienced ideas, images, feelings or bad dreams;
- *the Avoidance sub-scale* measures consciously recognised avoidance of certain ideas, feelings or situations, or conscious recognition of denial or repression.

It was found that the workers varied widely in the amount of stress they were experiencing, as measured by the IES. Some workers reported relatively low levels of subjective stress, while others reported relatively high levels. The stress levels for the 50 workers roughly approximated a normal distribution for the Avoidance sub-scale, the Intrusion sub-scale and the total IES. Because the authors used a different time period in which to measure the stress to that commonly used with the IES, direct comparisons cannot be made with other research which uses this scale.

The Apparent Distortion of Reality by Protective Workers

As noted in Chapter 7, political hostages often manage their experience of trauma by engaging in self-deception and distorting reality. This is commonly achieved through the engagement of mechanisms of defence. Indeed, the use of denial, a frequently used defence, is recognised as a response to many forms of trauma, as evidenced in the IES. Our results suggested that some workers appear to be using denial (the Avoidance sub-scale) at least some of the time. The authors examined this issue further to see whether the protective workers were engaging in reality distortion in relation to: the levels of violence associated with the child's family; the levels of violence to which the workers were exposed; and the levels of violence to which their colleagues were exposed.

Under-recall of violence within the families of children in their current case load

The workers were asked to reflect on whether nine forms of family violence were, or were not, present, in each of the families in their current case load. Each worker was, on average, responsible for 10 cases, totalling 484 cases surveyed. The workers consistently underestimated eight of the nine forms of violence reported in the current case files. Only sexual violence between adults significant to the child was not underestimated (see below). On average, violence was recorded in the file twice as often as that reported by the workers.

It is reasonable to assume that some of this discrepancy, between recalled and recorded rates, would be due to sampling error associated with the case files and memory error by the workers. However, the fact that the gap between the violence recalled and the violence recorded is both large and, with one exception, in the same direction, suggests that these results are being influenced by other factors. The authors suggest that one other factor may be that the workers are using denial and regulation of their conscious experiences in order to reduce their levels of stress.

Sexual violence between partners was the only form of violence that was not underestimated by the workers. It was slightly overestimated (3.2%) but was recorded in only 10% of the sample of files, considerably less than any other form of violence. The next highest was violence by the subject child to an adult, recorded in 32% of the sample, with the other seven forms of violence occurring in at least 50% of the files. It is likely that sexual violence is particularly disconcerting to women child protection workers, and this area requires further study.

Under-recall of fearful situations experienced by the workers

It was not only violence within the families that some workers were underestimating. Some also appeared to be under-recalling or displaying inconsistency in relation to memories of some of their own experiences of fear. One question in the interview asked workers about their worst experience in five different settings, in the past six months. The workers were asked to select the depth of their feelings from the following scale:

- no fear;
- slightly nervous;
- apprehensive;
- frightened; and
- really frightened.

The settings were: the office; a home visit during the day; a home visit at night; another location associated with work such as the Children's Court; and a non-work location. The answers to this question were compared with each worker's responses and comments in relation to other parts of the questionnaire. Twenty-three workers appeared to have problems, or inconsistencies, in relation to their recollection of concerning or fearful events. When asked to get in touch with their fearful emotions in this particular question, they appeared to 'forget' about some events, or 'forget' their depth of feelings about the event. The following examples illustrate this:

> 'The worker responded that she had not even experienced a slight nervousness in any of the settings. However, elsewhere in the interview she told the researcher how she had "felt frightened" during a home visit when she was in the kitchen and a person was using a knife in a very intimidating manner.' (Worker 1130)

> 'The worker responded that she had not even experienced a slight nervousness to any situation outside a work setting. She had elsewhere spoken of the fact that she was working with a "very cunning" person who may find out where her children were. The worker said, "about 12 months ago I realised the need to protect my children carefully".' (Worker 2330)

> 'The worker reported that she had no concern at all. However, elsewhere in the interview she had described an incident during a home visit where she had been locked in a house by a drunken woman who threw a coffee table and other things at her, and "lunged" at her. The worker had to call the police to release her from the house.' (Worker 2160)

> 'The worker responded that she had not even experienced a slight nervousness in any of the settings. However, elsewhere in the interview, the worker had spoken of how her son had been physically assaulted because of her work and a colleague had suffered a nervous breakdown, due in part to "out of hours" contact with work families. The interviewed worker had recently moved from a small country town to a bigger town, in order to obtain greater anonymity and to minimise the chance of the families of clients finding out where she lived.' (Worker 9160)

> 'The worker rated feeling "slightly nervous" about an incident, while elsewhere in the interview she had said about the same incident that she had been "really frightened".' (Worker 6620)

> 'The worker rated that she had not experienced any form of fear in "another work location". Elsewhere she had talked about an incident at a court hearing, saying "I had no fear because I notified security, but they didn't turn up . . . I could taste fear in my mouth. . . . Everyone else had backed away. Security arrived when it was all over." This worker made the following comments during the interview: "You have to keep suppressing a natural reaction so you can continue to work"; and, "we normalise when we should be more apprehensive than we are. I don't know why we do this".' (Worker 8120)

It is possible that some of these problems in recall may be due to 'normal' memory faults. However, the authors suggest that some may also be due to the operation of factors such as self-protective defences, which may be operational in hostage-like behaviour. Certainly, some workers appeared to be holding a duality of feelings, often an indicator of ego defences. It was interesting to note that a couple of the workers who had been temporarily responsible for another worker's case file appeared to have little trouble in recalling their feelings in relation to the case. This position was actually stated by one worker, who said:

> ' "I felt free to hate the person because I was not working with the person. It is different if it is your client. There was no way I was ever going near her again." ' (Worker 2180)

Under-recall of incidents of intimidation and/or violence to other workers

The authors found a similar underestimation of the frequency of intimidation and/or violence experienced by other protective workers. Twenty-nine workers said they personally 'often' experienced at least one form of intimidation and/or violence (see Chapter 6). However, only three workers believed that fellow protective workers in their office 'often' experienced intimidation and/or violence. This could perhaps be explained by the fact that workers do not talk about such events. However, 45 workers stated elsewhere in the interview that they 'often', or 'always', talked about distressing events with their colleagues. In relation to this, three workers volunteered the information that they believed that their work colleagues were 'distancing' themselves from them after each of them had experienced a particularly distressing incident.

Other evidence for distortion of reality

Some workers commented that they had suppressed feelings or had separated emotion from thinking, for example:

> 'The assault and/or neglect of a child ". . . has become more normal. Nothing really shocks me any more, as it once did. It's really sad, a part of life now." ' (Worker 6630)

> ' "I don't feel negative any more when I see kids being abused as it has become 'par for the course' now. I feel horrible, but don't walk out and classify it as negative experience." ' (Worker 5410)

> 'It becomes ". . . like water off a duck's back, but the long-term effect is drip, drip." ' (Worker 1180)

' "Two days ago someone rang and said they had put three plastic explosives in the workers' cars. It happens regularly. The trouble is it happens so often you take no notice." ' (Worker 6190)

How the Perpetrators are Viewed by Protective Workers

In Chapter 7, the personality and intent of the terrorist was described. It was noted that the terrorist generates fear in the victim as a method of control in order to achieve his or her desired outcome. In our Victorian study many workers described people who severely harmed children as having similar personality characteristics. Workers were asked to rate how commonly they believed each of 39 characteristics applied to those who assaulted, abused and/or neglected a child. The descriptors were approximately evenly divided between what could be described as 'positive' and 'negative' attributes. The rating scale choice was: 'never', 'rarely', 'sometimes', 'often' or 'always'.

Male perpetrators were overwhelmingly assessed as holding many negative characteristics which could lead to difficulties in interpersonal interactions. All but one worker rated male perpetrators as 'often' or 'always' controlling. At least half of the workers believed that male perpetrators also 'often' or 'always' displayed the following characteristics: manipulative (43 workers), impulsive (40 workers), authoritarian (40 workers), untrustworthy (37 workers), egocentric (35 workers), dominant, intimidating, threatening and dishonest. Only two workers rated male perpetrators as being 'often' or 'always' harmless.

In contrast, female perpetrators were overwhelmingly described as having victim and stress type characteristics. Over half of the workers believed that female perpetrators 'often' or 'always' held the following personality characteristics: stressed (47 workers), anxious (45 workers), a victim (44 workers), depressed (39 workers), deprived (39 workers), lonely (37 workers), impulsive, manipulative and misguided. Eight workers rated male perpetrators as 'often' or 'always' evil, while none of the workers believed female perpetrators to have this characteristic so frequently.

In response to another question, workers stated that male perpetrators were almost four times more likely than female perpetrators to instigate an event which they found distressing. Thus, male perpetrators are viewed as far more controlling and threatening than female perpetrators.

One of the case files surveyed revealed how one particularly difficult family attempted to exercise control over protective workers:

- The parents said they would only agree to cooperate with the worker if the child, not the parents, was regarded as 'the problem'.
- The parents stated that the children had told them that they only wanted to be interviewed by workers with the parents present.
- The parents would often not agree to meeting times, or agree, and then fail to attend.
- The parents demanded that some 'large' male friends remain during an interview with a protective worker, then complained about protective services breeching confidentiality.
- The mother threatened that she would kill herself if the children were removed.
- The family made a number of accommodation moves of considerable distance necessitating changes in the responsible child protection office, thus creating a pattern of postponing action. For example, after one move, an assessment of the children's welfare was delayed for five months.
- The parents demanded (and received) copies of the contents of the case files, including all reports written and received by the department.
- The parents often threatened legal action.

Although not recorded in the case file, the worker told the researcher of extensive intimidation and threats made by both the mother and father to protective workers, including death threats, and threats to the safety of a worker's own children.

Characteristics Displayed by the Workers

Helplessness

The workers stated that they experienced a range of feelings when working with a perpetrator, including feelings associated with helplessness. Most workers (39) 'never' or 'rarely' felt optimistic when working with a perpetrator. While 39 workers said they 'often' or 'always' felt professional, only 2 workers 'often' or 'always' felt competent. Indeed, 28 workers 'often' or 'always' felt exasperation (45 felt this 'sometimes' or more often); 19 'often' or 'always' felt pessimistic (44 'sometimes' or more often); 9 workers 'often' or 'always' felt inadequate (39 'sometimes' or more often); 5 'often' or 'always' felt despondent (30 'sometimes' or more often); and, 4 'often' or 'always' felt hopeless (24 'sometimes' or more often).

The fact that some workers sometimes describe feelings similar to helplessness was reflected in another question. They were asked about negative emotions they experienced in relation to a stressful event which may also extend beyond this event. Workers were asked to give two examples of events they found to be negative. The most frequently cited event (mentioned by 17 workers) related to intimidation or violence from clients or families. Other more commonly mentioned events related to lack of progress in a case, lack of support from the protective service organisation, and administration or supervision problems. Almost half of the workers (24) stated that they had negative emotional experiences, daily or more often.

The workers were asked to rate how commonly they experienced 40 possible responses to a negative event. Only those that relate to 'helplessness' are reported here. A significant majority of the workers (41) said that they 'often' or 'always' experienced frustration. Close to half of the workers (23) felt that they were not in control, 'often' or 'always'. Indeed, all the workers except one said that things were out of their control 'sometimes' or more frequently; 15 workers 'often' or 'always' felt helpless, 40 workers experiencing this 'sometimes' or more frequently; 16 workers 'often' or 'always' felt blocked about getting things done, 45 feeling this 'sometimes' or more frequently; 9 workers 'often' or 'always' felt unsure about their abilities as a protective worker, with 30 workers feeling this 'sometimes' or more frequently; and 11 workers 'often' or 'always' had difficulties making a decision, with a total of 37 experiencing this 'sometimes' or more frequently.

The findings suggest that feelings similar to helplessness and pessimism may be part of many workers' daily experiences.

High arousal

It has been noted (see Chapter 7) that traumatised people may experience high levels of arousal, which may be due to the person preparing to respond to the expectation of further trauma, e.g. the person may be getting ready to 'fight' or 'take flight'. Where a person has experienced repeated trauma, this high arousal may signify the presence of defences. As an example, being 'too busy to think' may enable some workers to avoid thinking about fears and perhaps enable them to avoid unpleasant memory intrusions.

Certainly, some workers displayed signs of high arousal. They appeared, as one senior worker described, to be 'hooked on the high of the work' and almost became dependent on the drama, the pressure, the overload and the crises. When asked about the good aspects of the job, 17 workers talked about the constant pace, the fact that work was full-on, pressured, addictive and unpredictable. When asked about their immediate response to positive or negative events, 38 workers stated that they experienced excitement 'sometimes' or more frequently, and 31 workers experienced exhilaration 'sometimes' or more often.

This chronic state of a 'hyperarousal–avoidance' cycle is often associated with high levels of fatigue, a factor also found in the Victorian study (Wilson 1989: 16). Thirty-two workers said that they 'often' or 'always' felt physically exhausted, and 31 'often' or 'always' felt emotional weariness. One worker said that in this job you 'get high on anything, if you don't, you cry'. Other examples of comments included:

' "It opened my eyes when I went overseas and worked. . . . It is only when you step outside, that you realise what you take. There is so much on, there is no time to think, just do it." ' (Worker 6220)

' "Because the work is high stress with adrenalin, it is difficult to let go at night. I can't wait to get back the next day. It is an addictive profession. It is only when you remove yourself for some time that you see the effects. [You become] guilty and despondent." ' (Worker 5280)

' "I don't fear for myself, but for my three children, I am cautiously alert." ' (Worker 1130)

'You ". . . feel differently when the person is likely to be violent . . . [You are] pumped up with adrenalin flowing, ready to run and looking for exits." ' (Worker 9110)

Drawing the Issues to Conscious Awareness

The interview process appeared to bring some issues to conscious attention, for some workers at least. Some workers expressed surprise, and often concern, about the extent of violence they had reported experiencing. One worker expressed 'amazement' as to why workers were not more frightened. She left the research interview, determined to report to the police a death threat she had received. Another said:

'The interview has ". . . highlighted how often I do deal with violence, it is something I take on board. When working with a family it is not that significant and maybe it should be." ' (Worker 2130)

Some workers showed an uncomfortable response to some questions. For example, one worker appeared to be a little shocked at the extent of the negative events she had experienced. Two workers did not wish to respond to some questions, one becoming quite distressed. One worker said after the interview that things were now a lot clearer to her. Three workers commented (as can be seen in the quote above) that it was only after leaving child protection for a time, that they realised how they had ignored, or taken for granted, the stress and threats.

THE ASSOCIATION BETWEEN TRAUMA, ISOLATION AND A HOSTAGE RESPONSE

In Chapter 6 we showed that some workers were exposed to violence and intimidation (trauma), and some workers experienced isolation. We have also discussed earlier in this chapter the findings that some workers appeared to be showing hostage-like behaviour. The researchers sought to determine whether there was a statistical association between these factors. In order to do this, a numerical 'score' was derived for each worker which represented her reported experience of violence and isolation, and a measure of hostage-like symptoms that she was experiencing.

The trauma score was derived from the type and frequency of violence and intimidation experienced by each worker (collated in Table 6.1, Chapter 6). Each form of intimidation or violence was given equal weight, but the value was increased as the frequency of the event increased. While it is recognised that each worker may not view all the forms of violence and intimidation as being of equal concern, this assumption was necessary, as it was not possible to consider the impact on each worker of each event. The derived trauma score for each worker ranged widely, with the group of scores for all the workers approximately resembling a normal distribution.

The isolation score for each worker was derived from a range of information relating to physical, emotional and intellectual isolation, the following issues being included:

- how useful they found theory;
- their view on resources available to address intimidation and/or violence;
- their satisfaction with staff development provided by the protective services organisation;
- the frequency, type, and their use of professional supervision;

- their perception of managerial support within the protective organisation;
- their view of support from the workers' families; and
- their feelings of isolation when working with an abuser, and after a stressful incident.

Each of these items was allocated equal numerical value, with the greater the perceived lack of support or isolation, the higher the value given. One exception to this was the measure of the frequency of professional supervision. This was judged by the authors to be the most important source of support for the worker and, as such, was given additional weight. Each item was added to give an isolation score for each worker. The total range of scores for all the workers again ranged widely, and again the range approximated a normal distribution.

The hostage response score for each worker was derived from the Intrusion sub-scale of the Impact of Event Scale (IES), discussed earlier in this chapter. The Intrusion sub-scale was judged to be a better measure of the hostage response than the complete IES. The IES was designed to measure the impact of a 'once-off' event. On the other hand, protective workers were subjected to repeated trauma, in a situation where the perpetrators of these incidents could seldom be physically avoided. Thus the 'intrusion' measures of the IES were thought to be a better measure of hostage-like behaviour.[1] Again, all items in the scale were given equal weight, with increased frequencies being given higher value.

A correlation matrix was derived using Pearson's coefficient of correlation, as shown in Table 8.1. The association between the addition of the trauma and isolation scores, and the hostage behaviour scores, for each worker, was examined. This association was found to be significant at the 1% level. Thus, those workers displaying higher levels of trauma and

---

[1] The IES was designed to measure the continuing impact on a person of a specific event that occurred in the past. The hostage effect is a response to trauma that is repetitive, continuing, and largely unavoidable. Thus, the IES does not directly measure the hostage effect. It measures intrusion and avoidance, in two sub-scales. The authors believe that people with a hostage response are less able to use avoidance as a stress reliever, as precursors and maintainers of the condition are ongoing trauma and isolation. In addition, a person is required to be consciously aware of avoidance, or have some recognition of denial, to complete the avoidance sub-scale component of the IES, while a large component of the hostage response appears to be unconscious. Horowitz et al. (1979: 218) state that where a person has 'massive denial or repression', there is a risk that the Avoidance sub-scale 'would be bound to include' some false negatives. Again, given the largely unconscious nature of the hostage response, there is a risk that this problem may occur. Thus, given these arguments, the Intrusion sub-scale, rather than the total scale, appears to be the better measure of a hostage response in the workers.

Table 8.1 Pearson's coefficient correlation matrix for scales measuring workers' Trauma, Isolation, Hostage-like behaviour (the Intrusion sub-scale), work Context, the Impact of Event Scale (IES), the Avoidance sub-scale and combinations of these scales, as examined in the Victorian study

	IES	Trauma +Isolation +Context	Trauma +Isolation	Trauma	Hostage	Context	Isolation	Avoidance
IES	1.000							
Trauma+Isolation +Context	0.423*	1.000						
Trauma+Isolation	0.379†	0.799*	1.000					
Trauma	0.246	0.382†	0.706*	1.000				
Hostage	0.923*	0.453*	**0.417***	0.298	1.000			
Context	0.325†	0.852*	0.367†	−0.023	0.339†	1.000		
Isolation	0.260	0.699*	0.623*	−0.114	0.255	0.540*	1.000	
Avoidance	0.927*	0.332†	0.286	0.159	0.710*	0.264	0.226	1.000

$* \ p < 0.01$ $† \ p < 0.05$

isolation were more likely to be showing hostage-like behaviour than those workers with lower levels of trauma and isolation.

As can be seen in Table 8.1, a number of other items were also included in the matrix. In particular, the inclusion of context scores needs to be mentioned. While not reported in detail in this book, apart from reference to some of the issues in Chapter 10, the research examined aspects of the environment or context that were likely to have an impact on the workers. This issue receives little attention in the literature reporting a 'typical' political hostage/terrorism situation. As discussed in the previous chapter, unlike many political hostages, the worker is likely to be engaged in a complex network of work-based and personal relationships and interactions. Trauma theory notes that a person who is already stressed is less able to deal with further stress (Herman 1992). Therefore, conversely, a person whose other experiences are positive, fulfilling and rewarding may have greater strengths to overcome some stressful experiences. Thus, the environment of a child protection worker may be a major influence on worker behaviour and, as such, should be taken into consideration.

As with the other factors, a score was calculated for each worker which reflected her degree of satisfaction with her work environment. The issues that were included in the development of this score were the worker's:

- satisfaction with work, office and professional conditions;
- satisfaction with the availability of resources for clients and their families;

- satisfaction with organisational changes;
- experience of discrepancies between what they would like to do at work and what they were actually doing;
- experience of positive and negative experiences at work; and
- actions taken to alleviate any stress they may experience.

As was found with the scores for trauma, isolation and hostage, the workers' views about the work context approximated a normal distribution. However, unlike these components, it was not possible to make the context measure entirely independent. Logically, the context cannot be entirely separated from issues such as isolation, so there is a small duplication of the factors that comprise these scores.

The addition of the context scores to the trauma and isolation scores slightly raises the correlation coefficient with the hostage scores (Table 8.1). This suggests that the addition of environmental stress in the work environment increases the likelihood that a worker will engage in hostage-like behaviour. This statistical association may partly be explained by the small sharing of items included in the scores but it may also be due to stress in the workplace increasing a vulnerability to a hostage response. This interpretation is supported by the fact that the association between isolation and hostage alone is not statistically significant, and the association between the context scores and the hostage scores is significant at the 5% level (Table 8.1).

A Word of Caution

The findings summarised here suggest that those workers who experience the higher levels of trauma and greater levels of isolation are more likely to display hostage-like behaviour. Hostage-like behaviour is even more likely to develop where the worker is also experiencing a stressful work environment. However, to derive these measures, it was necessary to make a number of assumptions in relation to what issues were important and, particularly, how these issues combined to impact on workers. For the purposes of analysis, it was assumed that the impacts could be combined in the form of linear addition. It is unlikely that all factors impacted in this way. For example, there may be a critical boundary of impact for particular workers. Certain issues which may be viewed as minor by some, may remind a worker of past trauma and cause extensive distress. Further research is urgently needed to clarify some of these issues. However, certain confidence in these findings can be taken from the fact that the statistical matrix (Table 8.1) is logically consistent, and that these findings are strongly supported by the workers' own accounts.

THE ASSOCIATION BETWEEN A HOSTAGE RESPONSE IN THE WORKERS AND PROTECTIVE FAILURE

Hostage theory proposes a link between hostage-like behaviour on the part of the protective worker and an increased risk of a failure to protect the child who has been maltreated. The study findings given in Chapter 4 reveal that many children who had been severely harmed were not protected from further harm. An ideal situation would enable this association to be examined statistically using a similar process to that outlined above in relation to trauma, isolation and hostage behaviour. Unfortunately this was not possible for a number of reasons. The events relating to particular children could often not be aligned with decisions made by particular workers. This was because of the extremely high turnover of workers. While those interviewed were the last workers responsible for the children in the 50 case files read, 45 files had more than one worker in the history of the file. These 45 files had an average of just over four (4.3) main workers sequentially responsible for each case, during the time each case was active (an average of 2.2 years). The true worker turnover was likely to be even higher, as information on the file as to who was the responsible worker was sometimes unclear. There were many reasons for this staff turnover. One reason, as told to the researchers, was case closure due to the disagreeable and/or menacing nature of the case.

The files mainly recorded events, only rarely documenting the reasons why decisions were made. The files also did not record workers' feelings. Frequently the worker felt the need to interpret the file for the researcher, as some highly stressful events were not recorded, even where this directly related to the child's safety. At times, fuller information was revealed in reports contained in the file which had been written by other professionals. As an example, in one file an attached report by a professional noted that a family member claimed that he had put out a murder contract on a protective worker. Many files had missing information and/or were not organised in chronological order – a problem experienced by other researchers (see, for example, Hunt et al. 1999). Finally, hostage-like behaviour is often unconscious, thus creating considerable measurement difficulties.

Thus, approaches other than statistical association were needed to examine the association between protection failure and hostage-like behaviour by the workers. Earlier in this chapter, findings were presented which showed that the workers consistently under-recalled the extent of violence associated with the families reported in the case files. It was also found that the workers under-recalled the physical assault, sexual and psychological abuse, and neglect of the children for whom they were responsible.

The workers reported that:

- 72% of their cases involved psychological abuse of a child;
- 43% of their cases involved physical assault of a child;
- 35% of their cases involved neglect of a child; and
- 26% of their cases involved sexual abuse of a child.

When these findings were compared with the sample (comprising just over 10%) of their files, which were examined in detail by one of the authors, the workers had consistently under-recalled the maltreatment experienced by the children. It was found that:

- psychological abuse was recorded in the files 1.4 times more frequently than the frequency recalled by the workers;
- physical assault was recorded in twice as many files than the frequency recalled by the workers;
- sexual abuse was recorded 2.2 times more frequently than the frequency recalled by the workers; and
- neglect was recorded 2.3 times more frequently than the frequency recalled by the workers.

Thus, the children from the workers' current case load were being subject to far greater maltreatment, indeed twice as many types of maltreatment, to that recalled by the worker. This level of under-recall by the workers was almost identical to that found in an earlier pilot study undertaken by the authors (Stanley & Goddard 1993b). The extent and consistency of this error of recall suggests an association between denial, associated with hostage-like behaviour, and protection failure.

Despite the difficulties referred to above, careful content analysis of the files sometimes suggested a link between decisions reminiscent of hostage-like behaviour and the failure to protect a child. The following are three brief examples of cases which serve to illustrate why the authors have drawn this conclusion.

In the first case, three children had been subjected to constant and severe abuse over a nine-year period. Although known to protective services over this period of time, the children remained unprotected. The maltreatment included almost daily physical assault, being burnt, dragged by their hair, poked with needles, being subjected to physical labour and food deprivation, being forced to remain confined and immobile and chained to objects. Sexual assault was strongly suspected. The file noted that the children's '. . . resistance appears to have been broken down by systematic and calculated physical punishment'. The parents had a long criminal history, as well as a history of domestic violence and drug use. They constantly obstructed, verbally harassed, and physically threatened protective workers with assault, death threats and threats to the workers' children.

After the research interview, the worker stated that she '. . . could now see that she had been a hostage to this family'. At a later date, a subsequent worker stated that she could see no grounds to remove the children from the family. However, one of the authors was told by a colleague that the worker was 'terrified . . . (and has) never been so scared'. The family continued to make 'strong' threats to workers, including death threats. The workers at the local office told the researcher that they accepted they were rendered powerless by the family and had 'decided not to perpetuate the pointless conflict' by visiting the family.

In a second example, the case file described five siblings as being subjected to severe and multiple forms of abuse. The children also appeared to be suffering from a number of physical stress symptoms, such as enuresis and encopresis. Domestic violence was reported by a minister of religion, and the children and their mother were restricted in outside contact by the children's father. In one extreme example, the mother did not receive immediate medical attention for a limb broken during an assault by the father, as she was not allowed out of the house without her husband accompanying her. The children reported hearing their mother being sexually assaulted. The 14-year-old girl, who had run away from home, described how she had been raped by her father over a number of years. She was concerned that her sister was also being raped.

The father was reported as being violent and intimidatory towards professionals. The file records that: the father made threats in a 'very violent and sexual way' towards a female welfare worker; a minister of religion reported to the police that he was fearful of assault; a child care agency put on extra staff for their own protection when they knew the father was visiting; and the school refused contact with adult family members.

The Children's Court decided to keep the remaining four siblings at home under a supervision order, with the condition that their parents attend joint and individual counselling. However, the file states that because of parental denial that any abuse was occurring, an agreement was made between protective services and the parents that they would accept weekly departmental visits instead of counselling. The file records only one home visit. The protective worker noted in the file that the father was 'a dangerous man', 'it's incredibly scary' and 'nobody is safe with him'. This protective worker for the family then left. The new worker recorded visiting the family three times in eight months but no information was provided about the children during this time. The worker wrote, however, that there is 'no point' in visiting as the parents do not cooperate. Despite many contrary opinions in the file, the worker recorded that she believed that only one child had any fear of the father. She recommended case closure, five months prior to the completion of the supervision order.

In the final example, concern was documented in the file, over a period of 22 months, about the welfare of two siblings who were suffering psychological abuse and neglect. The family had many concerning issues, including family violence, drug abuse and psychiatric illness. Members of the immediate and extended family were reported to be involved in a range of criminal activities and criminal networks. The mother claimed she had a store of guns and knives which she would use on any visiting protective worker. The father, although in jail on a long sentence, made threats to the effect that he had contacts outside the jail who would follow his instructions. Examination of the file revealed that: some police and court personnel expressed fear of the extended family; welfare agencies refused to work with the family; a placement officer, who was providing support to maintain the children at home, left because of 'an incident' (which was not further identified); and a male relative was too frightened to appear in a court hearing concerning the children.

There appeared to have been a departmental decision that the children should be removed from their mother's care, and the department made an unsuccessful attempt to implement this decision with the mother's agreement. The following is an extract from a report in the file which argued why the children should not be removed against the mother's wishes:

'Given the parents refusal to co-operate on a voluntary basis the question is now should we invoke our legal powers and face the possible hostility from a family notorious for crime and violence and who pride themselves on their reputation. Protective workers are rightly very anxious about the fact that their names are known to this family and are very hesitant to be involved in this case any further. . . . Should the children be removed the mother's well-being is placed in jeopardy given her husband's threats on the phone and the fact that he appears to be well aware of all movements at the home. . . . Up to now some voluntary agencies have been very reluctant to support Mrs ...... (mother) given the family's reputation. . . . The risk to the children we believe currently is more of an emotional nature than a physical one. Given Mrs ......'s (mother) fear of repercussions should the children be removed from her care it is our belief that she will not force the issue by overtly harming the children. We however need a close monitoring support system to ensure minimal harm to the children should we decide to leave them at home. It is the Protective Worker's assessment that if this was any other family it is highly likely that we would have seriously considered removing the children. It is the workers, team leader and manager's opinion that at this point in time on balance we could consider leaving the children with Mrs ...... (mother), but will have to make extra resources available to ensure regular support and monitoring. The rationale for this is that we believe that the children are not at immediate physical risk. Should we remove the children they will be caught up in a battle between ourselves and the family which will have a negative impact on the children as well. In addition workers by virtue of fear and intimidation will not be able to work effectively with this family and voluntary agencies will feel similarly. We also believe that Mrs ...... (mother) will work co-operatively with us given extra supports.'

The extract suggests that workers' fears for their own safety was an important factor in the decision not to remove the children. Rather than facing and addressing this barrier to protecting the children, the issue is skirted around and other reasons for not removing the children are provided. Despite the fact that workers are 'very anxious' about their safety, and that some voluntary agencies have been 'very reluctant' to be involved, the decision is made to provide 'regular support and monitoring'. It is easy to understand why the file was often inactive and why workers changed, on average, every two months.

The file subsequently documented further psychological abuse of the children in the form of exposure to violence and heavy drug use. One child, aged 9 years, was clearly in physical danger as the mother was threatening to kill her. It would appear that intimidation by a person in jail, in association with the apparent reluctance of other professionals to work with the mother, contributed to a reluctance by protective services to take action to ensure the welfare of these children.

CONCLUSION

We recognise that there are many possible causes of child protection failure. We also acknowledge that many complex factors are interconnected and may affect outcome in a variety of ways. It is apparent from the Victorian study that extensive violence may play a far larger role than has been acknowledged to date. Our research also suggests that child protection workers who experience the most intimidation and violence, and receive the least support, sometimes demonstrate hostage-like behaviour. This behaviour in turn may contribute to a failure to protect some children who have been seriously harmed.

9

BEYOND THE FIRING LINE: A BROAD PERSPECTIVE

INTRODUCTION

Up to this point we have drawn the reader's attention to a range of child protection issues which may create obstacles to the process of protecting children from further harm. These issues may be viewed and understood in the context of hostage theory. Given our present understanding of child abuse and child protection, it is neither feasible, nor desirable, to prescribe 'solutions' to address protection failures. Significant improvement in the welfare of children who have been seriously abused is only likely to be achieved through the provision of an environment which welcomes questioning and dialogue, and which involves the participation of all stakeholders, including protective workers. More research needs to accompany this process. As a first step in understanding the critical issues to be addressed, this chapter highlights the central themes from hostage theory and the Victorian child protection study findings. It needs to be pointed out that the reader will find some overlap in the following discussions due to the interrelated nature of the components which comprise hostage theory.

REPEATED CHILD PROTECTION FAILURES

It appears that there are major difficulties in protecting many children who have been seriously harmed and who are known to protective services. The Victorian child protection study indicates that for many children who have been severely assaulted, abused and/or neglected, abuse may be repeated. We examined the effectiveness of protection in terms of what could be judged as the absolute minimum standards of care of a child: the need for life without severe physical assault, sexual or psychological abuse, and for life with 'adequate' food, clothing, parenting behaviours and medical attention. The children in the study, however, were subjected to other abuses which were not considered in these re-abuse measures. For example, the files described children who witnessed siblings and parents being assaulted; children who lived with severely drug affected and/or mentally ill parent(s); and children who were homeless at 14 years of age.

As we have noted, the literature has concentrated on children who have died of assault or neglect. Commonly, these children were known to protective services prior to their death. The many examinations of the circumstances around a child's death contrast with the scant attention paid to the broader picture of a general failure to give adequate protection to many children who experience severe abuse. As we have noted in Chapter 3, the vast majority of children who suffer from further harm do not die. The impact of severe assault, abuse and/or neglect on some children may be profound, resulting in considerable physical, emotional and financial costs to the child and to society. The authors believe that whether the child dies, or experiences one or more adverse outcomes, may be due to a range of reasons, of which chance is one.

In the Victorian study, many of the case files of children who had been severely harmed revealed the repeated failure of protective services to prevent this harm from continuing. For example, provision of secure shelter is clearly a fundamental need for children, especially those children who have experienced severe abuse. Yet, at least 10% of the children in our study (aged from 1 to 17 years) were homeless, at the point of survey. The term 'at least' is used, as two other children were living with peers in what appeared to be a 'borderline' homeless situation, and the location of another two children could not be ascertained from their files.

The following case summary provides an example of repeated failure to protect the surveyed child, Delia, and her siblings. The case file recorded a history of physical assault, sexual abuse and neglect of Delia, who was almost 5 years of age at the time of our research. Some information about Delia's two younger sisters was also recorded in the file. Delia's mother had a lengthy history of physical and sexual abuse.

| 1991 | January | Delia was born, placed briefly in foster care, and returned home. |
| | February | Delia came to the attention of protective services again, on the grounds of neglect. A further, third |

		referral was made soon after this. Delia was found to be neglected and receiving inadequate nutrition.
1991	July	The file described Delia as suffering from failure-to-thrive and neglect (including medical neglect).
	September	Delia was placed in foster care for the second time.
	October	Delia was returned home. Soon after her return she was found to have suffered weight loss and general neglect, and had burns on her body. Severe violence was also found to be present in the family. Delia was placed in foster care for the third time.
	November	Delia was returned home.
1992	May	A referral was made to protective services about Delia's recently born sister, Robyn.
	July	Delia was again placed in foster care, but was soon returned home.
	August	Delia was found to have been physically assaulted and neglected.
1993	January	Delia was placed with her maternal grandmother and her file was closed.
	July	Following another referral to protective services, Delia was found to be neglected and receiving inadequate nutrition.
	November	Another sibling, Penny, was born.
	December	All files were closed.
1994	January	Delia and the new baby, Penny, were referred to protective services.
	April	Two more referrals were made about Penny, on the grounds of physical assault and neglect.
	May	Delia was found to have been physically assaulted.
	August	Penny was found to be neglected.
1995	January	Delia was once again placed with her maternal grandmother.
	February	The files on Delia and Penny were closed.
	March	Delia's file was reopened.
	April	A referral was made to protective services about the 'rape' of Robyn, aged 2 years.
	May	Another referral was made in relation to the neglect of Penny. Penny was found to be suffering from weight loss (as mother was 'forgetting' to feed her). She was left in dirty and wet clothes and bedding, and had a 'flat head' as a result of being left lying in her cot for long periods.

1995	June	Robyn was found to have been neglected, left out at night, and physically assaulted. All the children were described on the file as psychologically abused. The rape of Robyn was found to be 'unsubstantiated' but the file stated that she had been sexually abused.
	July	Penny was placed in foster care.
	August	Penny was returned home. Another referral was made about neglect of Penny. The case file reported that a relative had been 'violent' to Robyn and Penny.
	September	Mother's partner was said to have threatened Robyn with a knife.
	October	Penny was found to be failing-to-thrive. The maternal grandfather (who had sexually abused mother) was now living with the family, together with his male, intellectually disabled partner.
	November	Robyn's file was closed with an attached note indicating that it would not be reopened.
	December	Another referral in relation to the children was made to protective services.

The intervention of protective services clearly failed to protect these children.

THE TOTALITY OF VIOLENCE

It is still insufficiently recognised that violence may completely dominate families where there is severe assault, abuse and/or neglect of children. Violence is a very powerful, and often a very successful, means of controlling another person or a situation. The Victorian study found that the surveyed children were subjected to multiple forms of violence. Twenty-one of the 50 children were recorded as having experienced physical assault, sexual abuse, psychological abuse and neglect. A further 20 children were documented as having experienced harm within three of these abuse categories. The remaining nine children experienced psychological abuse, together with another form of harm. Many of these children experienced this harm at the hands of more than one person. Up to seven perpetrators were recorded in the case files.

People who are violent to children are often violent to other people. In every file examined in the Victorian study there was a record of at least one other form of family violence, or criminal activity within the community. At least half of the families had at least one record of a family member being involved in: verbal abuse between adults involved in the care of the surveyed child (41 families); physical assault between those partners (31 families); psychological abuse between those partners (25 families); and other forms of self-destructive behaviour such as suicide, self-mutilation or severe drug abuse (39 families). Further, in close to half of the families at least one member had been recorded as having psychiatric problems (24 families), alcohol problems (23 families) and drug abuse problems (23 families). It is clearly important that future research into severe harm to children should closely examine the totality of violence in these families in order to understand the true position of the child.

When a protective worker becomes involved with a violent family it is illogical to believe that the protective worker will be immune from this violence. The Victorian study demonstrates that the workers are not in fact exempt. Within a period of only six months, 9 of the 50 workers interviewed had been subjected to physical assaults, and four workers to assault by a person wielding an object. There were a total of 68 episodes of threatened assault. Thus, 35 of the 50 workers were victims of at least one major trauma, in the form of assault, attempted or threatened assault, a death threat, or another form of major intimidation (see Table 6.1).

Even without personally experiencing victimisation, the impact on the worker of being exposed to violence is likely to be significant. The worker may have to negotiate with a person who has a record of violence towards other people. In 20 families, at least one family member had physically assaulted someone outside the family. In 16 families, a member had sexually abused someone outside the family. The workers may be affected by violence in other ways. For example, as we discuss below, vicarious or secondary traumatisation, where the counsellor adopts symptoms of trauma, is documented in the literature (Herman 1992). In another possible impact of working with violence, Goodwin describes how this violence and abuse may be so terrifying and horrible, that there is a risk that the worker may place a limit on what she believes, in order to maintain 'a more sane and manageable world' (1985: 8).

A brief summary of one of the case files illustrates the extraordinary reality of violence:

'Mother had a history of severe abuse and neglect, an intellectual disability, psychiatric problems, drug and alcohol problems, self-mutilation and suicide attempts, a jail term, and two miscarriages due to domestic violence. She also had a sibling who was killed at four weeks of age. At the time of reading the file, the mother had five children, aged from 4 to 11 years. The case file recorded four male partners, all but one of whom were violent to her. The first male partner had alcohol problems and engaged in drug dealing. He was recorded as sexually abusing two of the children. The second male partner had an extensive criminal record involving drugs and violence. He was recorded as physically assaulting two children. There was little mention of the third male partner as this section of the case file was missing. The fourth male partner had a criminal record and drug problems. The file recorded him as sexually abusing two of the children. The file also recorded that the mother, two of her male partners, and two older children had been engaged in extensive intimidation of child protection workers.'

TAKING VIOLENCE AGAINST THE PROTECTIVE WORKERS SERIOUSLY

Violence against child protection workers is a significant part of the total picture of violence that may be present where children have been seriously harmed. The findings of the Victorian study on violence to workers were reviewed in Chapter 6. The workers were asked about actual violence, threatened violence and intimidation, in a time period of only six months. Despite this limited time period, the workers painted a grim picture.

At many levels society has been slow to respond to this violence to child protection workers. There are parallels with our understanding of child abuse and neglect itself. Less than 20 years ago, Finkelhor wrote that child sexual abuse was 'emerging' as a 'major' form of child abuse, and in the 1970s it was seen as 'rather uncommon' (1984: 1). It may be that our knowledge of the extent of violence against protective workers will undergo a similar process of recognition.

Certainly there are cautious signs for optimism. In mid-1999, *Community Care* introduced 'No fear: The campaign for safety in social work'. There were five main objectives in the campaign including recognition of the extent of violence against social workers, 'training' for staff, establishing targets for reducing violence, increasing public awareness of violence, and registering all violent incidents (see, for example, *Community Care*, 22 July 1999). What is particularly commendable about this campaign is the clear message that violence against workers is unacceptable. The resultant National Task Force (2001) report is examined in Chapter 11. For too long there has been a sense that violence is inevitable and therefore there is little that can be done. Some texts tend to reinterpret such violence. Balloch and colleagues, for example, suggest that when workers are subject to violence, attacks are not so much directed at them 'as individuals' but may be attacks 'on the authority or power they personify' (1995: 95). The truth is that, whatever the motivation, assaults are unacceptable.

Many workers in the Victorian study were the victims of criminal acts (see Table 6.1). Only 10 of the 50 workers, however, had *ever* made a statement to the police, with one worker making two statements. For two of these, the worker was not the source of the report. These involved damage to a car (pursued by protective services), and theft and use of credit cards (pursued by a bank). The police laid no charges in relation to five of the total of 11 reported incidents. The five reports not acted upon were an assault, two death threats, and two incidents of intimidation (one of which involved a gun).

The following summary provides an example of a case where an offence was not reported to the police:

> 'During one interview with a protective worker, the father became in-
> creasingly angry. At the end of the interview, he fiercely pushed a table into
> the worker's stomach. After discussion with her supervisor, the worker
> decided not to make a report to the police, as there was no bruising. The
> worker described how the incident "hit" her about a week later. She said
> she was in tears every day and did not want to go to work. The worker
> described the management response as "very good". She was given relief
> from her caseload but sought counselling outside protective services.'
> (Worker 9110)

Only 14 workers had *ever* made an official notification to management about a serious incident of any sort. Two of these related to concerns about procedural matters and three related to reports to police, men-tioned above. The great majority of workers 'coped' with the incident themselves. Nearly all the workers talked about the incident with their peers, 21 had undergone 'debriefing', and 20 took time off from work (10 doing this on more than one occasion). Of those taking time away from work, 15 workers used their annual holidays to recover from a stressful incident.

The apparent acceptance of much violence is serious at a number of levels. The failure to report criminal violence may reflect an element of hostage-like behaviour (see below). The failure to report is also of con-cern in relation to the message it gives to children and families. It may be that this failure gives the impression that actual (and threatened) violence can be overlooked and that there are no consequences for such behaviour.

THE FAILURE TO RECOGNISE HOSTAGE-LIKE BEHAVIOUR

The authors suggest that hostage-like behaviour is an important, yet largely unrecognised, dimension in child protection work. We have previously written how some children who have been assaulted, abused and/or neglected may behave like hostages (Goddard & Stanley 1994, Goddard & Tucci 1991, Stanley & Goddard 1995). Chapter 7 drew attention to the similarities between the personality and activities of some political terrorists and child abusers. The literature reports that some children who have been maltreated live in fear or terror and experience isolation (Stanley & Goddard 1995). While the literature rarely reports research on the child's perspective, it is reported that some children who have been maltreated respond with helplessness and use defence mechanisms, such as denial, disassociation and identification with the aggressor. They may form what the authors have described as a pathological attachment to the abuser and engage in hostage-like behaviour (Stanley & Goddard 1995).

The protective worker may also display such characteristics. In Chapter 8, we revealed that those workers who experienced both the greatest intimidation and/or violence and the least support, were more likely to be showing signs of trauma. Hostage theory draws attention to, and this study emphasises, the range of potentially concerning situations to which protective workers may be exposed. These are:

- the detailed histories of severely harmed children;
- accounts of other violence;
- exposure to the trauma of colleagues;
- threatened and actual harm to themselves;
- a lack of support; and
- exposure to other work-related stresses.

There is increasing evidence that people in high-risk occupations, such as the police, fire-fighting personnel and emergency workers, may suffer traumatic stress as a result of their exposure to trauma in others, and the possible risk to themselves (Paton & Violanti 1996). Of particular interest is a study where the Impact of Event Scale (IES) was administered to fire-fighters and social services populations (not further defined). While both groups had similar exposure rates, the social service group had double the IES score, or traumatic stress symptoms.

As we noted above, a person need not be directly exposed to trauma for it to elicit a stress response. Stress responses may be elicited solely by *indirect* exposure to trauma. Recent research into traumatic stress indicates that trauma can occur in those working with traumatised people. In such a situation, the protective worker may become a secondary victim (Iliffe & Steed 2000), subjected to what has been termed vicarious trauma or secondary trauma (Lee 1995, Wilson & Lindy 1994).

A recent Australian study confirms this. Iliffe and Steed (2000) explored the impact on counsellors of working with domestic violence clients. Although the sample was comparatively small (18), they found evidence of secondary traumatisation in the workers. The counsellors reported changes in their cognitive schema, especially in relation to safety and their 'worldview' (ibid.: 406). In addition, many of the respondents reported feelings of powerlessness, isolation and burn-out.

This study includes a number of other findings that are relevant. The counsellors did not work exclusively with domestic violence. On average, about half of their case loads (51%) were made up of domestic violence clients. Iliffe and Steed (2000: 408) suggest that:

> 'Counselors with high loads of trauma clients were found to experience more symptoms of vicarious trauma and more disrupted beliefs about themselves and others.'

The protective workers in our study, of course, had case loads made up exclusively of child abuse and neglect cases.

It also appears that the participants in Iliffe and Steed's study did not visit the homes of clients, or at least this aspect of their work is not reported. There is also no discussion of any actual or threatened violence directed at the counsellors. Nevertheless, listening to traumatic material provoked strong feelings of horror in the counsellors. Female workers experienced feelings 'more intensely and more frequently' (ibid.: 400), although Iliffe and Steed suggest that this finding may be related to the fact that females work more often with survivors. Finally, many of the counsellors 'reported that it was particularly difficult hearing about violence when children were involved and hearing about abuse when it was current' (ibid.: 401). A similar adverse impact was experienced by one of the authors when reading the case files for the Victorian study.

Child protection workers may experience secondary traumatisation from learning about what happened to the children for whom they are responsible, but their exposure to trauma is often much more than this. They may directly witness abuse and the physical and emotional scars of abuse. They may themselves become a victim of intimidation and violence. Some workers may experience this in an isolated and unsupportive environment and perhaps even in a setting where the worker is held responsible for the other person's criminal behaviour. As a result, some workers may adopt hostage-like behaviour. Thus, the authors understand hostage-like behaviour to be a far more profound response to a far more severe situation than one that may generate secondary traumatisation. Child protection workers may suffer direct, as well as secondary, traumatisation.

If protective workers feel isolated and powerless, if they feel constrained from displaying anger, or if they feel compelled to continue visiting families where violence is pervasive, we should not be surprised if those workers then discover that distortion of reality is the best, if not the only, option available. The following quotes from the authors' study appear to reflect such responses:

> ' "I am immune to the violence, . . . you develop an art where you can push the problem away . . .." ' (Worker 9120)

> ' "On the first home visit you are so nervous but when you are experienced, you don't realise the dangers you are taking." ' (Worker 6220)

> ' "You build a shield around yourself, don't take on feelings – you couldn't do the job if you did." ' (Worker 9130)

> 'The worker spoke about an armed hold-up at the protective services office and the harassment of staff by the offenders in the following weeks. She said, I have ". . . an understanding for the violence. I would expect people to be angry." ' (Worker 4120)

Such distortion of reality may be effective in reducing the perception, and the reality, of risk to the worker. A cooperating hostage does not continually need to be persuaded by extreme tactics to be 'convinced' of the position desired by the terrorist:

> 'The more I agreed with them, the more accepting of me they became and the more they left me alone to rest and to find some peace in this revolutionary maelstrom.' (Hearst 1982: 172)

> ' "Initially there were threats of violence but you get to understand each other after a while." ' (Worker 5210)

Hostage-like behaviour has probably prevented severe injury to, or saved the lives of, many political hostages, women trapped in violent relationships, children caught in families where they are assaulted, and possibly even protective workers who have to intervene in families steeped in violence. It may be difficult, however, for a person who is already a hostage to save another hostage. Past writers have not understood why some mothers fail to protect a child from violent males and yet many workers continue to place the responsibility for the child's protection with the child's mother. Like the mother of a child who has been mal-treated, the protective worker may find it very difficult to protect a child who has been maltreated from a determined aggressor. This difficulty will be compounded when the child is acting like a hostage and, as such, may be sabotaging the protective worker's actions to protect him or her.

The experience of trauma may affect a range of the worker's activities. A worker displaying some hostage-like behaviour may experience a reduc-tion in work capability. For example, there may be an impact on informa-tion processing, due to disturbances in time, memory and concentration, and the adoption of a helpless viewpoint (Herman 1995, Horowitz 1997, van der Kolk, van der Hart & Marmar 1996). A worker may find that hyperarousal may lead to difficulty in distinguishing between what is relevant and what is not, and dissociation may be used to deal with other stressful life experiences as well as trauma-related intrusions (van der Kolk, McFarlane & van der Hart 1996).

THE SIGNIFICANCE OF PSYCHOLOGICAL VIOLENCE

As we have noted, there has been a developing interest in violence to social workers and other care staff. This inquiry has largely been con-fined, however, to actual physical violence. Psychological violence and intimidation have rarely been considered (see, for example, Bulatao and VandenBos 1996). This omission is surprising, given that some authors suggest that psychological trauma may be, at least, equally as distressing as physical violence (Cameronchild 1980, Herman 1992, 1995). Other au-thors suggest that a fear that violence may occur can have a severe impact on a workforce (Norris 1990, Northwestern National Life 1993).

Psychological abuse would appear to be an essential component in the successful control of another person. Threats of harm are used more frequently than actual harm (Herman 1995).

> 'The methods of establishing control over another person are based upon the systematic, repetitive infliction of psychological trauma. These methods are designed to instil terror and helplessness, to destroy the victim's sense of self in relation to others, and to foster a pathological attachment to the perpetrator.' (Herman 1995: 92)

The terrorism literature documents how psychological intimidation is used as a method of control by reinforcing and reminding the victim of a physical act of violence, or even by only suggesting the possibility that a physical act of violence may occur. In the child protection context, this behaviour could involve threats about the protective worker's welfare, threats about the welfare of the worker's family or colleagues or, indeed, threats made to the protective worker suggesting harm to the child who has been maltreated.

The Victorian study found that psychological intimidation was often used by families who had severely harmed a child. For example, in a period of six months, most workers (86%) had experienced at least one episode of glaring and threatening looks. Over a quarter of the workers (28%) had experienced at least one episode of more severe intimidation in the form of having their exit blocked, having their car keys taken, or being followed.

Psychological abuse directed towards the worker may be more important than physical violence in influencing the worker's behaviour. The political terrorism literature states that the Stockholm Syndrome is less likely to occur in a situation where the hostage is physically injured (Strentz 1982). This may be because, when faced with the physical evidence of injury, it is hard to deny the violence, rationalise the events and identify with the aggressor. Moreover, when the child protection worker is injured, she is more likely to have greater external support, especially from the legal system. Ambiguity is removed and the authorities have stronger grounds for decisive protective action. Threatened rather than actual violence towards the worker may thus have a greater adverse impact on the worker's ability to protect the child.

SUPPORT FOR THE PROTECTIVE WORKER IS FUNDAMENTAL TO PROTECTION FOR THE CHILD

Our Victorian child protection study suggests that isolation is a crucial component in the formation of hostage-like behaviour. Isolation has been mentioned as an issue, especially in relation to the literature on stress and burn-out, in the 1970s and early 1980s, and again in some of the more recent literature on trauma. However, this complex concept has rarely been discussed in depth and remains largely under-researched.

The available literature concentrates on the importance of support in relation to recovery from trauma. Support is also said to have a major role to play in relation to prevention of stress and trauma (Proctor & Alexander 1992). We believe that issues relating to support and isolation, in the physical, emotional and intellectual sense, are relevant to many aspects of child protection. The central role of support, and indeed the complexities of the concept, can be seen in the following examples. Herman (1992) writes that a person has increased exposure to the terrorist or perpetrator's perspective when isolated from social supports. In an additional twist, she also notes that:

'The perpetrator's arguments prove irresistible when the bystander faces them in isolation.' (Herman 1992: 8)

She describes how isolation maintains the abuse:

'Without a supportive social environment, the bystander usually succumbs to the temptation to look the other way. This is true even when the victim is an idealized and valued member of society. . . . When the victim is already devalued (a woman, a child), she may find that the most traumatic events of her life take place outside the realm of socially validated reality. Her experience becomes unspeakable.' (Herman 1992: 8)

The organisational environment is important in the workers' experience of isolation or support. Tucci (1989: 10), in his examination of stress as a reason for high worker turnover in the Department of Human Services, Victoria, found that the workers' sense of anomie was an important factor in determining whether the workers stayed with, or left, the organisation. Bennett, Evans and Tattersall (1993: 41) found that child protection workers showing the highest stress were those who felt 'relatively under-supervised and isolated at work'.

The Victorian study found that the experience of trauma plus isolation was highly associated with hostage-like behaviour in protective workers. More research is urgently needed on the role and type of support needed to maximise the effectiveness of child protection work. Chapter 10 addresses this issue.

THE LACK OF POWER OF THE PROTECTIVE WORKER

The Victorian child protection study has led the authors to strongly question the apparent belief that the protective worker has the power to enforce change in established patterns of violent behaviour. We suggest that, in the face of non-cooperation, it is often the protective worker who may be forced to capitulate in order to maintain at least some form of contact with the family of the child who has been abused. As we described earlier in the book, there was a very strong perception, by all but one protective worker, that male perpetrators were controlling. There can be no doubt that protective services as an organisation is powerful, but the individual protective worker, in the home of a violent perpetrator of abuse, may have great difficulty utilising that power.

Barling (1996) draws attention to another issue important to understanding power in relation to protection work. He notes that those who experience and are exposed to workplace violence (to which, we would add exposure to other forms of violence):

> '. . . may now believe that they have lost the ability to control one of their most basic needs (i.e., the need for a safe and secure workplace).' (Barling 1996: 37)

Barling believes that this loss of control has substantial negative consequences. These include direct outcomes, such as a 'negative mood', 'cognitive distraction' and 'fear', and indirect outcomes, such as 'emotional exhaustion, depression, psychosomatic complaints, accidents [and] turnover intentions' (ibid.: 39). Some workers in the Victorian study reported these conditions: 31 workers said they 'often' or 'always' experienced emotional exhaustion; 21 workers 'sometimes', and 4 'often' or 'always', felt weepy for no apparent reason; 19 'often' or 'always' experienced headaches, nausea and/or tension; and 32 'often' or 'always' experienced physical exhaustion. It is difficult to view these workers as powerful.

Many workers felt helpless, an issue discussed in Chapter 8. A worker who feels unsupported and isolated may also feel powerless to change organisational behaviours that appear to be entrenched:

> ' "There is often no support from managers and the workers are made to feel devalued and deskilled." ' (Worker 4220)

> ' ". . . in this department, there is not much point about doing anything about anything. . . . You can talk to seniors who would listen and do nothing further. Not enough recognition of stress . . . very disempowering. You can't do anything, you feel anger and frustration." ' (Worker 2340)

> ' "Protection workers are at the bottom of the heap [and] . . . in a no-win situation." ' (Worker 4130)

> ' "I often feel gagged if my manager doesn't feed information up the bureaucratic line . . . they gate-keep." ' (Worker 6350)

THE NEED TO INVOLVE CHILD PROTECTION WORKERS

The final stage of the Victorian child protection study proposed to incorporate feedback of the results to the protective workers. This process was intended to facilitate discussion of the major implications of the study and to collate the workers' suggestions about actions required. This stage of the research proved to be difficult to complete.

It is possible to draw a number of conclusions from these events. As we discussed earlier in this book, the recent history of child protection has involved an increasingly procedural and bureaucratic response to child abuse. The demands for more detailed procedures arose from a series of inquiries into child deaths (see Chapter 3). They did not arise from research into serious abuse of children (nor from an examination of child protection practice in such cases), nor did they develop as a result of discussions with child protection workers. There is an urgent need to involve workers in future research.

FURTHER MESSAGES FROM THE WORK ENVIRONMENT

While there has been little research in the area, a strong association has been shown in the general workplace between job stress, workplace violence and intimidation (Northwestern National Life 1993). Job stress was found to be both a cause and an effect of workplace violence, with violence increasing with worker stress levels. The Victorian study produced a similar finding, those workers with higher work context stresses being more likely to display hostage-like behaviour (Chapter 8).

Chapter 2 documents the numerous, and often major, structural and policy changes that have taken place in the recent history of the Victorian government department responsible for child protection. These changes have often taken place in an atmosphere of conflict and there have been formal inquiries involving government, legal and academic leaders, together with extensive and influential media involvement. Within such an environment, protective workers were expected to continue their difficult, complex and emotionally demanding work.

The Victorian study found that many workers expressed difficulties in relation to their working facilities and conditions. Workers were asked to rate a number of issues on a five-point scale, which allowed for two levels of dissatisfaction, one neutral position, and two levels of satisfaction. About three-quarters of the workers expressed dissatisfaction with the number of protective workers and administrative staff. Dissatisfaction with the level of consultation between management and workers on policy and programme changes was expressed by 31 workers. Furthermore,

44 workers believed that organisational changes were adversely impacting on their work.

The lack of resources was also strongly criticised. Over half of the workers expressed dissatisfaction with their office facilities, in particular with the lack of suitable interviewing rooms:

> ' "The interview room has a buzzer, but I doubt if I could get over to it if in trouble. It's under the phone, so obvious to clients, who only have to stand in front of the wall." The worker said she preferred to conduct an interview with a potentially violent client in the hall, as "I've had enough of being pushed against walls".' (Worker 5410)

Only four workers expressed satisfaction with the availability of cars, many using words like 'shocking', 'the last straw', 'a nightmare', 'awful' and 'it impedes your ability to do the job properly'. For these workers, a positive work environment may have provided mitigating preventative and restorative influences in a highly stressful job. Instead, their work environment contributed to their stress. The following chapter offers further information about contextual stress in the workplace.

THE GULF BETWEEN THEORY AND PRACTICE

In Chapter 5 we suggested that there are still a number of important connections to be made, and contradictions to be resolved, in child protection practice. It would be comforting to assume that simple answers lie elsewhere but we do not believe that to be the case. There is a great deal more to discover. The literature on traumatic stress, for example, may make a contribution. There are, however, many shortcomings in that research. Nonetheless, there are parallels that need further exploration.

The traumatic stress literature is at least raising many important questions. One such question is what causes some people to transform some experiences into traumatic responses, while others do not (see, for example, van der Kolk et al. 1996). It is essential in such questioning not to blame the worker or to raise expectations that workers should cope with what is fundamentally unacceptable behaviour. With this proviso in mind, it is also important to examine whether workers who were abused as children will have especial difficulties with power and dominance in personal and/or professional relationships.

There are other deficits, however, in the traumatic stress literature. There is a common assumption that the stressful event or critical incident is discrete and time-limited (see, for example, Everly, Flannery & Mitchell

1998). Horwitz (1998), who writes of child protection workers experiencing psychological trauma from work experiences, also views the trauma-producing events as discrete and time-limited. As is common in the trauma literature, he emphasises that the protection worker must feel safe before healing can commence.

> 'Once safety has been achieved . . . [and] . . . After thoughts and feelings have been explored, trauma victims develop strategies for dealing with any remaining negative effects of the traumatic experience and return to their previous level of workplace functioning.' (Horwitz 1998: 369)

The Victorian study suggests that, for some workers at least, an ongoing experience of trauma may be their experience of 'normal' workplace functioning. Child protection workers, like hostages, may be subject to ongoing critical 'incidents'. Herman (1992: 118–122) argues that a 'new concept' is required for the 'chronically traumatized'. She proposes the term 'complex post-traumatic stress disorder' to describe the range of reactions to 'prolonged, repeated trauma' (ibid.: 119). Herman believes such a condition includes people who have been abused and/or exploited in domestic violence or as a child. While protective workers may not suffer from such profound stress, they may suffer stress from a number of sources simultaneously. Hostage theory may provide a framework that advances an understanding of the complexities of this area.

ADDRESSING HOSTAGE-LIKE BEHAVIOUR

Will Some Homes Always be Unsafe?

It is apparent that many of the children in our study were not protected after referral to protective services and after court-ordered intervention. The picture we have described is grim. The repeated return of some of the children to families racked by violence is difficult to comprehend. The problem of returning a child to an unsafe environment is not new, however. More than 10 years ago, Jones (1987: 409) suggested that:

> 'The idea that some families do not respond appears to be anathema to some practitioners and researchers alike. Yet the reality for those who work in the field of child abuse is that some families cannot be treated or rehabilitated sufficiently to offer a safe enough environment in which children can live.'

Jones proposed a number of reasons why some families fail to respond to the services offered:

1. There are some families who simply will not change. They do not intend or want to change.
2. Some parents persistently deny abusive behaviour in the face of clear evidence to the contrary.
3. Some families cannot change in spite of a will to do so. There may be a sub-group here of families who are willing to change but resources to help them are not available.
4. Some parents can change, but not 'in time' for their child's developmental needs. For example, a 6-month-old baby's abusive parent, who after two years becomes less impulsive and dangerous, but in the meantime whose baby has developed a strong attachment to a surrogate parent.
5. Similarly, other parents may change in time for their next child but not for the index one.
6. Finally there is the category of untreatable parents who fail to respond to one treatment approach but who may be amenable to another agency or approach.

Jones describes an 'untreatable family' as 'one in which it is unsafe to permit an abused child to live' (ibid.: 416). He makes it clear that this definition does not mean that such families should receive no help. He insists, however, that in these cases help should be directed at 'aiding relinquishment rather than reuniting the child and parent(s)' (ibid.: 416). Jones proposes that it is possible to summarise the characteristics of 'untreatable families' in five main groups:

1. *Parental factors associated with untreatability.* Parental factors associated with untreatability include a parental history of severe childhood abuse, a persistent denial of abusive behaviour, severe personality disorder (sociopathy or grossly inadequate personality), and mental handicap when associated with personality disorder.
2. *Parenting quality associated with poor outcome.* The parenting quality which most authors and clinicians find to be associated with poor outcome is a lack of empathic feeling for the child, either when victimised or in the present. Such parents fail to see their child's needs as separate or different from their own.
3. *Aspects of abuse associated with untreatable outcome.* Aspects of the abuse itself appear to be associated with an untreatable outcome, e.g., severe types of abuse such as fractures, burns and scalds.
4. *Dangerousness to child.* With respect to dangerousness, cases where the parent has perpetrated previous violent acts are more likely to prove untreatable. The greater the number of such acts the greater the risk of repetition.

5. *Type of professional response.* Lastly, there is a trend which links successful treatment outcome with the establishment of a helping relationship combined with an outreach component. Where this does not occur outcome seems less good.

Jones concludes by arguing that time limits must be set on any attempts to make a family safe.

Jones leaves out one very difficult and complex group of families who repeatedly harm their children. This is the group who not only harm one child but often harm all their children, as well as other family members and members of the community. When the violence is so all-pervasive, it is naïve to believe that a child has any hope of remaining safe. Serious and entrenched violence is rarely selective in its victims. Even in the unlikely event that the child who has been abused is not directly re-victimised, witnessing violence to others is in itself severely abusive. The child will be vulnerable to vicarious traumatisation unless all forms of violence are prevented. To be able to achieve adequate change in these families (if possible) would need extensive resources, beyond those currently available to protective services, at least in Victoria. Even given unlimited resources, it is doubtful if many of these families can change sufficiently to provide a safe environment for children.

One Approach towards Addressing Hostage-Like Behaviour in the Workers

In 1996 the New Zealand government department responsible for child protection undertook some policy and practice changes in response to information about hostage theory. These initiatives included:

- the establishment of Area Dangerous Situations Teams to '. . . act as a resource to the social worker managing the case, and to ensure that the effects of working in a dangerous situation are managed and minimised' (Doolan 1996);
- a systematic and regular review of situations of extreme violence and threat to workers;
- mandatory requirements of training (education) in relation to issues such as dangerous situations and hostage theory;
- the addition of personal worker safety to risk management reviews;
- debriefing conducted externally for all Dangerous Situation cases;
- a mandatory independent review of cases where three referrals are received within a 12-month period;

- access to legal advice in Dangerous Situation cases;
- the flagging of Dangerous Situation cases in protection record-keeping; and
- fast-tracking of access to specialist services in Dangerous Situation cases.

We await the results of the full evaluation of these changes. Implicit in these initiatives is a recognition that workers need far greater support if they are to attempt to work in the conditions we have described in our research.

CONCLUSIONS

In our view, reforms such as those undertaken in New Zealand are urgently required in Victoria and elsewhere. It is commonplace for research and theoretical development in fields such as child protection to emphasise the need for more research. The reality is that many of our efforts to protect children are failing and we need to know why. Whatever direction child protection takes in the future, supervision of child protection workers will be critical. For this reason, the following chapter examines supervision in some detail.

10

SUPERVISION: FROM PART OF THE PROBLEM TO PART OF THE SOLUTION

INTRODUCTION

Professional supervision is a vital source of support for the front-line worker. The Victorian child protection study examined in some detail many supervisory and organisational issues. This chapter commences with more information provided by the child protection workers. It then examines some of the literature on supervision, focusing particularly on supervision in child protection.

ISSUES ARISING FROM THE STUDY

What the Workers said about Supervision and their Supervisors

Of the 50 workers interviewed, 30 reported that they had at least one to two hours of formal supervision a fortnight. There were 20 workers who reported less supervision than this, with 10 workers having no formal supervision, or less than one hour each month. Some workers reported having informal supervision, but it was generally regarded as unsatisfactory. Comments included: 'no one sits down to talk'; we talk 'on the run'; and 'you have to catch her'.

The workers were asked about the quality of the supervision they received. Their opinions were fairly evenly divided, with 17 workers largely or totally dissatisfied and 20 workers largely or totally satisfied.

When asked how supervision time was spent, however, half of the workers reported that supervision was spent entirely 'going through' cases, reviewing decisions, meeting deadlines and following up administrative work:

> 'I am "not comfortable with this supervisor, so I only talk about the case load".' (Worker 9160)

> ' "... we zoom through cases, they don't want to know about other things".' (Worker 9140)

> ' "We go through cases. Not really anything else is done." ' (Worker 6350)

> ' "We spend time dealing with crises and going through cases." ' (Worker 6120)

> 'The role of the supervisor is ". . . allocating and pushing through cases".' (Worker 5210)

> ' "Supervision is for getting paperwork done and getting their backs covered." ' (Worker 2450)

> ' "The work has become more procedurally driven, supervision is more procedurally driven. You go through time checks with each case, the procedure is more important than the outcome for the child." ' (Worker 2340)

Supervision in this agency was almost exclusively on a one-to-one basis. The few team meetings that were held appeared to concentrate on disseminating information. Approximately one-third of workers would not make changes to current supervision practices but the others made a number of suggestions. One-third of the workers wanted more supervision, and almost one-third wanted more professional development and fewer changes in supervision. Changes in supervision were seen as a particular problem, with no opportunity to build trust, and time repeatedly wasted with repetitive discussion of cases.

> 'The worker said she had little supervision and described it as "spasmodic and of little use".' (Worker 8470)

> '. . . had four supervisors in the last month.' (Worker 9110)

> '. . . had three supervisors in the last six months.' (Worker 9130

> ' "My supervisor left. I went back to another, had another for a week, another for six weeks, and this person has just left." ' (Worker 6120)

> ' "I have learnt to be an isolated worker. If you open up, with personal issues and worries, then you are seen as personally incompetent." ' (Worker 5210)

> 'I get ". . . no support or understanding . . .".' (Worker 3320)

The following account describes a worker's struggle to function with little support after experiencing violence:

> 'The worker had no current cases as she was being "eased" back into work after stress leave as a result of repeated psychological violence. She had gone directly to child protection after completing her degree. The protective services induction course did not occur until weeks after she began seeing children and families, and she reported that she had a different supervisor every three weeks. The worker said she gradually "went down-hill", having panic attacks and feeling very traumatised by the work. The worker said that the problem ". . . should have been obvious. I got the impression that they just sat back and watched it happen." She said that, by chance, she found some people outside child protection who were able to help and she was still seeing a psychologist. After working one year she eventually took a long break from work, changed offices and began office-based work, doing tasks such as taking phone referrals. At the time of the interview the worker did not have a supervisor and the researcher privately felt that she was far from ready to return to work. The researcher subsequently learnt that the worker left the department a few weeks after the interview.' (Worker 8470)

What the Workers said about Management

As might be expected in a strongly bureaucratic structure, satisfaction with feedback on work issues decreased rapidly as the bureaucratic level got higher. While 28 workers said they were 'satisfied' with feedback about work at the office level, only eight reported satisfaction at regional level and only four at head office level. Workers were also asked about the support that they would receive if they experienced a stressful event. There was a clear trend for both an increase in the belief that workers would *not* be supported and an increase in uncertainty about whether they would be supported, as management seniority increased. For example, 70% believed supervisors would give automatic support, but only 21% believed that head office would do so. In fact, one-fifth of the workers volunteered the information that they believed they would be blamed if an adverse incident occurred.

> ' "The general procedure is to duck and weave. Left standing is the child protection worker. There is a culture of covering up your arse." ' (Worker 6130)

> ' "Workers take the blame in a public way and are not supported at all by head office . . . [Management] use workers to save the department . . . One day my numbers will come up." ' (Worker 2440)

> 'The worker had been subject to an inquiry into a case. She said she was blamed for system errors and human error at a senior level and that "front-

line workers were always blamed". She claimed that the measure of effectiveness used was whether the paperwork was up to date.' (Worker 2420)

'The worker spoke of how she took 10 months leave without pay following a court appeal that went very badly. She had to stay by herself for five days in a motel in Melbourne and said she had a torrid time with no support.' (Worker 1130)

The amount of stress perceived by the workers as being generated by the organisation itself should not be underestimated. (Other quotes were provided in Chapter 6 in relation to isolation within the organisation.)

'The worker talked of how workers were punished because they involved the union over workplace issues and because they were critical of management. She said she had been demoted as a result and that another worker who had been similarly demoted had resigned. She believed that the politics of the organisation was more stressful than working with clients and their families.' (Worker 5280)

' "I can cope with cases, but not the organisation . . . a defensive organisation. I feel devalued. . .." ' (Worker 2340)

' "There is system abuse to the client and also to the worker." '(Worker 6250)

'The worker expressed the view that there was often no support from management. She said she could deal with work and other associated issues but she had difficulty with the fact that the workers were made to feel "devalued and de-skilled".' (Worker 4220)

' "Acknowledgment of the stress of the job is only from fieldworkers. Management sees it as a myth. A piss-off. You are pressured to accepting more cases to get promotion." ' (Worker 9140)

' "Workers have no input to decision-making. Decisions are made further up irrespective of concerns by the staff [which were] totally peripheral to changes. Even if we were asked, it wouldn't make any difference anyway." ' (Worker 2440)

' "The department's direction is going out the window. . . . Senior management are more concerned with statistics than any reasonable interaction with the family." ' (Worker 1180)

What the Workers said about Peer Support

The study also examined other sources of support for the workers. All workers said that peer support was very important (90%) or important (10%). They used words like 'critical', 'vital', 'essential' and 'paramount' to describe interaction with their colleagues.

'Peer interaction is ". . . very, very, very important, a great source of support . . .".' (Worker 8430)

' "Interaction with colleagues is at least 40% of satisfaction with the job".' (Worker 4120)

'Peer interaction is ". . . extremely important as a stress reliever. It is good to know that other people are feeling the same way." ' (Worker 6630)

Peer support also featured in workers' descriptions of the positive aspects of the work.

What the Workers said about Support from their Families

Four workers did not answer these questions, one of whom said she did not wish to respond and another said she had no family. Of the 46 who responded, 9 (20%) believed that their families were not concerned about the worker's safety. Eight workers (18%) believed that their families showed considerable concern, and 29 (62%) believed that their families were concerned. The particularly interesting finding was that 39 workers (85%) reported that they censored what they told their families about their work, and all but three of these clearly indicated that they restricted what they said about threats to their safety and stress in order to protect their families from worrying. All those who did not censor the information had a partner in a related field of work or had been advised by a counsellor to share their experiences with their partner.

The Good and Bad Aspects of the Job

Workers were asked to nominate the good aspects of child protection work. (It should be noted that a number of workers reported more than one positive aspect.) Almost half (24) identified assisting in reducing abuse. Peer support (15), the variety of tasks and challenges (14), working with families (9), and developing professional skills (8) also featured prominently. Just over a quarter of the workers (13) reported that the constant pace, unpredictability and the pressure of the work was a positive feature of work. It is also interesting to note that, in response to this question on positive aspects, nine workers spoke predominantly of negative aspects, while one worker could not think of any positive aspects. The following are examples of worker responses:

'The work is addictive, never boring, gives you adrenalin rushes that I can't do without." ' (Worker 1180)

'It is good to be ". . . helping an innocent child, because childhood is meant to be the happiest time of your life . . . Every child has a right to a childhood." ' (Worker 5150)

'There is ". . . variety in work . . . It is always challenging . . . I live for the buzzes . . .." ' (Worker 3220)

'I like the ". . . variety of work and friendships with colleagues. I am committed to child protection." ' (Worker 6140)

'It is good ". . . being able to protect a child . . . the possibility of being able to make at least some changes in a family".' (Worker 1170)

' "I like holding at-risk families together and friendship with colleagues. I have a belief that children have a right to be safe." ' (Worker 4120)

The workers were also asked about the negative aspects of their work, and the discrepancies between what they do and what they would like to do. Two themes in particular stood out as being of the most concern. Firstly, more than half of the workers (29) reported that the lack of resources for clients was a major issue. When asked specifically about counselling resources, the workers showed considerable dissatisfaction with the counselling available for the child (40 dissatisfied), for the family (36), and for the abusive parent (47). The resources for placing children were a major cause of concern to the respondents with 36 workers dissatisfied with placement options.

The second major theme to emerge was the problem of work overload. Almost half (23) complained of too much work, while 31 complained of the hours worked and 34 were dissatisfied with their ability to escape work pressures.

' "We are like storm troopers, in and out so fast . . . issues of abuse are addressed in two visits . . . just get in and get out." ' (Worker 1180)

' "It comes down to working time and resources, no control of either." ' (Worker 3210)

High levels of dissatisfaction were expressed about the time available for client contact (38 workers), community liaison (41) and prevention work (46).

The workers were also asked about positive and negative emotional incidents at work. Only three workers experienced more positive incidents than negative incidents at work, 12 reported an equal number, while 35 experienced more negative events. The frequency of such events was also heavily dominated by negative experiences. Almost half

(24) stated that they had negative emotional experiences at work at least daily, seven of these stating that they had a positive experience every two weeks or less. Only seven workers had a positive experience on a daily basis.

Stress after Negative Experiences

The workers were asked about whether, and how often, they experienced a range of possible negative feelings after a stressful incident which may spill over to other situations. Findings relating to the intrusion and avoidance of emotions, and those relating to feelings of helplessness, are not reported here, as they are discussed in Chapter 8. Many of the workers stated they experienced a range of adverse outcomes. The most common negative feelings were workers 'often' or 'always' experiencing physical exhaustion (32) and emotional weariness (31). A significant minority of workers (13 to 19) 'often' or 'always' experienced: physical symptoms; anger; an increase in feelings of personal vulnerability; fear that the situation will be repeated; a need to 'steel' herself to get to work the next day; and an adverse impact on her private life and relationships. Only nine workers stated that stress at work never, or only rarely, had an adverse impact on their private life.

SUPERVISION IN CHILD PROTECTION

What the Supervisor has to Deal With

The issues reported above graphically illustrate the high demands placed on the roles of supervision and the supervisor. To these we must add the other factors described earlier in this book: threatened and actual violence against the child protection workers, the exposure to violence and trauma and the experience of isolation.

Some of these findings reflect earlier studies. The sense of alienation from management is evocative of Parsloe's image of a 'Berlin wall' between the team and the rest of the organisation (1981: 92). Parsloe also suggests that not only was the management hierarchy seen as invisible and remote but it was also perceived as ignoring the needs of the frontline workers and their teams. Similarly, but far more recently, Collings and Murray described supervision itself as potentially a further 'potent source' of stress for social workers (1996: 385). Again some 20 years ago, Cooper and Glastonbury (1980: 116) recognised a 'widening rift' between the practice of social work and the organisational structure. Perhaps the divide is greater than any of us have yet realised. Before reviewing the literature in some detail, however, it is essential to examine one other issue.

A Further Complicating Factor

The Victorian child protection study did not examine the personal characteristics of the workers. Because of the potential significance of the data, however, the workers were asked whether they had a history of abuse in their own backgrounds. Over half (26) believed that they had suffered child abuse as a child, one worker was unsure, and two stated that they did not wish to answer the questions. Psychological abuse, perpetrated by the parents, was most commonly reported. The most common methods of coping with the abuse were reported to be self-blame (eight workers), and acceptance of, or accommodation to, the abuse (eight workers). Helplessness was experienced by seven workers and disassociation by six. Barely a quarter (13) responded to the question as to whether work brought back memories of their own abuse. Eight said that it did, while two said that it did not. Three workers said they were unsure, as they had not dealt with a situation at work that was similar to their own experiences. Some 20 workers answered the question as to whether their own abuse had any impact on their work. Seven said it did not, while 13 said that it did. Seven of the latter group said that the impact was not necessarily negative as it allowed them to empathise with clients giving them hope that a resolution was possible.

> ' "I had to work at becoming more authoritarian . . . and become harder in the job. Not a negative effect, almost positive." ' (Worker 3110)

> ' "There are positive effects on work: you are made perceptive and given insight. I believe that is why I am here. Negative effects are where buttons are still pushed. I am not assertive enough at times with management and at times with clients, especially with very controlling and abusive males." ' (Worker 5210)

Uncertain Environments

A recurring theme in the interviews with child protection workers in our study was the procedural nature of supervision: 'dealing with crises', 'pushing through cases', 'getting paperwork done' and 'procedurally driven', are just some of the phrases noted above. These tensions, between the 'managerial' and the 'professional' aspects of supervision have been noted as a problem elsewhere (Payne 1994: 52). Both aspects, Payne notes, have repeatedly been identified as important – for example, in child abuse inquiry reports – but there are continuing deficits. Payne also writes of further problems in the supervision process:

> '. . . there is in some agencies a culture which emphasises the process of supervision (as a protection for the agency or for individual staff) rather than the outcome of better child care and more effective response for confident, capable social workers.' (Payne 1994: 52)

Almost without exception, the workers in our research clearly indicated that protection of the agency was seen as paramount. A 'new world' of social work practice (Taylor & Vigars 1993) with new legislation and new management styles is a common theme of reviews of supervision in child protection. Other writers, however, have argued that problems in staff supervision are not new but are more complex (see, for example, Davies (1988) writing of supervision in probation).

For the title and theme of their text, Hughes and Pengelly (1997) borrow the phrase 'turbulent environment' from Emery and Trist (1965). Hughes and Pengelly draw on writing from 20 years ago to emphasise that change has been occurring rapidly for many years, but they stress that the changes of recent years have occurred on 'an unprecedented scale' (1997: 7). The picture of rapid change in the UK painted by Hughes and Pengelly has been repeated in the child protection service we studied. The government department in which child protection services are located has even changed its name several times in the last 20 years (see Chapter 2).

Even taking account of the political, economic and organisational changes that have taken place does not do justice to the extent of change in child protection services throughout the Western world. The services put in place to deal with child abuse have found the problem to be increasing in size, changing in shape and growing in complexity. These changes in the problem itself have put unrecognised pressures on front-line workers and their supervisors. Services were implemented to respond to extreme physical abuse and neglect. Current definitions of abuse now include sexual abuse and emotional and/or psychological abuse. The 'discovery' of systems abuse has led to recognition that service responses may in themselves be abusive.

The Impossible in Pursuit of the Unattainable

Waters (1992: 41), in her study of supervision of child protection work, suggests that effective supervision may be 'an insurmountable task'. She usefully draws out the parallels between the difficulties faced in their work by child protection workers and the role of supervisor in wearing 'many hats: manager, teacher, supporter, and a source of knowledge and expertise' (1992: 41):

> 'Many would suggest that the roles adopted in supervision are incompatible, as is often said about the roles social workers need to adopt in carrying out child protection work.'

Waters identifies one of the problems inherent in both child protection and supervision of child protection workers as being the emotional impact of the work on the worker. She states that there has been little discussion of the emotional consequences of the job until very recently (a point with which we concur and we discussed in Chapter 5):

> 'Perhaps this reflects the historical and overriding view that to be "professional" is not to be involved or suffer any emotional reaction as a result of contact with human suffering.' (Ibid.: 31)

Waters' study also suggests very strongly that supervision does not provide child protection workers with the opportunities to 'recognise, acknowledge, and begin to deal with the stress and anxieties . . .' (ibid.: 97).

Payne (1994: 44) reviews the aims of supervision in theory and draws upon the work of Kadushin (1992) who identifies three elements of supervision: the administrative or managerial; the educative; and the expressive, supportive and leadership functions. Payne himself, however, follows other writers and links the last two aspects, reducing the division to managerial and professional supervision. It is in this reductionism that part of the problem may lie: the stresses of child protection work experienced by child protection workers have both professional and personal impacts. If the personal costs of the work are subsumed under the professional discourse of supervision then they may get lost altogether. Waters (1992: 11), on the other hand, clearly identifies four main functions of supervision and describes them all as 'essential' if the best possible service is to be forthcoming: administrative; educational; supportive or enabling; and professional.

Differences in the descriptions of the functions of supervision are more than differences in emphases. The roles of supervision, as outlined by

Richards, Payne and Shepperd (1990: 13–14), for example, acknowledge the management, educational and supportive functions but add a fourth: mediation. They describe this function as necessary

> '. . . to represent staff needs to higher management, to negotiate what services need to be co-ordinated, or to clarify to others outside the agency the legal or resource constraints or requirements within which the team is operating.' (Richards et al. 1990: 14)

Our findings suggest that this is a vital element.

The nature of child protection work influences the supervision process, according to Richards and colleagues. They emphasise particular features of the work: it is 'emotionally charged'; it involves high levels of stress; high risk is involved in decision-making; the conflicts between care and control; the complex legal frameworks; potential cross-cultural issues; and, interdisciplinary and inter-agency activities (Richards et al. 1990: 14). Again, actual or threatened violence towards workers is apparently overlooked.

A strength of Richards and colleague's work, however, is their recognition of the 'primitive and painful feelings' that may be triggered in the worker (ibid.: 39). Richards and her co-authors recognise that the 'most ordinary natural response to pain' is to attempt to avoid it altogether, but such avoidance may lead to decisions that are 'collusive or without concern for those who may suffer in the process' (ibid.: 39). Some of the strategies used in avoiding painful and confronting situations are also summarised by Richards. These include denial, professional distancing, ritual behaviour, and projection. The parallels with hostage theory are clear. Denial, or 'reluctance to rock the boat' is understood to be all pervasive (ibid.: 39):

> 'Children are reluctant to tell, or to say no; parents are reluctant to hear. Workers are reluctant to act; seniors rely on procedures; everyone is fearful of the consequences if the pain is confronted head-on. These fears might be real or imagined, but frightening nevertheless.'

Richards and colleagues reinforce their arguments by drawing on the much-cited description of a child abuse case conference by Bacon (1988) who describes the strategies used by professionals to avoid placing a child in danger on the register of children 'at risk'. It is very interesting to note that, in Bacon's article, the workers also avoided confronting the parents with their concerns about the child, perhaps because of the violence that is only briefly mentioned.

Towards a Broad View of Supervision

Just as hostage theory has its origins beyond the normally accepted realms of social work, in the area of supervision of protective workers it is perhaps necessary for supervisors, and those writing about supervision, to examine what is being done outside social work. In arguing that closer attention should be paid to the personal support of protective workers we are, in part at least, merely reflecting what is happening elsewhere. The role of supervisors in businesses has changed (Rabey 1997). Hopkins (1997), for example, describes the recognition that supervisors in organisations should play a role that extends beyond an emphasis on efficient production (in child welfare terms, the rapid turnover of cases) and encompasses the view that workers may require personal support. Work environments beyond protective services report that workers feel overloaded, suffer stress and other personal and family problems (Hopkins 1997). The response, according to Hopkins (1997: 1217), has been 'the increasing expectation' that supervisors in corporations are responsible for both the professional and personal well-being of their workers. The world of large corporations, when examining the problems of open communication between staff, recognised the contribution that the literature close to social work can provide. Gabarro (1983), for example, draws on the work of Carl Rogers in attempting to deal with the strong feelings and tensions generated in teams of sales managers.

The 'discovery' of child abuse has created many other problems for child protection workers. Increasing recognition of child abuse occurred at a time when other research was demonstrating that institutions had deleterious effects. One of the major 'solutions' to the problem of child abuse – the removal of the abused child to a children's home – was therefore no longer available or became an action of last resort. Similar complexities are apparent when supervision is examined more closely.

Hopkins, for example, writes that, from the 1970s onward, as employers become more aware of and concerned about the problems of their workers, many organisations introduced programmes to provide assistance to 'troubled workers' (1997: 1217). Child protection, from the 1970s onwards, can be judged as travelling in the opposite direction. The work, as we have observed, has become dominated by procedural requirements as a result of the particular focus of child death inquiries reviewed in Chapter 3. Supervision, in response to this, has in turn become dominated by a need to ensure that workers are adhering to these procedures. As a consequence, the workers' personal and professional experiences and needs are discounted. There are other complex factors that contribute to these pressures on supervision, not the least the expectation that social workers are able to form helping relationships with all clients (see Chapter 5). When workers are unable to meet these expectations about relationships, they may be reluctant to discuss them in supervision if they are framed as professional failures. As we have stressed, it is unrealistic to expect child protection workers to form relationships and work in partnership with clients (usually men) who are extremely violent. Procedural requirements might therefore be used as an avoidance technique by the worker as well as by the supervisor.

Denial and the avoidance of pain, referred to above in the quotation from Richards and colleagues (1990: 39), can and does occur in supervision just as it does in other responses to child abuse. There are clear parallels here with the attempts to integrate organisational and psychodynamic theories. Neumann and Hirschhorn (1999: 685), for example, assert that:

'A fundamental assumption of psychodynamic theories is that sources of energy and motivation frequently are inaccessible to the conscious mind of those people involved even though behaviour and emotions are being affected.'

Conversely, they stress that organisational theorists rarely regard individuals as 'the central actors' (ibid.: 685):

'Most social scientists applying organizational theory concern themselves with the design, management, and charge of the structures and processes involved in linking subsystems, organizations and their environments.'

The child protection worker, however, is very much the central actor in the protective process. We observed early in this book that there has been little research on work with seriously abused children. Similarly, there has been very little research on the supervision of protective workers. Rushton and Nathan (1996: 359) also argue that we need to know a great deal more about the quality and content of supervision and whether or not it is beneficial to the child:

'No studies have identified methods and styles of supervision that are predictive of a reduction of risk to children.'

Supervision is recognised as important in a number of child abuse inquiry reports (as we noted above): child protection is described as 'the use of personal skills within a structured supervisory context' (Department of Health 1991: 28) and supervision is described as 'an integral part of case management' (ibid.: 30). It is tempting to observe, once again, that the difficult task of clearly delineating exactly what is required is avoided as in the repeated exhortations to work in partnership with parents (see Chapter 5). Rushton and Nathan identify two 'significant strands of thought' in the child abuse inquiry reports and, rightly in our view, draw attention to their potentially incompatible nature. On the one hand, supervision is required to be 'inquisitional' and conducted in a 'purposive and structured fashion' (Rushton & Nathan 1996: 358–359). On the other hand, the supervisor must 'deal effectively with the highly emotional nature of the work (ibid.: 359).

Other writers have noted the similarities between the social worker–client relationship and the supervisor–social worker relationship. Rushton and Nathan draw out one aspect in particular in the above description. Just as the protective worker is given the unenviable task of balancing care and control, so the supervisor is expected to both control and care for the child protection worker.

Protective services are not alone in facing such conflicts. Willshire (1999) explores the idea that some facets of the work carried out by psychiatric services are impossible to achieve. In a useful analysis of organisational, interpersonal and societal elements of the work, she argues that the very act of acknowledging the impossibility of some of the work may make the stresses more bearable rather than something that has to be controlled or completely denied.

Protective workers and their supervisors are both operating in circumstances where not knowing and not understanding may be regularly present in their work every day. Not completely knowing and not completely understanding the families that they work with is an omnipresent factor in protective work (as it is in mental health services). Omniscience, however, sometimes appears to be the expectation. Willshire's theme is that while we believe a 'definitive solution' is waiting to be found, such a belief will lead to 'continual movement' and change, a response evident in the protective services we studied (Willshire 1999: 798). Willshire recognises that there are dangers in such a view, and that identifying the impossible elements might in itself be seen as some form of solution. We do not go as far as Willshire; we believe that there are elements in her analysis that are too pessimistic. We do, however, have to acknowledge that there are many aspects of child protection work that we do not yet fully understand.

As Brashears (1995) emphasises, supervision is as old as social work itself. She reports that academics and practitioners have argued, throughout the comparatively short history of social work, about how to define social work supervision. Brashears argues that supervision should be reconceptualised as social work practice. As a consequence the values of advocacy, self-determination and empowerment should not only apply to clients but also to the supervised social workers themselves (Brashears 1995: 697). This is, we believe, a fundamental consideration.

Towards Integration

Brown and Baume (1996), in a particularly helpful text on supervision, identify a number of problems in the literature and in practice. They suggest that there is a broad dissatisfaction with the standard of supervision, little material available to supervisors, and relatively little acknowledgement of the importance of a value base in supervision. They see these factors in a context of rapid change and emphasise the importance of supervision in maintaining worker morale and high quality services (ibid.: 5). The chapter on the supervisor's response to the worker's stress and trauma is particularly central to our work.

The first case study describes a worker involved in a complex child abuse case. The case re-awakens feelings from the worker's own childhood, results in him being threatened by the child's father, and provokes difficulties in his relationships at home and work (ibid.: 107). Brown and Baume recognise the effects on the team and examine in detail the worker's possible reactions to stress. Of particular importance is Brown and Baume's recognition that:

> '. . . traumatic stress is primarily maintained by internal rather than external stressors. These internal stressors originate from re-experiencing some of the effects of the traumatic incident that happened at an earlier time.' (Ibid.: 118)

The Victorian child protection study found that workers were experiencing intrusions of traumatic experiences, as we described in Chapter 8.

Furthermore, Brown and Baume (1996: 118) emphasise another complexity:

> 'The distinguishing feature determining whether a person becomes traumatised by an incident is not the size of the incident, but whether it challenges a person's core beliefs about both themselves, and the way they see the world. It is important to note that it is the worker's subjective experience that is all-important, not the specific nature of the incident triggering their reaction. Thus in some circumstances being spat at may be experienced as more traumatic than being threatened with a knife.'

Hostage theory recognises that small incidents may have a cumulative impact and may be of extreme significance to an individual worker.

Brown and Baume (1996: 122–123) describe some very useful responses that the supervisor can make to the traumatised worker. These include what they term 'mediative responses', which include taking an 'executive role' dealing with practical issues, ensuring that colleagues are fully informed of the incident, and assisting colleagues to respond appropriately. Brown and Baume also provide important information about 'restorative responses'. These include maintaining contact even if the worker is absent on sick leave as a result of the incident, offering information about common reactions to trauma, and offering de-briefing which may be undertaken elsewhere if the worker prefers. An important aspect of hostage theory recognises how isolation compounds trauma.

Brown and Baume describe in detail the central aspects of debriefing and we provide a summary of these. The worker is asked to talk the supervisor through the incident in detail while being told that this process can be painful. They are given an explanation that without this process there are aspects that may become 'buried' only to return (for example, as flashbacks and nightmares). The supervisor is encouraged to acknowledge the worker's distress and to assist the worker in expressing his or her fears about what occurred. Apparent gaps in the account of the incident should be explored, as these may signify important feelings. The account of the incident should take the worker up to the present time, identifying problems since the incident, and exploring supports and the need for counselling. (For a more detailed account see Brown and Baume 1996: 124–125.)

Brown and Baume are to be commended for addressing the issue of post-traumatic stress in protective workers. There is much in their work that will ameliorate the problems of the protective worker. They recognise that supervisors may 'inherit' workers who are already traumatised and that such trauma can be re-awakened. Our reservations centre on the repeated focus on a traumatic 'incident'. In child sexual abuse there is now an acceptance that such abuse is more than an 'incident'. Sexual abuse is in fact a process, and a similar understanding needs to be applied to the traumatisation of workers who may be subject to traumatic stress on a regular basis, as our research has shown. We have further concerns that, while it is important that we fully recognise insights into worker traumatisation, such a prescriptive approach may be counter-productive while there are still major deficits in our understanding of these processes.

Group Supervision

Brown opens his book on consultation with the following words:

'The social worker's job is complex and demanding. It is often stressful. The first priority is to survive. After that, the aim is to be as effective as possible in responding to the needs of the people who come, or are sent or referred, to the agency.' (Brown 1984: ix)

At first sight, such words appear to contradict much of what is written about social work activity. Yet in order to assist abused children and their families, the protective worker must be able to perform efficiently and effectively. This need to survive is a theme that is also found in other texts. Dale, Davies, Morrison and Waters (1986: 205), for example, dedicate a chapter to 'professional survival'.

A great deal of the supervision described by the workers in our study can be described as defensive. Child protection work itself has been described as defensive and the description appears to be used in a number of ways. There is the mechanism of denial:

'. . . the wish not to see, hear or identify anything suggesting abuse or risk of abuse because it is either personally unacceptable or emotional reserves just cannot take any more.' (Waters 1992: 39)

Defensive practice is also said to occur when following detailed procedures works against the best interests of the child (Harris 1987). Defensive work, however, can be positive and negative, according to Harris.

Both aspects of defensive practice appear to apply to supervision in our study. The child protection workers reported that supervision was concerned with conforming to the procedures and that much of the emotional context of the work was denied. As in Waters' (1992) UK study, the structure and organisation of the child protection service itself appeared to be part of the problem. Waters argues for increased professional autonomy but accepts that the need for public accountability is likely to prevent such changes. There are, however, other ways of at least enhancing a sense of respect for front-line workers in large organisations. A number of workers expressed a wish for group supervision. The introduction of group supervision has a number of advantages (see, for example, Hawkins & Shohet 1989). It can be perceived positively, because many of the workers themselves are requesting it. It is time and cost-effective with experienced supervisors able to contribute to the supervision of a number of workers at the same time. As Hawkins and Shohet (1989) observe, it can provide supportive peer group experiences for workers. The workers in our study regarded peer group support as essential.

A third advantage, according to Hawkins and Shohet (1989: 95), is that group supervision is enhanced by the workers:

> '. . . receiving reflections, feedback, sharing and inputs from their colleagues as well as the group supervisor. Thus potentially this setting is less dominated by the supervisor, with the concurrent dangers of over-influence and dependency.'

This is a particularly important facet of group supervision when dealing with the effects of threatened and actual violence. The hostage-like effects we have described in this book are more likely to be present in the worker who experiences trauma and isolation. While at first sight it might appear unlikely that workers would reveal concerns about violence in a group in preference to a one-to-one session, this has not been borne out in our experience working with groups of workers. There is inevitably at least one worker who is prepared to reveal the impact of violence. The sharing of a sense of vulnerability by one worker triggers similar revelations by others.

Hawkins and Shohet (1989: 96) also suggest that there are other advantages provided by group supervision; a group provides not only a broader range of experiences but also 'a greater empathic range not just on the gross level of gender, race or age range, but also of personality types'. A fifth advantage they propose is that group supervision provides opportunities to re-enact sessions with clients, and to use techniques such as sculpting and role-reversal. Hawkins and Shohet discuss group supervision as an alternative to individual supervision. We stress that we are suggesting it as a means of enhancing individual supervision rather than replacing it entirely. They also differentiate team supervision and peer supervision from group supervision. We are endorsing the collective activity involved rather than prescribing membership which may vary according to organisational structure and other factors.

Waters (1992) also proposes group supervision as a means of surmounting some of the deficits in individual sessions. Although using the term 'peer group supervision', she includes the manager as a potential participant and identifies another potential benefit in such an arrangement: it allows the manager or supervisor to act as part of the group rather than as an individual with responsibility. Waters (1992: 115) outlines a number of other benefits: such as group supervision 'allows a greater potential for sharing ideas, airing practice difficulties, fostering supportive relationships and for learning'. These aspects are also stressed by Brown who particularly emphasises the notion of 'mutual aid' where each member of the group may take 'the helper and helped role at different times' (1984: 79).

Other Supervision and Consultation

Another proposal for change suggested by Waters (1992) is the use of supervision or consultation from workers other than the line manager. She starts from the perspective that supervision in child protection is basically used as a managerial 'tool' to enforce accountability, a finding clearly supported by our study. Waters proposes the use of other supervisors or consultants as a means of overcoming the dilemma of supervisors primarily acting as control agents. The use of consultation would also allow the creation of more 'open' and 'trusting' supervision relationships (Waters 1992: 116). Other advantages of such an initiative, according to Waters, would be the increased understanding that can be generated in complex cases where the worker and supervisor may find themselves 'stuck' (ibid.: 116). Even more importantly, in our view, the use of outside supervision may overcome the possibility of collusion and denial on the part of worker and supervisor that exists in the current context (Waters 1992).

Other writers endorse the use of supervisors other than line managers. The question of accountability is frequently raised. While Waters does not see the problem as insurmountable, there are clear difficulties if the relationships created are not clearly delineated (Hughes & Pengelly 1997). This is an issue that concerns us. While accepting that the increase in managerial and procedural tasks has reduced the time available for close analysis of individual cases, and similarly recognising that consultation has long been used, Hughes and Pengelly emphasise the need for clear communication between the case consultant and the line manager.

They also express concern that the use of other supervisors or consultants has been seen as a way of avoiding confronting the lack of performance in the line manager. Our major concerns are related to this point. The workers in our study were highly stressed by their work. The organisation has to accept responsibility for this and it is essential that the use of other consultants or supervisors is not seen by the organisation as a means of escaping this responsibility.

There are other related issues of accountability in such arrangements. Hughes and Pengelly (1997) identify the problems that may arise where the consultant, especially an external consultant, does not have the authority to ensure that the suggestions that are made are actually put into practice.

Helping the Supervisor

Everything we have written so far in this book stresses the complexity of child protection work. If child protection work is complex, then the task of supervising the protective worker is doubly so. Much of the writing about developing skills in supervision uses the word 'training' (see, for example, Hawkins & Shohet 1989) rather than the term 'education'. The term 'education' more appropriately emphasises the complexity of the task.

Just as the protective workers we interviewed appeared at times to be overwhelmed by the extent and nature of the violence with which they were expected to deal, it is clear that the supervisors/line managers also struggle with the care and control dilemmas that they face. It is not surprising that denial appeared to feature predominantly in the responses that the protective workers reported. Management requirements must at times appear to them to be incompatible with the workers' needs.

Our study did not involve interviewing the supervisors but it is essential to acknowledge that, if protective workers need more assistance to understand and respond to the challenges of their work, then the supervisors will need similar assistance. Clear understandings of the functions and the limitations of supervision will assist both supervisor and front-line workers. Other changes – for example a greater focus on the need for support for, and care of, workers – will place greater challenges on the role of supervisor.

Inherent in such changes is the need for evaluation of the supervision process. Drake and Washeck stress the need for workers to be able to provide feedback on the supervision they receive. They propose that this is particularly important because supervisors can give precedence to the demands of management in preference to the demands of workers which may be 'delayed or set aside' (Drake & Washeck 1998: 73). Such developments may be seen as placing greater stress on supervisors.

Supervisors themselves will require responses to their needs and these can only be achieved through recognition of the central role supervision should play in protecting children. If protective services are to value their workers, then supervisors have a central role in such changes and must be helped to prepare for and carry out the improvements. Supervisors should have access to quality supervision themselves. They should have the opportunity to undertake further education both to enhance their supervision and to better understand child abuse and child protection. Supervisors also require assistance in addressing the moral and ethical issues that arise from the extent of protection failure, as shown in our study.

These demands require particular skills and personal characteristics on the part of the supervisor. Central to these will be a willingness to accept that threatened and actual violence may require new supervision skills, for example, skills in debriefing, if the needs of the worker (and ultimately the child) are to be appropriately addressed. Supervisors will need assistance in bringing the workers' emotional responses, such as fear and anxiety, into supervision sessions. They will also need assistance in acting as advocates for the workers in the larger organisation, as discussed above.

CONCLUSION

Writing of the future of supervision in social work, Payne outlines a number of possible scenarios. His third scenario, and in his words the 'most horrific', is a situation where the professional aspects of supervision have been ignored and there is:

> '. . . a descent into unthinking adherence to politically and bureaucratically defined roles, implemented procedurally rather than through professional discretion and creativity, and enforced by managerial sanctions and crude quality assurance mechanisms.' (Payne 1994: 55)

Payne is rightly concerned about what such a vision of the future might mean for the clients, the 'most oppressed and disadvantaged members of society' (ibid.: 55).

While we share his concerns, we have others. According to some of the protective workers we interviewed, Payne is not describing an imaginary future but a very real present. Furthermore, the workers are also 'oppressed and disadvantaged' by the structures within which they are expected to operate.

Supervision is frequently referred to as the 'key' to effective practice in social work (see, for example, Ross 1992). The metaphor implies a number of things: that there is a lock, and that the lock, once unlocked, will allow us access to where we want to go. The protective workers who contributed to our research were subject to multiple and interrelated stressors and received little recognition of their plight, let alone offers of assistance from the organisation in which they were working. Changes to supervision can accomplish a great deal but interventions that address only one relationship are unlikely to be sufficient. Broader contributions to theoretical and conceptual development are required.

11

THE FIRING LINE REVISITED

INTRODUCTION

This chapter revisits the story of Robert originally described in Chapter 1, and provides an interpretation of events in the light of the research presented in this book. The material derived from the case file is in *italics*.

ROBERT REVISITED

Robert was 10 years old at the time of our research. His case file describes only the last year of child protection intervention. Robert had previously been subject to a court order but his earlier files are missing. Information contained in his current file suggests that he has been subject to physical assault, sexual and psychological abuse, and neglect. The following account is taken from his current case file.

The information about Robert was incomplete. The lost files may have given the workers important information about Robert's situation and clues to aid the workers' judgements about his future welfare. The protective workers were completely isolated from an historical perspective, which would have facilitated clear assessment and case planning. This missing information may also have enabled the workers to be forewarned about, and thus better prepared for, the family's propensity for violence and intimidation. The case file examined had no assessment by protective services as to what they believed had happened to Robert and on which to base protective action. Despite this, it is clear that he had been harmed in many ways.

*   *   *

About a year earlier, Robert told his mother that he was being sexually abused by his step-father. His mother said that there was nothing that she could do about it. In total, Robert reported this history of abuse to five professionals. He rang a telephone 'help-line' on two occasions, and was 'strapped' by his step-father for doing so. He told his local doctor. He rang child protection services. He also confirmed the abuse during the eventual police interview. Shortly after the police interview, however, Robert wrote a detailed retraction of his statement to the police about the abuse. Some months later, he wrote another retraction.

Robert's mother was unable to protect him from harm. The many professionals from whom Robert sought help were unable to offer him protection. Indeed, Robert was physically assaulted by his step-father when he found that Robert had sought help. Robert's behaviour in retracting the statement about his abuse suggests that Robert himself may have been adopting hostage-like behaviour. Our knowledge of Robert's punishment for previously disclosing abuse tends to confirm this view. The file contained no explanation or assessment about these retractions, nor was there any further record in the case file of Robert describing events or giving his opinions.

*   *   *

There was little detailed information on the file about Robert's mother. She had had a previous relationship with a man who was described as a 'heavy drinker' and a 'very violent person', who repeatedly 'bashed' and 'threatened' her. Robert's mother had attempted to leave her current relationship on several occasions, sometimes taking the children with her but at other times leaving them with her partner. In addition to these regular separations the family changed accommodation frequently. When she left her partner on the last occasion, mother was threatened with violence by her partner's relatives if she did not return. When she finally went back to the house, she was 'severely' beaten by her partner who told her that she would be 'killed' if she left him again. In spite of this extreme violence, mother stated that her partner was a 'loving man' who respected her. She excused his aggression and violence on the grounds that she had been 'flirting' with another man. Mother did say that she was 'always nervous', however, but she did not understand why. She categorically denied to authorities that Robert had been sexually abused by her partner.

The file recorded extreme physical and psychological violence perpetrated towards mother from a previous partner, and from the current partner and his relatives. The connections between domestic violence and child abuse were clear. Mother had effectively been silenced by her partners' violence. Indeed, she denied that Robert had been sexually abused. The children's exposure to such violence against mother was in itself extremely abusive. The assaults on mother also served as a reminder to the children of the power of the step-father and his relatives. The violence also clearly demonstrated to the children what was likely to happen if family loyalty was betrayed.

Mother's comments were suggestive of her own hostage-like situation. She was forced to deny reality and rationalise her partner's violence. She herself described her own state of constant anxiety. Isolated and intimidated, Robert's mother could not acknowledge the extent of Robert's abuse nor meet his emotional and psychological needs. The frequent changes of accommodation further isolated Robert and his mother from friends and the community. These moves also served to increase the likelihood of changes in those attempting to work with the family, thus reducing the chances of professionals gaining a clear picture of the disturbed behaviour.

*   *   *

There was also surprisingly little information on the file about Robert's step-father, the alleged perpetrator. He was described as a 'heavy drinker'. There had been police involvement on a number of occasions as a result of his assaults on Robert's mother. He had been intimidating and verbally abusive to protective workers, and had also threatened to 'blow up' the local protective services office. The step-father's brother and sister also lived in the same house. Robert's mother had been threatened by them and they had also made threats of violence towards the protective workers. Robert had a younger brother and sister but there was no evidence on the file of any assessment of their welfare.

There was a lack of detailed information about Robert's step-father. His violent behaviour was exacerbated by the heavy use of alcohol. This factor would have been likely to increase his unpredictability, a factor, as noted in Chapter 7, which served to increase his power over others. It would also have created an additional source of anxiety and fear on the part of other members of the household. There had been considerable police involvement concerning assaults on Robert's mother. Although it was not clear how the police became involved, this highlights the common differential response to domestic violence and child abuse. There was no record of the police attending the household in response to child abuse. In spite of a number of police interventions for domestic violence, however, there was no record on the case file of any prosecution of Robert's step-father for the assaults on Robert's mother.

The step-father, together with the step-father's brother and sister, had all made threats against individual protective workers. The step-father had also threatened to 'blow-up' the protective services office. There was no record on the file of any report to the police or any police response to these threats. It is hard to believe that such pervasive threats of, and actual, violence would not have a major impact on all those involved. There was no record on Robert's case file of any investigation of the safety of Robert's siblings. Such an investigation would also have assisted in clarifying Robert's situation. The undertaking of such an assessment, however, would have risked provoking further threats of violence.

*   *   *

The family vigorously contested all court proceedings relating to Robert. There was tension within protective services as a result of one court hearing. In this, protective services' own legal representatives came to an agreement with the family's solicitor to return Robert to his home, in spite of opposition from the protective workers themselves. Robert was returned under a legal order which required the workers to supervise his well-being at home with his mother and step-father. The magistrate at the court hearing was 'aggressive' in the face of the protective workers' opposition to the supervision order.

Attempts at intervention appeared to unite the family against any perceived threat from outside. In the Children's Court, the child protection workers were completely overruled by their own legal representatives. The magistrate, in turn, failed to respond adequately to the workers' concerns about the safety of the home. Robert was returned to the household under a supervision order. As a result of this order, the workers were legally required to supervise Robert's safety. The child protection workers, in effect, were forced to work with the adults who were threatening them. The court hearing must have reinforced any sense of powerlessness in the workers. It must also be suggested, in reviewing this case, that the outcome of the court case might have been different if other steps had been taken. Firstly, the court report from the protective workers did not provide the full detail of all the threatened and actual violence that had occurred in the case. Secondly, as we noted above, there was no evidence on the file that the extremely serious threats made against the protective workers had ever been reported to the police.

*   *   *

There was also extreme tension between the police and protective services. The police had planned to complain formally about protective services' initial handling of Robert's reports of abuse. In turn, protective services expressed 'serious concern' that the police had arrived at Robert's school in uniform to interview him without protective services, or any other support person, being present during the interview. The police decided not to prosecute Robert's step-father for any offences.

Major conflicts between the police and protective services were evident on the case file. The police planned to complain about protective services, while protective services had already 'expressed concern' about the manner in which the police intervened.

The difficulties inherent in interdisciplinary practice have been a recurrent theme in much child protection research. While this was not a specific part of the Victorian child protection study, it is our sense that the tensions between professionals and organisations understandably are often greater when multiple forms of violence are present. Both the criminal justice system and the child protection system completely failed Robert. The results might have been different if all those involved had recognised all the violence, responded to it appropriately, and were prepared for its effects on individuals and organisations.

*   *   *

Robert reported the sexual abuse by his step-father to the family's general practitioner. In his statement to the court, the GP stated that he did not believe Robert was capable of writing his initial retraction without substantial adult 'assistance'. The doctor received a 'threatening' letter from the family's solicitor, and he and his colleagues had also been threatened with violence by the step-father. The GP clearly stated that he was not prepared to visit the home on his own.

The step-father, in particular, had successfully isolated Robert from many possible sources of professional assistance. The GP clearly stated that, in his view, Robert's retraction was at least assisted by an adult. As a result of his report, the doctor received a letter from the family's solicitor. The GP, in the face of threats of violence to himself and colleagues, also asserted that he was not prepared to visit the home on his own. This refusal to undertake home visits is an option rarely exercised by protective workers. There was no evidence on the file of the GP or any other community professionals reporting any of these threats of violence to the police.

*   *   *

Robert's mother, step-father, and step-father's siblings had all made numerous complaints, principally about protective services, to a number of senior politicians and government officials, who in turn instigated official inquiries. They had also written to complain about police involvement in the case. In all these complaints they denied that Robert had ever been abused.

By using a strategy of repeated complaint, the step-father and his siblings succeeded in turning part of the protective service system against itself. This strategy may have had a number of effects. Firstly, it is difficult for protective services to remain focused on Robert's safety when the interventions being used are themselves subject to investigation. Secondly, when the front-line workers are subject to such inquiries by management, they may become further isolated. The management system that is supposed to provide supervision and support is instead being used to investigate the workers. Finally, the strategy further enhanced the sense that the violent step-father was also capable of thwarting the efforts of entire organisations.

*   *   *

There was some information on the file about the family's involvement with the broader community. One neighbour reported that she had seen Robert 'cringe like a beaten dog' in the presence of his step-father. She also reported that all three children were rarely allowed outside the home. The neighbour expressed fears for her own safety if the step-father found out that she had given any information. Another neighbour reported that Robert's mother was completely 'dominated' by the step-father and his relatives. After Robert retracted his reports of abuse, he and his mother visited neighbours and other people in the community to allow Robert to apologise for accusing his step-father.

The step-father was able to intimidate members of the wider community, further isolating Robert, his mother and siblings, and protective workers, from support. These reports by community members, their apparent fear of the step-father, and the highly unusual behaviour of a child 'apologising' to others for accusing his step-father of abuse, were apparently considered of little significance in the case for Robert's protection.

*   *   *

During this protective service involvement, Robert spent a period of one week with a foster family. The foster father reported to the police that he was terrified of the step-father and his relatives and that they had threatened to assault him and leave him with serious injuries. The foster father received a letter from the family's solicitor threatening defamation proceedings if he continued to 'talk'. A court hearing returned Robert to his home on an interim basis with the condition that the step-father leave the family home. However, following a visit two weeks later by protective services, the step-father was apparently living at home in contravention of the court order. Prior to the next court hearing, Robert was placed in a motel overnight.

The foster father did report the step-father's extreme threats of violence to the police. There was no indication on the file that any charges were laid as a result of this report. It does appear, however, that there was some action by the police in response to the report because, soon after his complaint to the police, the foster father received a letter threatening legal proceedings from the family's solicitor.

It was difficult to ascertain from the file the rationale for Robert's two brief placements. Once again, the sense is that step-father was entirely controlling events. The step-father's complete disregard for the system and any consequences was most clearly depicted in his utter disregard for the court order forbidding him to live at home.

*   *   *

Two psychologists assessed Robert. The first reported to the court that he believed that Robert had been sexually abused and that he was suffering from an 'accommodation syndrome'. The second assessment confirmed that Robert had been physically assaulted and emotionally abused. This psychologist reported that Robert was suffering from 'a fairly high level of fear'. This report recommended that the step-father, and his brother and sister, receive counselling, and that the step-father specifically receive counselling for 'sexual problems'. Two referrals were made apparently as a result of these psychological assessments. The first agency advised protective services that they were 'unable to take on this family'. The second agency declared that this family was not suitable for any available counselling and that it was not appropriate that they see Robert as he was still living with the perpetrator of abuse. It appeared that neither Robert nor any other member of the household received any counselling.

Confirmation by two professionals that Robert had experienced abuse was still insufficient to enable decisive action to be taken to ensure Robert's protection. Counselling services were understandably reluctant to become involved with this family, thus further isolating protective workers. Again, the violence of the step-father appeared to entirely control the course of events. Not only was Robert left at home with the alleged perpetrator, he was denied contact with professional agencies who may have provided another opinion on his situation in the home. Putting aside Robert's need for counselling in relation to abuse, he would also have been in need of counselling to address the traumatic upheaval to his life associated with his allegations and retractions of abuse.

*   *   *

There was clear evidence on the file that the assessment of the protective workers changed as time passed. The initial assessment concluded that Robert was 'at risk of significant emotional harm due to sexual abuse'. Subsequent assessments found that there was 'the likelihood of significant physical harm'. The workers, however, concluded on the file that a thorough family assessment was not possible because of the 'adversarial' nature of any meetings with the family.

The last visit recorded on the file graphically described the aggression experienced by the worker. At one point, she found herself sitting in a chair with three adults 'standing in close proximity'. They were aggressively making 'derogatory' remarks about protective services and the worker herself. The worker described this on the file as 'an intimidating, verbally abusive scene'. She recorded that she was upset and felt 'extremely intimidated and overpowered'. The file recorded seven changes of key protective workers in one year. At the time of the research, the eighth worker had just resigned. The researcher was told that another worker had resigned specifically because of this family. The final record on the file stated that access to the house had been denied on the last attempted visit. There was no evidence on the file that any further contact had been made with Robert for five months. There were no indications on the file that any other action was planned to protect Robert in the future.

The file recorded the details of some of the intimidation suffered by some of the eight protective workers who were responsible for Robert's protection over the course of a year. The language used to summarise the intimidation frequently appeared to understate the fuller descriptions elsewhere in the file. The situation where the worker felt 'extremely intimidated and overpowered' is described as an 'adversarial' meeting.

This censorship on the case file was most pronounced when court reports were examined, as in the situation noted above. None of the reports for court gave any sense of the totality of violence created by Robert's step-father. When such censorship occurs, important information is lost and decisions are made by people (for example, the children's court magistrate) who are not in full possession of all the facts. Information may also be lost on the full extent of the harm suffered by the child.

Some Further Lessons from Robert's File

We chose to review Robert's case for a number of reasons. Firstly, although it is apparent that severe intimidation took place, there was no

record of any of the threats against the protective workers, other professionals, or members of the community actually being carried out. All
these people, professionals and neighbours alike, were in fear of step-
father. Many knew of his assaults on family members. Many were
aware of other people's fear of step-father. Some would have known
that others in the community refused to become involved in the family.
Some would have known that step-father appeared to be able to flout a
court order with absolute impunity. The power of psychological intimidation is apparent. Actual violence against any of the workers was not
necessary.

Secondly, it is too rarely recognised that intimidation and violence may
have a clear purpose. Writing of terrorism, Thackrah (1989: 37) states
that:

> '. . . it is not mindless violence. . . . A terrorist campaign that causes a
> significant threshold of fear amongst the target population may achieve its
> aims.'

As Crayton (1983: 33) succinctly states:

> 'Terrorism is an attempt to acquire or maintain power or control by intim-
> idation, by instilling a fear of destruction or helplessness . . ..'

The campaign of psychological intimidation conducted by Robert's
step-father was completely effective if his aim was to totally isolate
Robert, Robert's siblings and mother. To return to Thackrah's description of terrorism, the intimidation may not have been 'irrational' or
'mindless' but rather 'a deliberate means to an end' with 'clear objectives' (1989: 38).

The evidence that Robert had been seriously abused and his mother had
been seriously assaulted was overwhelming. Robert himself said to many
people, including the police and protective services, that he had been
sexually abused and physically assaulted by his step-father. The police
had been called a number of times in response to domestic violence. Two
psychological assessments concluded that Robert had been abused. In
spite of this evidence, the protective services assessment moved from
sexual abuse to the 'likelihood' of physical harm.

Thirdly, when Robert was returned to live with his mother and step-
father, the child protection workers were left in an impossible situation.
Robert's welfare could only be supervised with the cooperation of the
adults present. He was, however, living with people who denied that
abuse had ever occurred and who actively opposed any intervention. It is

perhaps not surprising that, in the face of threatened violence and over-whelming odds, the next child protection worker modified her view of what was happening and reduced the recorded risk to Robert. By doing this, the step-father could be avoided. In such a situation it is understand-able how a protective worker, as reported in Chapter 8, may feel helpless and frustrated.

Fourthly, although we did not have access to police records, it is interest-ing to speculate what might have been different if the incidents of domes-tic violence had been met with the full force of the law. It is clear that there were a number of opportunities to forcefully intervene but, for whatever reasons, no decisive action appeared to be taken. Future re-search into such serious cases must be multidimensional, examining events and actions from more than one perspective.

Finally, early in the book we alluded to the importance of language. Interest is growing, for example, in the language used by the media and others to describe children and child abuse (Goddard & Saunders 2000, Saunders & Goddard in press). It is our view that similar studies of child protection files would prove fruitful. Although it was not part of our research, it was noticeable that in many files there were references to the needs or wishes of the 'family'. It is difficult to understand what common needs or wishes there might be in circumstances such as Robert's. Robert and his siblings needed a safe environment. Robert's mother also re-quired protection from her partner. While the 'family' might be a useful shorthand, there are clear dangers in failing to disaggregate the needs of the individuals in the household. Robert's 'family', made up of his mother, his siblings, his step-father, and step-father's own siblings, was a very dangerous and damaging place.

This case has been used to illustrate some of the important messages from the Victorian child protection study. Robert did not die but was severely, repeatedly harmed. If he had died, his circumstances would have been closely but, in all probability, narrowly examined. The child protection workers were required to form a relationship with an ex-tremely violent man. The violence appeared to permeate every signifi-cant relationship, both within the family and within the community. The protective workers themselves were subject to threats of extreme vio-lence. They became isolated as the family united against any interven-tion. Tensions between agencies, apparently instigated or exacerbated by the intimidatory behaviour, resulted in repeated protection failure for Robert. In the midst of this turmoil, Robert withdrew his allegations. The workers themselves withdrew, isolated and apparently powerless to protect Robert. It is our contention that these events can only be

understood if all the threatened and actual violence is fully acknowledged and taken seriously.

ESCAPING THE FIRING LINE

There are many other issues that arise from an analysis of Robert's and
other children's circumstances in this study. As we noted early in the
book, attempts to understand child abuse in all its forms, and the planning of responses in the form of child protection services, are comparatively recent processes. In such circumstances, it is probable that
there will be a lag in the development of theoretical approaches to understanding the field.

It is easy to dismiss the response to Robert's plight as merely bad practice.
As we noted in Chapter 1, the media in the UK and elsewhere gave
extensive coverage to the terrible death of Victoria (known as Anna)
Climbie. A statutory inquiry and an internal investigation by Harringey
Council had been ordered. While it is too early to form a judgement on
this particular case, it appears that many assumptions had already been
made:

> 'It seems clear that there were some major errors made . . . Misunderstand-
> ings surrounding cultural differences have been cited, alongside criticisms
> of inexperience, lack of training and unfeasibly high case loads. That there
> were instances of appalling communication between different agencies is
> obvious . . ..' (Winchester 2001:10)

Other writers have made similar assertions about Victoria Climbie's
death. Hirst, for example, argues that another inquiry is not necessary
because 'we should already know the answers – from 50 or so similar
inquiries' (2001: 10).

Our research suggests that there is a great deal more to learn. It is our
assertion that, in any attempt to prevent future child protection failures,
we must seek a better understanding of relationships between protective
workers and the people with whom they work. It may be asking too
much of child protection workers (or anyone else) to maintain a sense of
equilibrium in the face of the trauma inflicted by some people (for example, Robert's step-father). Child protection workers are particularly
vulnerable but other workers may also be subject to hostage-like responses. Special emphasis needs to be placed on the vulnerabilities of all
workers. Supervision will need to provide empathetic and non-
judgemental support. The role of management will be crucial.

In spite of so much negative media coverage, there are some grounds for cautious optimism. There is much to commend in the National Task Force (2001) report. There is the statement that violence against social care workers is completely unacceptable, and that employers have 'a duty . . . to keep social care workers from harm' (p. 7). There is a recognition that more information sharing is required, and that staff require greater support from the police. There is the encouraging acknowledgement that the 'threat and impact' of violence against field workers:

> '. . . can be very severe because they are often alone and a long way from support when it happens and it is totally unexpected.' (National Task Force 2001: 13)

While verbal abuse and threatening behaviour are recognised, there is still a preoccupation with 'incidents' of violence. The National Task Force, recognising the difficulties caused by inconsistency, adopts the following definition (2001: 17):

> 'Incidents where persons are abused, threatened or assaulted in circumstances relating to their work, involving an explicit or implicit challenge to their safety, well-being or health.'

Such definitions risk overlooking the all-pervasive and cumulative atmosphere of violence that may involve many people, and the subsequent effects on practice.

It is clear, however, that far more research is required if we are to fully understand the nexus between violence against child protection workers and child protection failures. No amount of 'training' of social care workers will prevent all unconscious reactions to trauma, just as no amount of revision of procedures will prevent all deaths caused by child abuse. As the editorial in *Community Care* (2001b: 17) stated, in response to the National Task Force report: 'Now starts the real task.'

CONCLUSION

This book has suggested that hostage theory provides at least a partial explanation of the difficulties inherent in protecting children who have been severely assaulted, abused and neglected. We do not claim that this theoretical approach to child protection failure provides all the answers to the many questions raised in this book and elsewhere. The Victorian child protection study, however, has provided detailed information on the totality of violence in serious cases of harm to children. It is our assertion that it is only through rigorously examining all violence (including actual and threatened violence to the workers themselves) together with providing more intensive supervision and support for workers, that we will make more successful interventions in these serious cases.

We observed in Chapter 2 that social and political forces shaped responses to child abuse in Victoria and elsewhere. The Victorian child protection system has similarities to child protection systems in place elsewhere but, inevitably, there are some differences. For this reason alone, we cannot claim that our results can be generalised to systems elsewhere. It is clear, however, that while research has enhanced our understanding of child assault, abuse and neglect, our current approaches to child protection have been too narrow. Similar views have been expressed in the UK and the USA (see, for example, Speight & Wynne 2000). Hostage theory may assist us in gaining the deeper understanding that we so urgently require if we are to be more successful in our efforts to protect children from harm.

APPENDIX: THE
VICTORIAN STUDY

The Child Abuse and Family Violence Research Unit undertook the Victorian study between 1993 and 1997. Some of the findings of this research are reported in the text of this book. The Victorian department responsible for protective services provided the information for the research. This government-run organisation services the state of Victoria, in Australia, covering a major urban area (population approximately four million), smaller urban areas and a widely spread rural population. A brief overview of the study method follows.

Interviews were conducted with a random sample of 50 child protection workers. This sample represented approximately one-third of the total population of protective workers (as at August 1993) who worked with, and had face-to-face contact with, protective clients. The numbers of protective workers have subsequently considerably expanded.

The second major source of information came from protection files on 50 children. These files were drawn at random from the current cases of the 50 interviewed protective workers. The criterion for inclusion in the study was that the children were presently under, or had been under, a legal protection order. Thus the sample comprised the more severely assaulted, abused and/or neglected children. The 50 cases represented approximately 1.3% of the total population of children in Victoria who were under a legal protective order at the time of the survey.

The sample of workers

The research sample comprised 50 protective workers, selected at random from workers responsible for cases open for over three months. Two-thirds of the sample of workers were based in Melbourne, a major metropolitan area, and one-third were based outside Melbourne, within the state of Victoria. This distribution reflected that found in the total population of protective workers. Of the 50 workers, 27 were qualified social workers; the remainder were qualified in social welfare (11) and psychology (7), or held a general degree (5). Twenty-two workers also held an additional degree and 4 were in the process of further study. Almost half (24) had been a protective worker for under two years, 22 had been in the position for between two and five years, and 4, for six years or over. Two workers had experience in child protection prior to joining this organisation. Just over two-thirds of the workers (34) joined as new graduates.

The sample comprised 8 male and 42 female protective workers. This approximated the distribution of males/females in the population group of direct service workers. Just over half of the sample of workers (26) was between 25 and 35 years of age, 5 workers being under 25 years; 19 workers were aged 36 or over.

The workers' cases

The study examined 50 protection case files, randomly drawn from the longer-term case load of the interviewed workers. This sample represented, on average, 10% of each worker's current total case load of family groups. The majority of children in the sample (40) were on a legal protection order, which ranged in time from six months to two years. Four children were on an interim protection order, and one child was on a permanent protection order. Although on an order when selected for the sample, the files on four children were closed when read by the researcher, and for one child the protection order had expired.

The sample of children

There were 24 males and 26 females in the sample of children. They represented all age groups up to 17 years, with slightly more children in the early teenage years of 13, 14 and 15. The children had been known to protective services (as measured from the first referral to when the file was either closed for the last time, or read by the researcher) from under three months to 15 years. Twenty-nine children were known to protective services for under three years and 15 children were known for over five years, the average time being 3.6 years. However, some files had periods when they were not active, for example, they were closed and reopened, not allocated to a worker, or there was no contact for a period of two months or longer. When these times are deducted, the average contact time for each of the children was 2.2 years. This figure is only approximate because for eight children, one or more volumes in their files were unavailable to the researcher, were missing, or were unable to be comprehended.

Only seven children appeared to have both natural parents present at home as their most common experience of 'family'. Most children (34) were raised by a single parent, usually their mother, and frequently this also included one, or a series of, mother's partners. For nine children, their predominant experience of 'family' did not appear to include either natural parent.

When the file was read, almost half of the children (24) were located in their usual family household. Five were with other family members outside their usual household and one was with an adult friend. Six children were in a foster home placement and five in an institutional setting. Five of the children were homeless and two were living with peers. The researcher was not able to ascertain from the files the location of two children.

REFERENCES

Adams, D. (1996; 23 January) Exorcism led to stabbing, court is told. *The Age* 3.

Angus, G. & Hall, G. (1996) *Child abuse and neglect: Australia 1994–95*. Australian Institute of Health and Welfare, Canberra.

APA (1980) *Diagnostic and statistical manual of mental disorders* (3rd edn). American Psychiatric Association, Washington, DC.

APA (1994) *Diagnostic and statistical manual of mental disorders* (4th edn). American Psychiatric Association, Washington, DC.

Arches, J. (1991) Social structure, burnout, and job satisfaction. *Social Work* 36(3): 202–206.

Artley, A. (1993) *Murder in the heart: A true-life psychological thriller*. Hamish Hamilton, London.

Auditor General, Victoria (1996) *Protecting Victoria's children: The role of the Department of Human Services*. Government Printer, Melbourne.

Bacon, R. (1988) Counter-transference in a case conference: Resistance and rejection in work with abusing families and their children. In G. Pearson, J. Treseder & M. Yelloly (Eds) *Social work and the legacy of Freud: Psychoanalysis and its uses*. Macmillan, Basingstoke, 185–201.

Baldwin, N. & Harrison, C. (1994) Supporting 'children in need' – the role of the social worker. In T. David (Ed.) *Working together for young children: Multiprofessionalism in action*. Routledge, London, 104–118.

Balloch, S., Andrew, T., Ginn, J., McLean, J., Pahl, J. & Williams, J. (1995) *Working in the social services*. The National Institute for Social Work, London.

Bandura, A. (1990) Mechanisms of moral disengagement. In W. Reich (Ed). *Origins of terrorism: Psychologies, ideologies, theologies, states of mind*. Cambridge University Press, Cambridge, 161–191.

Barling, J. (1996) The prediction, experience, and consequences of workplace violence. In G.R. VandenBos & E.Q. Bulatao (Eds) *Violence on the job: Identifying risks and developing solutions*. American Psychological Association, Washington, DC, 29–49.

Barnes, G.B., Chabon, R.S. & Hertzberg, L.J. (1974) Team treatment for abusive families. *Social Casework* 55(10): 600–611.

Barnett, O.W. & LaViolette, A.D. (1993) *It could happen to anyone: Why battered women stay*. Sage, Newbury Park.

Bennett, P., Evans, R. & Tattersall, A. (1993) Stress and coping in social workers: A preliminary investigation. *British Journal of Social Work* 23(1): 31–44.

Bialestock, D. (1966) Neglected babies: A study of 289 babies admitted consecutively to a reception centre. *Medical Journal of Australia* 2: 1129–1133.

Biestek, F.R. (1957) *The casework relationship*. Loyola University Press, Chicago.

Birrell, R.G. & Birrell, J.H. (1966) The 'maltreatment syndrome' in children. *Medical Journal of Australia* 2: 1134–1138.

Birrell, R.G. & Birrell, J.H. (1968) The maltreatment syndrome in children: A hospital survey. *Medical Journal of Australia* 2(23): 1023–1029.

Blatt, S.J. (1990) Interpersonal relatedness and self-definition: Two personality configurations and their implications for psychopathology and psychotherapy. In J.L. Singer (Ed.) *Repression and dissociation: Implications for personality theory, psychopathology, and health.* University of Chicago Press, Chicago, 299–333.

Boreham, G. (1993; 24 November) Top PS man blasts media and unions. *The Age* 7.

Bowie, V. (1989) *Coping with violence: A guide for the human services.* Karibuni Press, Sydney.

Brashears, F. (1995) Supervision as social work practice: A conceptualization. *Social Work* 40(5): 692–699.

Braye, S. & Preston-Shoot, M. (1995) *Empowering practice in social care.* Open University Press, Buckingham.

Brazier, J. & Carter, J. (1969) Coordinated services for the maltreated child in Western Australia. *Australian Journal of Social Work* 22(4): 14–21.

Briar, S. & Miller, H. (1971) *Problems and issues in social casework.* Columbia University Press, New York.

Brieland, D. (1974) Children and families: A forecast. *Social Work* 19(5): 568–580.

Bright, M. & McVeigh, T. (2001; 14 January) Why did no one try to save this bright, happy girl? *The Observer,* 8–9.

Brown, A. (1984) *Consultation: An aid to successful social work.* Heinemann, London.

Brown, A. & Baume, I. (1996) *The social work supervisor: Supervision in community, day care and residential settings.* Open University Press, Buckingham.

Brown, R., Bute, S. & Ford, P. (1986) *Social workers at risk: The prevention and management of violence.* Macmillan, Basingstoke.

Brown, D. & Fromm, E. (1986) *Hypnotherapy and hypnoanalysis.* Laurence Erlbaum, Hillsdale, New Jersey.

Buchanan, A. (1996) *Cycles of child maltreatment: Facts, fallacies and interventions.* John Wiley & Sons, Chichester.

Bulatao, E.Q. & VandenBos, G.R. (1996) Workplace violence: Its scope and the issues. In G.R. VandenBos & E.Q. Bulatao (Eds) *Violence on the job: Identifying risks and developing solutions.* American Psychological Association, Washington, DC, 1–23.

Burgess, A.W. & Holmstrom, L.L. (1974) Rape Trauma Syndrome. *American Journal of Psychiatry* 131(9): 981–986.

Caffey, J. (1946) Multiple fractures in the long bones of children suffering from chronic subdural haematoma. *American Journal of Roentgenology and Radium Therapy* 56: 163–173.

Cameronchild, J. (1980) An autobiography of violence. In G.J. Williams & J. Money (Eds) *Traumatic abuse and neglect of children at home.* The University Press, Aberdeen, 293–306.

Carney, T. (1984) *Child welfare practice and legislation review: Equity and social justice for children, families and communities* (The Carney Report). Government Printer, Melbourne.

Carvel, J. (2001; 13 January) NSPCC calls for complete overhaul of child protection procedures. *The Guardian.* Special report: Child protection, internet edition.

Clarke, J. (Ed.) (1993) *A crisis in care? Challenges to social work.* Sage, London.

Clarke, J. (1996) After social work? In N. Parton (Ed.) *Social theory, social change and social work.* Routledge, London, 36–60.

Clough, S. (2001a; 13 January) Failures left tragic Anna to cruel fate. *The Daily Telegraph* 1.

Clough, S. (2001b; 14 January) Murdered by her carers. *The Sunday Age* 11.

Collings, J.A. & Murray, P.J. (1996) Predictors of stress amongst social workers: An empirical study. *British Journal of Social Work* 26(3): 375–387.

Collins, S. (2000; 1 July) Never again: How we all failed James Wakaruru. *The New Zealand Herald*, internet edition.

Community Care (2001a; 11–17 January) Comment: Anna's tragedy, 17.

Community Care (2001b; 25–31 January) Comment: Now starts the real task, 17.

Compton, B.R. & Galaway, B. (1984) *Social work processes* (3rd edn). The Dorsey Press, Homewood, Illinois.

Connaway, R.S. & Gentry, M.E. (1988) *Social work practice*. Prentice Hall, Englewood Cliffs

Conte, J. (1985) The effects of sexual abuse on children: A critique and suggestions for further research. *Victiminology: An International Journal* 10(1–4): 110–130.

Cooper, D.M. & Glastonbury, B. (1980) The dilemma of the professional employee. In B. Glastonbury, D.M. Cooper & P. Hawkins (Eds) *Social work in conflict: The practitioner and the bureaucrat*. Croom Helm, London, 116–125.

Cooper, L. (1993) A word salad: Enterprise based competencies in child protection. *Children Australia* 18(2): 26–30.

Corby, B. (1987) *Working with child abuse: Social work practice and the child abuse system*. Open University Press, Milton Keynes.

Corby, B. (1993) *Child abuse: Towards a knowledge base*. Open University Press, Buckingham.

Crayton, J.W. (1983) Terrorism and the psychology of the self. In L.Z. Freedman & Y. Alexander (Eds) *Perspectives on terrorism*. Scholarly Resources, Wilmington, Delaware, 33–41.

Crelinsten, R.D. (1987) Terrorism as political communication: The relationship between the controller and the controlled. In P. Wilkinson & A.M. Stewart (Eds) *Contemporary research on terrorism*. Aberdeen University Press, Aberdeen, 3–23.

Critchley, C. (1996; 11 November) System is a 'monster'. *Herald Sun*, 12.

Dale, P., Davies, M., Morrison, T. & Waters, J. (1986) *Dangerous families: Assessment and treatment of child abuse* (2nd edn). Tavistock Publications, London.

Daro, D. (1988) *Confronting child abuse: Research for effective program design*. The Free Press, New York.

Davies, J. (1996; 20 October) Did the state fail baby Dillion? *The Age* 1, 2.

Davies, J. (2000; 20 October) Crisis in child protection network: Abused children may face years of itinerant lifestyle. *The Age* 1.

Davies, J. (2001; 23 January) State wards at risk: Report. *The Age* 1.

Davies, M. (1988) *Staff supervision in the probation service: Keeping pace with change*. Avebury, Aldershot.

Davies, R. (Ed.) (1998) *Stress in social work*. Jessica Kingsley, London.

Dawe, K. (1975) Help for maltreated children and their families. *Australian Social Work* 28(2): 17–27.

Department of Health (1991) *Child abuse: A study of inquiry reports 1980–1989*. HMSO, London.

Department of Human Services (1996; 12 March) Advertisement: Appeal to staff of the department of H&CS. *The Age* A2.

Department of Human Services (1997) *The redevelopment of Victoria's Youth and Family Services: Strategic directions*. Department of Human Services, Victoria.

Department of Treasury and Finance (2000) *2000–01 Budget estimates: Budget paper No. 3*. Author, Victoria.

Dingwall, R., Eekelaar, J. & Murray, T. (1983) *The protection of children: State intervention and family life*. Basil Blackwell, Oxford.

Dobash, R.E., Dobash, R.P. & Noaks, L. (Eds) (1995) *Gender and crime*. University of Wales Press, Cardiff.

Dobash, R.P., Dobash, R.E., Cavanagh, K. & Lewis, L. (1995) Evaluating criminal justice programs for violent men. In R.E. Dobash, R.P. Dobash & L. Noaks (Eds) *Gender and crime*. University of Wales Press, Cardiff, 358–389.

Dominelli, L. (1996) Deprofessionalizing social work: Anti-oppressive practice, competencies and postmodernism. *British Journal of Social Work* 26: 153–175.

Doolan, M. (1996) *A strategy to support workers deal with dangerous situations*. Unpublished departmental document, Children and Young Persons Service, New Zealand.

Drake, B. & Washeck, J. (1998) A competency-based method for providing worker feedback to CPS supervisors. *Administration in Social Work* 22(3): 55–74.

Drake, F.M. (1971) On change. *British Journal of Social Work* 1(1): 63–71.

Dykstra, C. (1995) Domestic violence and child abuse: Related links in the chain of violence. *Protecting Children* 11(3): 3–5.

Edelwich, J. & Brodsky, A. (1980) *Burn-out: Stages of disillusionment in the helping professions*. Human Services Press, New York.

Eitinger, L. (1982) The effects of captivity. In F.M. Ochberg & A.D. Soskis (Eds) *Victims of terrorism*. Westview Press, Boulder, Colorado, 73–94.

Emery, F. & Trist, E. (1965) The causal texture of organisational environments. In F. Emery (Ed.) *Systems thinking 1: Selected readings*. Penguin, Harmondsworth, 241–257.

Everly, G.S., Flannery, R.B. & Mitchell, J.T. (1998) *Critical Incident Stress Management (CISM): A review of the literature*. Paper presented at the ACISA Conference, March. Auckland, New Zealand.

Farmer, E. & Owen, M. (1995) *Child protection practice: Private risks and public remedies. Decision making, intervention and outcome in child protection work*. HMSO, London.

Farouque, F. (1996; 16 August) Kennett defends child protection. *The Age* A2.

Fields, R.M. (1982) Research on the victims of terrorism. In F.M. Ochberg & A.D. Soskis (Eds) *Victims of terrorism*. Westview Press, Boulder, Colorado, 137–148.

Finkelhor, D. (1984) *Child sexual abuse: New theory and research*. The Free Press, New York.

Flynn, E.E. (1987) Victims of terrorism: Dimensions of the victim experience. In P. Wilkinson & A.M. Steward (Eds) *Contemporary research on terrorism*. Aberdeen University Press, Aberdeen, 337–355.

Fogarty, J. & Sargeant, D. (1989) *Protective services for children in Victoria: An interim report*. Government Printing Office, Melbourne.

Ford, D.A. & Regoli, M.J. (1993) The criminal prosecution of wife assaulters: Process, problems and effects. In N.Z. Milton (Ed.) *Legal responses to wife assault: Current trends and evaluation*. Sage, Newbury Park, 127–164.

Form, W.H. (1975) The social construction of anomie: A four-nation study of industrial workers. *American Journal of Sociology* 80: 1165–1191.

Frederick, C.T. (1994) The psychology of terrorism and torture in war and peace: Diagnosis and treatment of victims. In R. Liberman & J. Yager (Eds) *Stress in psychiatric disorders*. Springer Pub. Co., New York, 140–159.

Freedman, L.Z. (1983) Terrorism: Problems of the polistaraxic. In L.Z. Freedman & Y. Alexander (Eds) *Perspectives on terrorism*. Scholarly Resources Inc, Wilmington, Delaware, 3–12.

Freud, S. (1926) Inhibitions, symptoms and anxiety. In *The standard edition of the complete psychological works of Sigmund Freud* (Vol. 20). Hogarth, London, 77–175.

Gabarro, J.J. (1983) Understanding communication in one-to-one relationships. In L.A. Schlesinger, R.G. Eccles & J.J. Gabarro (Eds) *Managing human behavior in organizations: Text, cases, readings*. McGraw-Hill, New York, 131–141.

Garrett, A. (1958) Modern casework: The contributions of ego psychology. In H.J. Parad (Ed.) *Ego psychology and dynamic casework: Papers from the Smith College School of Social Work.* Family Service Association of America, New York, 38–52.

Germain, C. (1970) Casework and science: An historical encounter. In R.W. Roberts & R.H. Nee (Eds) *Theories of social casework.* University of Chicago Press, Chicago, 3–32.

Gibbons, J., Conroy, S. & Bell, C. (1995) *Operating the child protection system: A study of child protection practices in English local authorities.* HMSO, London.

Gibson, F., McGrath, A. & Reid, N. (1989) Occupational stress in social work. *British Journal of Social Work* 19(1): 1–16.

Gil, D.G. (1975) Unraveling child abuse. *American Journal of Orthopsychiatry* 45(3): 346–356.

Gillan, A. (2001; 18–24 January) For Anna, a new life ended in pain, fear and filth. *The Guardian Weekly* 8.

Gillan, A. & Carvel, J. (2001; 13 January) Urgent inquiry into repeated failures. *The Guardian.* Special report: Child protection, internet edition.

Gleeson, M. & Coffey, M. (1996; 24 October) When will it end? *Herald Sun*, 2, 3.

Goddard, C.R. (1980) Child abuse: The safety of the home. *Australian Child and Family Welfare* 5(3): 3–5.

Goddard, C.R. (1988a) *Victoria's protective services: Dual tracks and double standards.* Victorian Society for the Prevention of Child Abuse and Neglect, Melbourne.

Goddard, C.R. (1988b) Social worker's responses to repeated hostility in child abuse cases: The traditional social worker–client relationship or a new approach to hostage theory? *Facing the future: Proceedings of the first Victorian Conference on Child Abuse, Victorian Society for the Prevention of Child Abuse and Neglect, Melbourne, Victoria,* 146–163.

Goddard, C. (1989) *The social worker–client relationship: A missing link in child abuse cases.* Paper presented at 10th Anniversary Conference of the British Association for the Study and Prevention of Child Abuse and Neglect, York, England.

Goddard, C. (1994) Governing the 'Family': Child protection policy and practice and the 'Children of God'. *Just Policy* 1: 9–12.

Goddard, C. (1996a) Read all about it! The news about child abuse. *Child Abuse Review* 5: 301–309.

Goddard, C. (1996b) *Child abuse and child protection: A guide for health, education and welfare workers.* Churchill Livingstone, Melbourne.

Goddard, C. (1996c; 19 June) The kids out of luck. *Herald Sun* 19.

Goddard, C. (1996d; 21 June) The child care challenge. *The Age* A13.

Goddard, C. (1996e; 11 November) An agenda for change. *Herald Sun* 19.

Goddard, C. (2000; 26 October) The neglectful state. *The Age* 15.

Goddard, C. (2001) A media case study: The life and death of Daniel Valerio. In *Out of sight: NSPCC report on child deaths from abuse* (2nd edn). NSPCC, London, 168–170.

Goddard, C. & Carew, R. (1988) Protecting the child: Hostages to fortune? *Social Work Today* 20(16): 12–14.

Goddard, C. & Carew, R. (1989) Social work: Mechanical or intellectual? *Social Work Today* 19th January: 22, 23.

Goddard, C. & Carew, R. (1993) *Responding to children: Child welfare practice.* Longman Cheshire, Melbourne.

Goddard, C. & Liddell, M. (1995) Child abuse fatalities and the media: Lessons from a case study. *Child Abuse Review* 4: 355–364.

Goddard, C.R., Liddell, M.J. & Brown, T. (1990) A fresh or flawed approach to child protection in Victoria, Australia? *Child Abuse and Neglect* 14(4): 587–590.

Goddard, C. & Saunders, B. (2000) The gender neglect and textual abuse of children in the print media. *Child Abuse Review* 9: 37–48.

Goddard, C., Saunders, B., Stanley, J. & Tucci, J. (1999) Structured risk assessment procedures: Instruments of abuse? *Child Abuse Review* 8: 251–263.

Goddard, C.R. & Stanley, J.R. (1994) Viewing the abusive parent and the abused child as captor and hostage: The application of hostage theory to the effects of child abuse. *Journal of Interpersonal Violence* 9(2): 258–269.

Goddard, C.R. & Tucci, J. (1991) Child protection and the need for the reappraisal of the social worker–client relationship. *Australian Social Work* 44(2): 3–10.

Goodwin, J. (1985) Creditability problems in multiple personality disorder patients and abused children. In R.P. Kluft (Ed.) *Childhood antecedents of multiple personality*. American Psychiatric Press, Washington, DC, 1–20.

Greenland, C. (1987) *Preventing CAN deaths: An international study of deaths due to child abuse and neglect*. Tavistock, London.

Hacker, F.J. (1983) Dialectic interrelationships of personal and political factors in terrorism. In L.Z. Freedman & Y. Alexander (Eds) *Perspectives on terrorism*. Scholarly Resources, Wilmington, Delaware, 19–32.

Hamilton-Byrne, S. (1995) *Unseen unheard unknown: My life inside the family of Anne Hamilton-Byrne*. Penguin, Australia.

Harris, N. (1987) Defensive social work. *British Journal of Social Work* 17(1): 61–69.

Hawkins, P. & Shohet, R. (1989) *Supervision in the helping professions: An individual, group and organizational approach*. Open University Press, Milton Keynes.

Healy, K. (1998) Participation and child protection: The importance of context. *British Journal of Social Work* 28(6): 897–914.

Hearst, P.C. (1982) *Every secret thing*. Pinnacle Books, New York.

Herman, J.L. (1992) *Trauma and recovery*. Basic Books, New York.

Herman, J.L. (1995) Complex PTSD: A syndrome in survivors of prolonged and repeated trauma. In G.S. Everly Jr & J.M. Lating (Eds) *Psychotraumatology: Key papers and core concepts in post-traumatic stress*. Plenum Press, New York, 87–100.

Herrenkohl, R.C., Herrenkohl, E.C., Egolf, B. & Seech, M. (1979) The repetition of child abuse: How frequently does it occur? *Child Abuse and Neglect* 3(1): 67–72.

Hester, M. (1994) Violence against social services staff: A gendered issue. In C. Lupton & T. Gillespie (Eds) *Working with violence*. Macmillan, Basingstoke, 153–169.

Hindmarsh, J.M. (1992) *Social work oppositions: New graduates' experiences*. Avebury, Aldershot.

HMSO (1975) *Report of the committee of inquiry into the provision and co-ordination of services to the family of John George Auckland*. HMSO, London.

HMSO (1979) *The report of the committee of inquiry into the actions of the authorities and agencies relating to Darryn James Clarke*. 1979; HMSO, London.

HMSO (1995) *Child protection: Messages from research*. Author, London.

Hirst, J. (2001; 22 January) Another crumbling public service. *New Statesman* 10–12.

Hopkins, J. (1987) No words just tears: Stress and distress amongst staff working in child abuse cases. *Child Abuse Review* 3(2): 3–8.

Hopkins, J. (1997) Meeting the care needs of staff in the PSS. *Social Work Today* 16: November.

Horowitz, M. (1979) Psychological response to serious life events. In V. Hamilton & D.M. Warburton (Eds) *Human stress and cognition: An information processing approach*. John Wiley & Sons, Chichester, 237–265.

Horowitz, M.J. (1997) *Stress response syndromes: PTSD, grief, and adjustment disorders* (3rd edn). Jason Aronson Inc., Northvale, New Jersey.

Horowitz, M.J., Markman, H.C., Stinson, C.H., Fridhandler, B. & Ghannam, J.H. (1990) A classification theory of defence. In J.L. Singer (Ed.) *Repression and dissociation: Implications for personality theory, psychopathology, and health*. The University of Chicago Press, Chicago, 61–84.

Horowitz, M.J., Wilner, N. & Alvarez, W. (1979) Impact of Event Scale: A study of subjective stress. *Psychosomatic Medicine* 41(3): 209–218.

Horwitz, M. (1998) Social worker trauma: Building resilience in child protection social workers. *Smith College Studies in Social Work* 68(3): 363–377.

Horwitz, S. & Higham, S. (2000; 22 April) Brianna report cites chaos in 7 D.C. agencies. *Washington Post*, A01.

Howe, D. (1996) Surface and depth in social-work practice. In N. Parton (Ed.) *Social theory, social change and social work*. Routledge, London, 77–97.

Howitt, D. (1992) *Child abuse errors: When good intentions go wrong*. Harvester Wheatsheaf, Hemel Hempstead.

Hughes, G. (1993; 25 September) Ministers step up attack on child protection report. *The Age* 3.

Hughes, L. & Pengelly, P. (1997) *Staff supervision in a turbulent environment: Managing process and task in front-line services*. Jessica Kingsley, London.

Hugman, R. (1991) *Power in caring professions*. Macmillan, Basingstoke.

Humphreys, R. (1995) *Sin, organised charity and the Poor Law in Victorian England*. Macmillan, Basingstoke.

Hunt, J., Mcleod, A. & Thomas, C. (1999) *The last resort: Child protection, the courts and the 1989 Children Act*. The Stationery Office, London.

Iliffe, G. & Steed, L.G. (2000) Exploring the counselor's experience of working with perpetrators and survivors of domestic violence. *Journal of Interpersonal Violence* 15(4): 393–412.

Irvine, E.E. (1979) *Social work and human problems: Casework, consultation and other topics*. Pergamon Press, Oxford.

Israel, J. (1971) *Alienation: From Marx to modern sociology*. Allyn & Bacon, Boston.

Johann, S.L. (1994) *Domestic abusers: Terrorists in our homes*. Charles C. Thomas, Springfield, Illinois.

Johnson, J. (1991) *What Lisa Knew*. Bloomsbury Publishing Ltd, London.

Jones, D. (2000; 25 March) Inside the house of hell. *Daily Mail*, 8–9.

Jones, D.P.H. (1987) The untreatable family. *Child Abuse and Neglect* 11(3): 409–420.

Jones, D.N., Pickett, J., Oates, M.R. & Barbor, P. (1987) *Understanding child abuse* (2nd edn). Macmillan Education, London.

Jones, F., Fletcher, C., Ibbetson, K. (1991) Stressors and strains amongst social workers: Demands, supports, constraints, and psychological health. *British Journal of Social Work* 21: 443–469.

Kadushin, A. (1992) *Supervision in social work*. Columbia University Press, New York.

Kardiner, A. & Spiegel, H. (1947) *War, stress, and neurotic illness: The traumatic neuroses of war* (rev. edn). Hoeber, New York.

Kempe, C.H., Silverman, F.N., Steele, B.F., Droegemuller, W. & Silver, H.K. (1962) The battered child syndrome. *Journal of the American Medical Association* 181: 17–24.

Kempe, R.S. & Kempe, C.H. (1978) *Child abuse*. Fontana/Open Books, London.

Korbin, J.E. (1989) Fatal maltreatment by mothers: A proposed framework. *Child Abuse and Neglect* 13: 481–489.

Krystal, H. (1971) Trauma and affects. In H. Krystal & W. Neiderland (Eds) *Psychic traumatization : After effects, individuals and communities*. International Psychiatry Clinics, USA, 81–116.

Kutek, A. (1998) No health, no service . . . In R. Davies (Ed.) *Stress in social work.* Jessica Kingsley, London, 33–46.

Lazarus, R.S. (1991) *Emotion and adaption.* Oxford University Press, New York.

LBB (1985) *A child in trust: The report of the panel of inquiry into the circumstances surrounding the death of Jasmine Beckford.* London Borough of Brent.

Leat, D. (1975) Social theory and the historical construction of social work activity: The role of Samuel Barnett. In P. Leonard (Ed.) *The sociology of community action.* University of Keele, Keele.

Lee, C.S. (1995) *Secondary traumatic stress in therapists who are exposed to client traumatic material.* Unpublished doctoral dissertation, The Florida State University College of Human Sciences, Florida.

Leonard, P. (1966) *Sociology in social work.* Routledge & Kegan Paul, London.

Levine, M. & Levine, A. (1992) *Helping children: A social history.* Oxford Press, New York.

Levy, A. (2001; 14 January) Children must have the protection they deserve. *The Observer,* 9.

Liddell, M. (1993) Child welfare and care in Australia: Understanding the past to influence the future. In C. Goddard & R. Carew (Eds) *Responding to children: Child welfare practice.* Longman Cheshire, Melbourne, 28–62.

Liddell, M. (1997) Social work influencing outcomes. In *Association of Australian Social Work, Proceedings of the 25th National Conference,* Vol. 1: 415–422. Australian Association of Social Work, Canberra.

Liddell, M. & Goddard, C. (1995) *Victorian child welfare: A continuing crisis of policy and provision.* Paper presented to the 1995 National Social Policy Conference, July. Social Policy Research Centre, University of New South Wales, Sydney.

Liddell, M. & Liddell, M. (1999) Being a 'Good Parent': The role of the state in child welfare. In J. Tucci, C. Goddard, B. Saunders & J. Stanley (Eds) *Agenda for change: Solutions to problems in Australian child protection systems. Selected conference papers, Kids First Conference 2–3 April 1998, Australians Against Child Abuse & the Child Abuse and Family Violence Research Unit.* Monash University, Melbourne, 106–120.

Lishman, J. (1994) *Communication in social work.* Macmillan, Basingstoke.

Loane, S. (1988; 2–7 July) Our children, our shame. *The Age.*

Loane, S. (1997) The view from the other side: A journalist's perspective. *Child Abuse Review* 6: 55–59.

Lupton, C. & Gillespie, T. (Eds) (1994) *Working with violence.* Macmillan, Basingstoke.

Lynch, M. (1992) Child protection – have we lost our way? *Adoption and Fostering* 16(4): 14–22.

Lyon, C. & de Cruz, O. (1993) *Child abuse* (2nd edn). Family Law, Bristol.

McGuire, C. & Norton, C. (1992) *Perfect victim: The true story of 'the girl in the box'.* Virgin Pub, London.

Markiewicz, A. (1996) The child welfare system in Victoria: Changing context and perspectives 1945–1995. *Children Australia* 21(3): 32–41.

Midwinter, E. (1994) *The development of social welfare in Britain.* Open University Press, Buckingham.

Mikulincer, M. (1994) *Human learned helplessness: A coping perspective.* Plenum Press, New York.

Milburn, C. (1994; 29 October) Public critics, private warnings. *The Age* 17, 27.

Milburn, C. (1996; 7 November) Call for national probe on children. *The Age* A3.

Miller, A.H. (1980) *Terrorism and hostage negotiations.* Westview Press, Boulder, Colorado.

Miron, M.S. & Goldstein, A.P. (1978) *Hostage*. Behaviordelia Inc., Kalamazoo, Michigan.

Mitchell, B.J. (1996) *Report from America: Child welfare and child protection services*. St Anthony's Family Service, Victoria.

Mitchell, J.T. & Everly, G.S. Jr, (1997) The scientific evidence for critical incident stress management. *Journal of Emergency Medical Services* 22: 87–93.

Mottram, M. (1996a; 18 August) The lost generation. *The Age*, News 13.

Mottram, M. (1996b; 7 January) Children in care 'disgrace'. *The Age* 1.

National Task Force on Violence Against Social Care Staff (2001) *Report and national action plan*. DoH, London (internet version).

Neumann, J.E. & Hirschhorn, L. (1999) The challenge of integrating psychodynamic and organizational theory. *Human Relations* 52(6): 683–695.

Norris, D. (1990) *Violence against social workers: The implications for practice*. Jessica Kingsley Publishers, London.

Northwestern National Life (1993) Fear and violence in the workplace: A survey documenting the experience of American workers. In G.R. VandenBos & E.Q. Bulatao (Eds) *Violence on the job: Identifying risks and developing solutions*. American Psychological Association, Washington, DC, 385–397.

NSWCDRT (New South Wales Child Death Review Team) (1997) *Annual report 1996–1997*. Author, Sydney.

Ochberg, F.M. (1982) A case study: Gerard Vaders. In F.M. Ochberg & A.D. Soskis (Eds) *Victims of terrorism*. Westview Press, Boulder, Colorado, 9–36.

O'Hagan, K. (1996) Competence in child protection. In K. O'Hagan (Ed.) *Competence in social work practice: A practical guide for professionals*. Jessica Kingsley Pub, London, 86–107.

O'Hagan, K. (1997) The problem of engaging men in child protection work. *British Journal of Social Work* 27(1): 25–42.

O'Hagan, K. & Dillenburger, K. (1995) *The abuse of women within childcare work*. Open University Press, Buckingham.

Overmaier, J.B. & Seligman, M.E.P. (1967) Effects of inescapable shock upon subsequent escape and avoidance learning. *Journal of Comparative and Physiological Psychology* 63: 28–33.

Painter, J. & Martin, L. (1996; 26 March) Report alert on staff crisis. *The Age* 1.

Parsloe, P. (1981) *Social services area teams*. George Allen & Unwin, London.

Parton, N. (1991) *Governing the family: Child care, child protection and the State*. St Martin's Press, New York.

Parton, N. (1996) Social theory, social change and social work: An introduction. In N. Parton (Ed.) *Social theory, social change and social work*. Routledge, London, 4–18.

Parton, N. & Small, N. (1989) Violence, social work and the emergence of dangerous-ness. In M. Largan & P. Lee (Eds) *Radical social work today*. Unwin Hyman, London, 120–139.

Paterson, J. (1990) *Community Services Victoria: Annual report 1989/90*. L.V. North, Melbourne.

Paton, D. & Smith, L.M. (1996) Psychological trauma in critical occupations: Methodological and assessment strategies. In D. Paton & J.M. Violanti (Eds) *Traumatic stress in critical occupations: Recognition, consequences and treatment*. Charles C. Thomas, Springfield, Illinois, 15–57.

Paton, D. & Stephens, C. (1996) Training and support for emergency responders. In D. Paton & J.M. Violanti (Eds) *Traumatic stress in critical occupations: Recognition, consequences and treatment*. Charles C. Thomas, Springfield, Illinois, 173–205.

Paton, D. & Violanti, J. (Eds) (1996) *Traumatic stress in critical occupations: Recognition, consequences and treatment*: Charles C. Thomas, Springfield, Illinois.

Payne, M. (1994) Personal supervision in social work. In A. Connor & S. Black (Eds) *Performance review and quality in social care*. Jessica Kingsley, London, 43–58.

Pease, L. (1992) *Survivors of incest speak: A qualitative research study*. Unpublished thesis, Monash University, Melbourne.

Pegler, T. (1996a; 19 February) Child protection hits crisis point. *The Age* A2.

Pegler, T. (1996b; 21 June) Life of crime for one in five wards. *The Age* A5.

Pegler, T. & Martin, L. (1996; 8 March) Work bans hit children at risk. *The Age* A3.

Perlman, H.H. (1957) *Social casework: A problem-solving process*. The University of Chicago Press, Chicago.

Perlman, H.H. (1979) *Relationship: The heart of helping people*. The University of Chicago Press, Chicago.

Philp, M. (2001; 20 February) Children's aid staff face burnout. *The Globe and Mail*, A20.

Pirrie, M. (1993; 10 November) Abuse workers launch bans. *Herald Sun* 2.

Pirrie, M. (1994; 19 May) Child abuse reports leap. *Herald Sun* 4.

Pirrie, M. (1996; 29 June) Death of an angel. *Herald Sun* 1, 4.

Polkowski, M. (1993) *The defence mechanism of dissociation as used by an adult survivor of childhood sexual abuse trauma: A case study*. Unpublished thesis, Monash University, Melbourne.

Post, J.M. (1987) Group and organisational dynamics of political terrorism: Implications for counterterrorist policy. In P. Wilkinson & A.M. Stewart (Eds) *Contemporary research on terrorism*. Aberdeen University Press, Aberdeen, 307–317.

Post, J.M. (1990) Terrorist psycho-logic: Terrorist behavior as a product of psychological forces. In W. Reich (Ed.) *Origins of terrorism: Psychologies, ideologies, theologies, states of mind*. Cambridge University Press, Cambridge, 25–40.

Pratt, L.I. & Barling, J. (1988) Differentiating between daily hassles, acute and chronic stressors: A framework and its implications. In J.R. Hurrell, L.R. Murphy, S.L. Sauter & L.C. Cooper (Eds) *Occupational stress: Issues and developments in research*. Taylor & Francis, London, 41–53.

Preston-Shoot, M. (1989) Time for positive action on dementia. *Social Work Today* 11(2): 12–14.

Preston-Shoot, M. & Agass, D. (1990) *Making sense of social work: Psychodynamics, systems and practice*. Macmillan Education, London.

Prins, H. (1975) A danger to themselves and to others. *British Journal of Social Work* 53: 297–309.

Proctor, J.L. & Alexander, D.A. (1992) Stress among primary teachers: Individuals in organizations. *Stress Medicine* 8(4): 233–126.

Rabey, G.P. (1997) *Workplace leadership: Moving into management today*. The Dunmore Press, Palmerston North.

Reder, P., Duncan, S. & Gray, M. (1993) *Beyond blame: Child abuse tragedies revisited*. Routledge, London.

Reder, P. & Lucey, C. (1991) The assessment of parenting: Some interactional considerations. *Psychiatric Bulletin* 15: 347–348.

Rhodes, M. (1986) *Ethical dilemmas in social work practice*. Routledge & Kegan Paul, Boston.

Richards, M., Payne, C. & Shepperd, A. (1990) *Staff supervision in child protection work*. National Institute for Social Work, London.

Richmond, M. (1917) *Social diagnosis*. Russell Sage Foundation, New York.

Ross, J.W. (1992) Editorial: Clinical supervision: Key to effective social work. *Health and Social Work* 17(2): 83–85.

Rowett, C. (1986) *Violence in social work: A research study of violence in the context of local authority social work*. University of Cambridge Institute of Criminology, Cambridge.

Rushton, A. & Nathan, J. (1996) The supervision of child protection work. *British Journal of Social Work* 26: 357–374.

Sackeim, H. (1983) Self-deception, self-esteem and depression: The adaptive value of lying to oneself. In J. Masling (Ed.) *Empirical studies of psychoanalytical theories*, Vol. 1. The Analytic Press, Hillsdale, New Jersey, 101–158.

Sanders, R. (1999) *The management of child protection services: Context and change*. Ashgate/Arena, Aldershot.

Sanders, R., Colton, M. & Roberts, S. (1999) Child abuse fatalities and cases of extreme concern: Lessons from reviews. *Child Abuse and Neglect* 23(3): 257–268.

Saul, J.R. (1997) *The unconscious civilization*. Penguin Books, Australia.

Saunders, B.J. & Goddard, C.R. (in press) The textual abuse of childhood in the English-speaking world: The contribution of language to the denial of children's rights. Childhood.

Saunders, L. (1987) *Safe and secure in Surrey? Violence to staff of the Social Services Department*. University of Birmingham, Birmingham 5/6: 32–55.

Schecter, S. & Edleson, J.L. (1995) In the best interest of women and children: A call for collaboration between child welfare and domestic violence constituencies. *Protecting Children* 11(3): 6–11.

Schornstein, S.L. (1997) *Domestic violence and health care: What every professional needs to know*. Sage, Thousand Oaks.

Scott, P.D. (1973) Fatal battered baby cases. *Medicine, Science and the Law* 12(3): 197–206.

Seeman, M. (1972) The signals of '68: Alienation in pre-crisis France. *American Sociological Review* 37: 385–402.

Seligman, M.E.P. & Maier, S.F. (1967) Failure to escape traumatic shock. *Journal of Experimental Psychology* 74: 1–9.

Silver, L.B., Dublin, C.C. & Lourie, R.S. (1971) Agency action and interaction in cases of child abuse. *Social Casework* 52(3): 164–171.

Singer, J.L. (1990) Preface: A fresh look at repression, dissociation, and the defences as mechanisms and as personality styles. In J.L. Singer (Ed.) *Repression and dissociation: Implications for personality theory, psychopathology, and health*. The University of Chicago Press, Chicago, 1–32.

Skinner, A.E. & Castle, R.L. (1969) *78 battered children: A retrospective study*. NSPCC, London.

Smale, G., Tuson, G., Biehal, N. & Marsh, P. (1993) *Empowerment, assessment, care management and the skilled worker*. HMSO, London.

Smith, S.M., Hanson, R. & Noble, S. (1973) Parents of battered babies: A controlled study. *British Medical Journal* 4: 388–391.

Smith, S.M., Honigsberger, L. & Smith, C. (1973) EEG and personality factors in baby batterers. *British Medical Journal* 3(870): 20–22.

Social Welfare Department (1970) *Annual report*. Victorian Government, Melbourne.

Solomon, S.D. (1986) Mobilising social support networks in times of disaster. In C. Figley (Ed.) *Trauma and its wake*, Vol. 2. *Traumatic stress theory, research and intervention*. Brunner/Mazel, New York, 232–263.

Soskis, D.A. & Ochberg, F.M. (1982) Concepts of terrorist victimization. In F.M. Ochberg & A.D. Soskis (Eds) *Victims of terrorism*. Westview Press, Boulder, Colorado, 105–136.

Speight, N. & Wynne, J. (2000) Is the Children Act failing severely abused and neglected children? *Archives of Disease in Children* 82(3): 192–126.

Stanley, J. & Goddard, C. (1993a) The association between child abuse and other family violence. *Australian Social Work* 46(3): 1–8.

Stanley, J. & Goddard, C. (1993b) The effect of child abuse and other family violence on the child protection worker and case management. *Australian Social Work* 46(4): 1–8.

Stanley, J.R. & Goddard, C.R. (1995) The abused child as a hostage: Insights from the hostage theory on pathological attachment and some developmental implications. *Children Australia* 20(1): 24–29.

Stanley, J.R. & Goddard, C.R. (1997) Failures in child protection: A case study. *Child Abuse Review* 6: 46–54.

Stevenson, O. (1971) Editorial. *British Journal of Social Work* 1(1): 1–3.

Stevenson, O. (1974) Editorial. *British Journal of Social Work* 4(1): 1–3.

Stordeur, R.A. & Stille, R. (1989) *Ending men's violence against their partners: One road to peace.* Sage, Newbury Park.

Strentz, T. (1982) The Stockholm Syndrome: Law enforcement policy and hostage behaviour. In F.M. Ochberg & D.A. Soskis (Eds) *Victims of terrorism.* Westview Press, Boulder, Colorado, 149–163.

Summit, R.C. (1983) The child sexual abuse accommodation syndrome. *Child Abuse and Neglect* 7: 177–193.

Swift, K.J. (1995) *Manufacturing 'bad mothers': A critical perspective on child neglect.* University of Toronto Press, Toronto, 21–39.

Symonds, M. (1982) Victim responses to terror: Understanding and treatment. In F.M. Ochberg & D.A. Soskis (Eds) *Victims of terrorism.* Westview Press, Boulder, Colorado, 95–104.

Taylor, M. & Vigars, C. (1993) *Management and delivery of social care.* Longman, Harlow.

Teitelbaum, S. (1991) Countertransference and its potential for abuse. *Clinical Social Work Journal* 19(3): 267–276.

Thackrah, R. (1989) Terrorism: A definitional problem. In P. Wilkinson & A.M. Stewart (Eds) *Contemporary research on terrorism.* Aberdeen University Press, Aberdeen, 24–44.

The Age (1995; 27 May) Sanctions on child labor a threat to trade. 6.

The Age editorial (1996a; 26 March) Avoiding the point. 12.

The Age editorial (1996b; 22 June) When the state plays parent. A22.

The Age (1996c; 13 November) UN agency condemns plight of child slaves. A11.

The Sunday Age editorial (1991; 10 November) How many deaths before action? 14.

The Violence Against Children Study Group (1999) *Children, child abuse and child protection: Placing children centrally.* John Wiley & Sons, Chichester.

Thoburn, J. & Lewis, A. (1992) Partnership with parents of children in need of protection. In J. Gibbons (Ed.) *The Children Act 1989 and family support: Principles into practice.* HMSO, London, 49–62.

Thompson, N., Murphy, M. & Stradling, S. (1994) *Dealing with stress.* Macmillan, Basingstoke.

Timms, N. (1962) *Casework in the child care service.* Butterworth, London.

Timms, N. & Timms, R. (1977) *Perspectives in social work.* Routledge & Kegan Paul, London.

Tinklenberg, J. (1982) Coping with terrorist victimization. In F.M. Ochberg & D.A. Soskis (Eds) *Victims of terrorism.* Westview Press, Boulder, Colorado, 149–163.

Tossell, D. & Webb. R. (1986) *Inside the caring services.* Edward Arnold, London.

Tucci, J. (1989) *Conceptualising the high turnover rate of pre-court child protection workers: A new framework and study of determinants.* Presented at Victorian Society for the Prevention of Child Abuse and Neglect Conference, Melbourne.

Tuohy, W. (1995; 3 February) God and demons battle for Mandy's soul. *The Age* 3.

Tuohy, W. & Freeman-Greene, S. (1995; 30 January) 5000 youths go homeless. *The Age* 1.

Turnell, A. & Edwards, S. (1999) *Signs of Safety: A solution and safety oriented approach to child protection casework*. W.W. Norton & Co, New York.

Ungoed-Thomas, J. & Collcutt, D. (2001; 14 January) Social work bosses backed bungling that let child die. *The Sunday Times*, 4.

USABCAN (United States Advisory Board on Child Abuse and Neglect) (1995) *A nation's shame: Fatal child abuse and neglect in the United States*. Department of Health and Human Services, Washington, DC.

Valentine, M. (1994) The social worker as 'bad object'. *British Journal of Social Work* 24(1): 71–86.

van der Kolk, B., McFarlane, A.C. & van der Hart, O. (1996) A general approach to treatment of Posttraumatic Stress Disorder. In B. van der Kolk, A.C. McFarlane & L. Weisaeth (Eds) *Traumatic stress: The effects of overwhelming experience on mind, body, and society*. The Guilford Press, New York, 417–440.

van der Kolk, B., van der Hart, O. & Marmar, C. (1996) Dissociation and information processing in posttraumatic stress disorder. In B. van der Kolk, A.C. McFarlane & L. Weisaeth (Eds) *Traumatic stress: The effects of overwhelming experience on mind, body, and society*. The Guilford Press, New York, 303–327.

van de Ploerd, H.M. & Kleijn, W.C. (1989) Being held hostage in the Netherlands: A study of long-term aftereffects. *Journal of Traumatic Stress* 2: 153–170.

Vaughan, P.J. & Badger, D. (1995) *Working with the mentally disordered offender in the community*. Chapman & Hall, London.

VCDRC (Victorian Child Death Review Committee) (1997) *Annual report of inquiries into child deaths: Protection and care*. Author, Melbourne.

VCDRC (Victorian Child Death Review Committee) (1998) *Annual report of inquiries into child deaths: Protection and care*. Author, Melbourne.

Walker, L.E.A. (1979) *The battered woman*. Harper & Row, New York.

Walklate, S. (1995) *Gender and crime: An introduction*. Prentice Hall/Harvester Wheatsheaf, London.

Wardlaw, G. (1982) *Political terrorism: Theory, tactics and counter-measures*. Cambridge University Press, Cambridge.

Waters, J.G. (1992) *The supervision of child protection work*. Avebury, Aldershot.

Wattam, C. (1992) *Making a case in child protection*. Longman, UK.

Whittington, R. & Wykes, T. (1989) Invisible injury. *Nursing Times* 84(42): 30–32.

Wilding, P. (1982) *Professional power and social welfare*. Routledge & Kegan Paul, London.

Willshire, L. (1999) Psychiatric services: Ongoing impossibility. *Human Relations* 52(6): 775–804.

Wilmot, C. (1998) Public pressure: private stress. In R. Davies (Ed.) *Stress in social work*. Jessica Kingsley, London, 21–32.

Wilson, J.P. (1989) *Trauma, transformation, and healing: An integrative approach to theory, research, and post-traumatic therapy*. Brunner/Mazel, New York.

Wilson, J.P. & Lindy, J.D. (1994) Empathic strain and countertransference. In J.P. Wilson & J.D. Lindy (Eds) *Countertransference in the treatment of PTSD*. The Guilford Press, New York, 5–30.

Wilson, J.P. & Walker, A.J. (1989) The psychobiology of trauma. In J.P. Wilson (Ed.) *Trauma, transformation, and healing: An integrative approach to theory, research, and post-traumatic therapy*. Brunner/Mazel, New York, 21–37.

Winchester, R. (2001; 25–31 January) Is the child protection system good enough? *Community Care* 10–11.

Wolmar, C. (2001; 14 January) How did it happen again? *The Independent*, internet edition.

Wykes, T. (Ed.) 1994 *Violence and health care professionals*. Chapman & Hall, London.

Wykes, T. & Whittington, R. (1991) Coping strategies used by staff following assault by a patient: An exploratory study. *Work and Stress* 5: 37–48.

Yallop, R. (1996; 26–27 October) Kennett snubs judge's call for child deaths inquiry. *The Weekend Australian* 6.

Young, L. (1964) *Wednesday's child: A study of child neglect and abuse*. McGraw-Hill, New York.

Youth and Family Services (1999) *The redevelopment of Victoria's Youth and Family Services: Purchasing specifications*. Department of Human Services, Victoria.

Zilbert, N.J., Weiss, D.S. & Horowitz, M.J. (1982) Impact of Event Scale: A cross-validation study and some empirical evidence supporting a conceptual model of stress response syndromes. *Journal of Consulting and Clinical Psychology* 50(3): 407–414.

INDEX